Austerity

Austerity

When It Works
and
When It Doesn't

Alberto Alesina, Carlo Favero, and Francesco Giavazzi

Princeton University Press

Princeton and Oxford

Copyright © 2019 by Princeton University Press

Published by Princeton University Press
41 William Street, Princeton, New Jersey 08540
6 Oxford Street, Woodstock, Oxfordshire OX20 1TR

press.princeton.edu

LCCN 2018959619
ISBN 978-0-691-17221-7

British Library Cataloging-in-Publication Data is available

Editorial: Joe Jackson and Jacqueline Delaney
Production Editorial: Kathleen Cioffi
Text Design: Leslie Flis
Jacket Design: Matt Avery / Monograph
Production: Erin Suydam
Publicity: James Schneider
Copyeditor: Theresa Kornak

This book has been composed in MinionPro and Gotham

Printed on acid-free paper. ∞

Printed in the United States of America

1 3 5 7 9 10 8 6 4 2

To Eva, Giovannella, and Susan

CONTENTS

ACKNOWLEDGMENTS

We have been working on the topic of this book for many years. Our very first paper on austerity (by Giavazzi) dates from 1990, almost three decades ago. Since then the three of us, as a group, separately and with other coauthors have written many papers on fiscal policy and austerity. This volume offers a broad perspective that no single paper can give and also includes new recent results and reflections on hotly debated topics like the recent austerity in Europe.

The list of individuals to whom we have to be grateful is long. First of all, we need to thank all the coauthors of various papers which helped us develop our thinking, which led to this book. They include Silvia Ardagna, Gualtiero Azzalini, Omar Barbiero, Marina Benedetti, Dorian Carloni, Tullio Jappelli, Giampaolo Lecce, Armando Miano, Marco Pagano, Matteo Paradisi, Roberto Perotti, Fabio Schiantarelli, and Jose Tavares.

Many colleagues and friends gave us comments, including Alan Auerbach, Antonio Afonso, Olivier Blanchard, Marco Buti, Fabio Canova, Jacopo Cimadomo, Daniel Cohen, Giancarlo Corsetti, John Driffill, Vitor Gaspar, Domenico Giannone, Ethan Ilzetzki, Oscar Jordà, Eric Leeper, David Leigh, Greg Mankiw, Marco Maffezzoli, Karel Mertens, Tommaso Monacelli, Gernot Müller, Evi Pappa, Giorgio Primiceri, Valerie Ramey, Morten Ravn, Lucrezia Reichlin, David Romer, Luca Sala, Lawrence Summers, Guido Tabellini, Vito Tanzi, Alan Taylor, Harald Uhlig, Carlos Vegh, Charles Wyplosz, and participants in seminars and conferences. Various cohorts of students suffered through early versions of our papers and helped us make them more intelligible.

Given the large amount of data work, we are especially grateful to our research assistants, who put in long hours of painful and often tedious work. Some of them also became coauthors of various papers: we thank Gualtiero Azzalini, Omar Barbiero, Igor Cerasa, Francesco Furno, Giulia Giupponi, Daniele Imperiale, Madina Karamysheva, Danila

Maroz, Pierfrancesco Mei, Armando Miano, Matteo Paradisi, Jacopo Perego, Lorenzo Rigon, and Giorgio Saponaro.

We often asked for help from economists at the IMF, the OECD, the ECB, and many national central banks and treasury departments to clarify details of the data. We cannot list them all, but thanks to all of you!

Donna Zerwitz was phenomenal at turning our first draft written in "italinglish" into intelligible English and to clarify our convoluted sentences. We (and the readers) should be enormously grateful to her.

Our editor at Princeton University Press, Joe Jackson, has provided a steady and calm guidance through the process. Kathleen Cioffi made sure every detail worked as planned. Two anonymous referees were extraordinarily helpful.

We gratefully acknowledge the support of IGIER at Bocconi University and of the Italian Ministry for Research and Universities through the 2015 PRIN grant # 2015FMRE5X. Some of the work of this book was written while Alesina was visiting Bocconi University: he is grateful for the generous support.

Austerity

CHAPTER ONE

Introduction

AUSTERITY

The term "austerity" indicates a policy of sizeable reduction of government deficits and stabilization of government debt achieved by means of spending cuts or tax increases, or both. This book examines the costs of austerity in terms of lost output, what types of austerity policies can achieve the stated goals at the lowest costs, and the electoral effects for governments implementing these policies.

Why Austerity?

If governments followed adequate fiscal policies most of the time, we would almost never need austerity. Economic theory and good practice suggest that a government should run deficits during recessions—when tax revenues are low and government spending is high as a result of the working of fiscal stabilizers such as unemployment subsidies—and during periods of temporarily high spending needs, say because of a natural calamity or a war. These deficits should be balanced by surpluses during booms and when spending needs are low. In addition, forward-looking governments might want to accumulate funds for "rainy days" to be used when spending needs are temporarily and exceptionally high. If governments followed these prescriptions, austerity would never be needed.

Instead, periods of austerity are relatively common, for two reasons. First, most governments do not follow the foregoing prescriptions: deficits often accumulate even when the economy is growing and the deficits produced during recessions are not compensated for by surpluses during booms. As a result, many countries have accumulated large public debts even in perfectly "normal" times. Italy,

Belgium, and Ireland built up large debts in the late 1970s and 1980s when gross domestic product (GDP) growth was relatively strong (more than 2% per year on average in all three countries). Greece accumulated an enormous debt at the beginning of this millennium when its growth was skyrocketing, at around 5% per year. Various political distortions may lead governments to not tax enough or, especially, to overspend.

The second reason why austerity may be needed is that sometimes exceptionally large amounts of government spending (for example, because of a war or a major disaster), perhaps even larger than anticipated, create so much debt that it cannot be reduced simply with economic growth. In some cases countries have grown out of debt, but this is not always possible. In the immediate aftermath of the Second World War growth and inflation were high enough to reduce the debt accumulated during the war years. But in recent decades this has not generally been the case. In fact, high debt itself is sometimes an impediment to growth, for instance because of the high taxes needed to finance the interest payments on the debt. The combination of high debt and low growth often leads to debt crises as investors lose confidence in the government's ability to service the debt. Austerity policies are then introduced in the attempt to restore confidence.

At times these two reasons—excessive accumulated debt and crisis—interact. Consider, for instance, the latest round of austerity, from 2010 to 2014, after the Great Recession. At the beginning of the financial crisis, several countries (for example, Italy and Greece) had already accumulated high levels of debt for no good reason. In other countries (Spain and Ireland), debt was relatively low thanks to temporarily and exceptionally high tax revenues originating from a bubble in the real estate sector. But as soon as the housing boom collapsed this fiscal bubble also exploded. The financial crisis generated a debt crisis because it hit economies in which past fiscal errors had resulted in high and dangerous debt levels.

The bottom line is that austerity measures sometimes are required because of past policy mistakes, or a combination of policy mistakes and unexpected negative shocks. The latter are fortunately relatively rare, so austerity is almost always the result of poor foresight and overspending relative to tax revenues.

Which Austerity ?

Discussions about the relative benefits and costs of the austerity policies implemented following the financial crisis that started in 2007 have been toxic, often taking a very ideological, harsh, and unproductive tone. One side argued that austerity, whether in Europe, the United States, or in any other Organisation for Economic Co-operation and Development (OECD) country was unnecessary. What these economies needed was more government spending and more time to recover from the financial crisis and grow out of the recession. Deficits and debts should have been allowed to grow even larger and for a longer time. The anti-austerity front argued that austerity was counterproductive because it resulted in increases, rather than reductions, in the debt over GDP ratio: it generated falls in the denominator of this ratio that more than offset the gains in the numerator. The most extreme version of this argument is that doing nothing, rather than engaging in any form of austerity, would have resulted in a lower debt over GDP ratio. The opposite side argued that rapidly rising levels of government debt, especially in some European countries, would have led to defaults and bank collapses, as many banks held large amounts of sovereign debt. This in turn would have generated a second round of financial crisis and an even harsher and longer recession. Many feared the breakdown of the euro, with unpredictable but potentially dramatic economic and political consequences. Furthermore, the accumulation of even larger debts would have made the future austerity even more severe. The markets did not seem convinced of the anti-austerity view: in countries with rapidly increasing debt such as Greece, Italy, Spain, and Portugal spreads skyrocketed and reversed only when austerity measures were implemented and when the European Central Bank (ECB) stepped in with unconventional monetary measures.

The main message of this book is that in order to understand the effects of austerity, one needs to recognize that there are two different types of it. One is based on increases in taxes, direct or indirect: in OECD economies with already high tax rates, further tax increases have exactly the effects that anti-austerity commentators fear. They are deeply recessionary in the short to medium run (up to 3 or 4 years after they are introduced), inducing large declines in GDP. On the other hand, austerity policies based on spending cuts, at least in OECD countries over the past three decades, have had the opposite effects of those predicted by anti-austerity commentators. Their costs, in terms of output losses, have been very low, on average close to zero. Austerity based on tax hikes has often resulted in an increase in the debt over GDP ratio. Whether or not the debt over GDP ratio would have gone up even more without those tax hikes is hard to say. Instead, austerity based on spending cuts has often resulted in significant reductions in the debt over GDP ratio. This difference between the effects of tax increases and spending cuts depends on two factors. One is the different effect of the two policies on the denominator of the debt over GDP ratio. The other is that spending cuts, particularly those that reduce the rate of growth of automatic entitlement programs, have a more permanent effect on deficits than tax hikes do. This is because taxes will eventually need to catch up with the automatic increases of various spending programs, if the latter are not tackled. If taxes keep rising they will slow down GDP growth, thus affecting the denominator of the debt over GDP ratio; if they do not the numerator will increase because spending goes up and taxes do not.

What could explain these remarkable differences between expenditure-based and tax-based austerity? We explore various alternative explanations. One "theory" is that the difference is simply due to a systematic heterogeneity in accompanying policies: accompanying monetary policy, exchange rate devaluations, and supply-side reforms all could "help" expenditure-based austerity more than tax-based austerity. We will show that this is not the case. A second more promising explanation has to do with expectations and confidence. Imagine a situation in which an economy is on an unsustainable path with an exploding public debt. Sooner or later a fiscal stabilization has to occur. The longer this is postponed, the higher the taxes that will need to be raised or the spending to be cut in the future. When the stabilization occurs it removes the uncertainty about further delays that would have increased even more the costs of the stabilization. The beneficial effects of the removal of uncertainty are more likely to occur with spending cuts than with tax hikes. This is because the latter does not address the automatic growth of entitlements and other spending programs; thus it does not produce a long-lasting effect on the budget. The result is that taxes will need to be constantly increased to cover the increase in outlays. Thus the confidence effect is likely to be much smaller for tax hikes, as expectations of future taxes will continue to rise. Spending cuts produce the opposite effects. Our findings on the behavior of business confidence during episodes of austerity support this view.

Another set of explanations relates to the supply side of the economy, which reacts very differently to tax hikes or spending cuts. Tax hikes and spending cuts have different demand and supply side effects. Increases in labor taxes, for instance, reduce the labor supply and raise labor cost for firms and thus prices. They also reduce aggregate demand of consumers, lowering disposable income. Spending cuts reduce aggregate demand directly but, especially if perceived as permanent, they reduce the expected future burden of taxation for consumers and may also influence their labor supply, since taxes are expected to go down. These interactions of demand and supply generate "general equilibrium effects" that are often overlooked in the journalistic analysis of fiscal policy. As we shall see later, a critical factor that explains these interactions is whether or not the changes in fiscal policy are expected to be permanent or transitory. We return in more detail to these issues in Chapter 7.

Can Austerity Be Expansionary?

Yes, it can. Expansionary austerity occurs when reductions in government spending are accompanied by increases in other components of aggregate demand (private consumption, private investment, and net exports), which more than compensate for the reduction in government expenditures. We shall see how the role of private investment is especially important. Because the idea of expansionary austerity has raised a few eyebrows, it is worth clarifying from the very beginning what we posit. The possibility of expansionary austerity does not mean that every time a government reduces public spending the economy expands. The term instead implies that in certain cases the direct output cost of spending cuts is more than compensated for by increases in other components of aggregate demand.

More precisely, what does it mean that austerity can be "expansionary"? One definition could be that austerity is expansionary when growth is positive during the period of austerity or in the immediate aftermath. This would be a rather weak definition. Imagine that austerity occurs in a period when most countries are experiencing a boom and the country with austerity performs worse than average but still with positive growth. The opposite argument applies when a country implements austerity in a period of worldwide recession. An alternative definition implies that austerity is expansionary when it is accompanied by output growth above a certain threshold, say near the top of the distribution of growth, in comparable countries at that time. This is the definition that we adopt in our descriptive analysis. A cursory look at the data suggests some examples of expansionary austerity: Austria, Denmark, and Ireland in the 1980s; Spain, Canada, and Sweden in the 1990s. In the aftermath of the financial crisis the two countries that did better with austerity were Ireland and the United Kingdom, despite huge banking problems in the former. Both countries used mostly spending cuts. We illustrate some of these "expansionary" episodes, and others, in detail in Chapters 3 and 8 for those before and after the financial crisis respectively, and of course we include them all in our statistical analysis in Chapters 7 to 10. In our statistical simulation, expansionary austerity occurs when the fiscal adjustment leads to higher growth than in the alternative scenario with no policy change. According to this definition expansionary austerity may occur only in cases of spending cuts.

When Austerity?

Governments should implement austerity policies when their potential cost is lowest. One might think that this is the case when the economy is growing, not when it is in a recession. This intuition is reasonable. Note that in our sample we have more cases of austerity that started in a recession than in a boom. This is in part by construction, since we exclude cases of spending cuts or tax increases occurring to cool down the economy. By doing so we "err" on the side of excluding cases of austerity that "took advantage of" a situation in which the economy was expanding. These considerations suggest that if a country could choose to implement austerity when not in a recession, then our estimates of the costs of austerity would be lower. In particular, spending cuts would have even lower costs than those, already very low, that we find; and expansionary austerity would be more likely to occur.

The issue of whether multipliers (i.e., the effects of tax hikes or spending cuts on output) are higher in a recession is complicated, as we will see in Chapter 9. A variety of subtle issues are at play in these comparisons. First, when an economy is in a recession it may already have put in motion its adjustment forces; the opposite is true in a boom, which may already nurture the forces of its reversal. Second, governments, typically because of past mistakes, often do not have the luxury of waiting. Consider the recent episodes of austerity in Europe. During 2010–11 the collapse of confidence in sovereign European debt and the explosion of interest rates on government bonds in some countries (Italy, Spain, Greece, Portugal) led to a situation that was close to a debt-induced financial crisis. Could the governments of these countries have waited, postponing austerity to when the recession was over? Hard to say. We do not know what would have happened absent austerity. What we can say, however, is that even in these cases, namely when austerity policies are implemented during a recession, the differences between the two types of austerity described in the foregoing still hold: tax-based austerity plans have been much more costly than spending-based plans. A related question is the timing of the introduction of an austerity plan, given what a country's trading partners are doing. If a group of trading partners all implement austerity policies at the same time, these may be more costly in terms of output losses because of negative spillovers through the channel of international trade.

The second characteristic of the recent round of austerity is the zero lower bound. That is, austerity policies were introduced when short-term interest rates were already so low that monetary policy could not help by pushing them even lower. Obviously this was not the case for those countries where term spreads and spreads over the yields on safe bonds had increased during the crisis, raising long-term interest rates to levels above 6%: they were not at the zero lower bound, at least on long-term interest rates. Austerity helped to reduce those high rates. We shall discuss the ways in which the recent round of austerity is different from previous ones. Our basic finding on the different effects of tax-based and expenditure-based austerity continues to hold, even in these cases of austerity at zero lower bound.

Is Austerity a (Political) Kiss of Death?

The president of the European Commission at the time of this writing, Jean-Claude Juncker, famously remarked a few years ago "We all know what are the policies which we should follow, but we do not know how to introduce them and then be re-elected." He was referring to fiscally prudent policies, geared toward reducing deficits. In academia and in policy circles the idea, vastly held as obvious, is that voters always punish incumbents who raise taxes or cut spending to reduce deficits. But if one looks at the data more closely, this view is much less supported by the evidence than one may think, even outside of traditionally fiscally conservative countries like Germany. Many governments that have implemented tight fiscal policies and reduced deficits have been reelected, and the other way around, fiscally careless governments were punished by the voters. More generally, especially in multiparty political systems, it is not easy to predict electoral outcomes based purely on economic policies, and fiscal policy is only one of them. The evidence does not support Juncker's statement: many governments have been able to implement austerity policies and be reelected. Of course this does not mean that governments that cut spending or raise taxes are always reelected: it means that reality is much more subtle and complex than what Juncker's statement implies.

FOUR CONTRIBUTIONS OF THIS BOOK

This book makes four contributions to the literature on fiscal policy. First is the data. We have documented in detail close to 200 multiyear austerity plans carried out in 16 OECD economies (Australia, Austria,

Belgium, Canada, Denmark, Finland, France, Germany, Ireland, Italy, Japan, Portugal, Spain, Sweden, the United Kingdom and the United States) from the late 1970s to 2014. To reconstruct these plans we have consulted original documents (some produced by national authorities, some produced by organizations such as the OECD, the International Monetary Fund (IMF) or the European Commission) concerning about 3,500 individual fiscal measures. We have classified these measures in 27 categories, then aggregated into 15: among them Transfers are classified separately from other government spending, Direct Taxes separately from Indirect Taxes, Tax Credits and Deductions separately from other tax revenue, and so on. In our statistical analysis, however, we used a coarser level of aggregation because, given the size of our sample, it is difficult to identify the effects of such a large number of components. However, this higher level of disaggregation can be used in future research to investigate the effects of finer plans than the ones analyzed in this book. The documentation we provide is very extensive, allowing other researchers to improve on our classification and exogeneity judgment calls. A link to the data available in a form which is ready to use is at https://press.princeton.edu/titles/13244.html. Since the coverage of this dataset is very large, although in retrieving the data we have consulted a number of experts, mistakes and imprecisions are always possible. Thus, suggestions on how our data could be improved are welcome.

Our second contribution is methodological. The standard approach evaluates fiscal policy period by period, studying individual shifts in taxes or spending, what is often referred to as "fiscal shocks." This approach overlooks two important points. One is the multiyear nature of fiscal adjustments. When legislatures decide to launch a fiscal consolidation program, this rarely consists of isolated shifts in this or that tax, or in this or that spending item; instead, what is adopted is typically a multiyear plan with the objective of reducing the budget deficit by a certain amount every year. To the extent that expectations matter for the planning of consumers and investors, the multiyear nature of a fiscal adjustment, and the announcements that come with it, matter. The second observation is that the decisions of how much to cut spending and how much to raise taxes are interconnected through the deficit reduction target and cannot be assumed to be independent of one another. Once these considerations are taken into account, the year-by-year, instrument-by-instrument analysis of fiscal policy appears to be incomplete and statistically misleading. We address these concerns by constructing multiyear fiscal plans and describing their effects on the economy.

The results of the analysis constitute our third contribution. We document a sharp difference between adjustment plans based mostly on tax increases and plans based mostly on expenditure reductions. The first, tax-based plans, are significantly more recessionary than expenditure-based plans throughout, and particularly in the 2 years after the start of a fiscal adjustment plan. This finding suggests that there is no "austerity" as such: the effects of austerity policies are sharply different depending on the way they are implemented.

Finally, and this is the fourth contribution of the book, we ask whether austerity is the "kiss of death" for governments that adopt these policies. We conclude that it is not, or at least not necessarily.

THE PUNCHLINE IN A NUTSHELL

In developing our argument we need to overcome three major obstacles The first is the so-called "endogeneity" problem, namely the interaction between fiscal policy and output growth. Suppose you observe a reduction in the government deficit and an economic boom. It would be highly questionable to conclude that policies that reduced deficits have generated growth, as it could easily be the other way around: other factors (not fiscal policy) may have increased growth and by doing so raised tax revenue for given tax rates and reduced spending for unemployment compensation or welfare, thus reducing deficits. We address the endogeneity problem by considering only policy changes motivated not by the state of the business cycle but only by a desire to reduce deficits. The former would be a reaction to the cycle and not necessarily the "cause" of GDP fluctuations. Once exogenous fiscal adjustments episodes have been identiifed, then the calculation of their impact on the economy requires the specification of an empirical model. The simpler the model the easier it is to calculate the effects of taxes and spending,

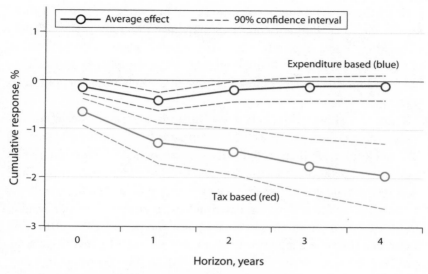

Figure 1.1. Response of GDP to two different austerity plans.

but the simpler the model the more likely it is that important relations among variables are missed. One faces a trade-off between simplicity and accuracy.

Second, major episodes of austerity often are accompanied by changes in other policies: monetary policy, exchange rate, labor market reforms, regulation or deregulation of various product markets, tax reforms, and so on. In addition, austerity is sometimes adopted at times of crisis because of runaway debt, not in periods of "business as usual." Third, virtually all austerity programs are multiyear plans announced in advance and then revised along the way: we need to take these announcements into account.

Two key figures summarize our results and hopefully will motivate the reader to follow our detailed explanation of how they were constructed.

The first is Figure 1.1, which shows the effect on GDP of tax-based versus expenditure-based austerity plans. The word "plans" is important because we will embrace in our empirical analysis the fact that austerity is almost always conducted through multiyear policy packages involving immediate policy changes, announcements for the future, and implementation of past announcements. We will consider all three factors in modeling the economic effects of austerity, thus taking into account the expectations of consumers and investors. We will also allow for the fact that different countries may have different "styles" of policymaking. Some typically adopt frontloaded plans, in which most of the fiscal adjustment is implemented when the plan is announced; others adopt a set of measures but postpone their implementation to subsequent years.

Figure 1.1 shows the effects of two austerity plans, one based mostly on spending reductions (the blue line) and one based mostly on tax hikes (the red line). Both plans reduce the primary deficit by 1% of GDP. The blue and red paths describe the response of GDP relative to the path GDP would have followed in the absence of the fiscal plan. The figure reflects the average of the effects simulated on all 16 countries of our sample and is based on parameters estimated over the period 1978–2014. The difference between expenditure-based and tax-based plans is striking, and they are statistically different from one another (confidence intervals are such that the simulated response lies within the interval with a 90 percent probability). Tax-based plans lead to deep and prolonged recessions, lasting several years. Expenditure-based plans on average exhaust their very mild recessionary effect within two years after a plan is introduced. This average is the result of cases with more pronounced recessions and cases of expansionary austerity, namely cases in which, following the introduction of an adjustment plan, between 1978 and 2014, GDP grew faster than its average growth rate. We shall explore in more detail the results of Figure 1.1 in Chapter 7, where we shall also distinguish the effect of cuts in expenditure on goods, services, and investment and cuts in transfers, showing that the results are broadly similar, although cuts in transfers imply even lower costs in terms of GDP growth. The component of aggregate demand that mostly drives the heterogeneity between tax-based and expenditure-based austerity is private investment. We shall also discuss which "theory" could explain these findings.

Chapter 8 shows that these results apply also to the austerity plans adopted by a number of European countries after the financial crisis that started in 2007. On this point our results stand in contrast with those widely publicized by Blanchard and Leigh (2014). They argue that austerity post-2008 looks different from before; namely, it was

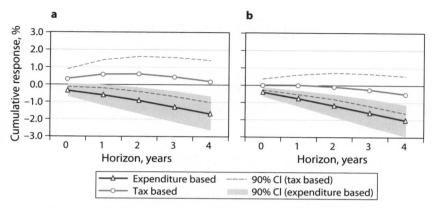

Figure 1.2. Debt dynamics. (a) High debt (to GDP)—high cost of debt. (b) Low debt (to GDP)—low cost of debt.

more costly per unit of austerity than what was predicted based on past experiences. We argue that this is probably not the case.

Figure 1.2 shows the response of the government debt over GDP ratio to the two types of austerity, tax based and expenditure based. To measure these effects it is necessary to reconstruct the debt dynamics which depends on the inherited debt ratio, the rate of growth of GDP, and the pattern of inflation, which, together with the average interest cost of the debt, determine how much government revenue is needed to service the debt. Figure 1.2 shows the response of the debt ratio to adjustment plans in the case of a high level of debt (around 120% of GDP) and relatively high cost of debt servicing and in the case of a low level of debt (around 60% of GDP) and relatively low cost of debt servicing. The figure reports the difference between the pattern of the debt ratio in the presence of austerity and the same pattern absent austerity. In the high debt–high cost of debt scenario an expenditure-based (blue) plan has a stabilizing effect on the debt dynamics differently from a tax-based (red) plan; in the low debt–low cost scenario the expenditure-based adjustment remains stabilizing, while the effect of a tax-based plan is neutral. The blue and red paths describe the response of the debt ratio to a plan relative to the path that the ratio would have followed in the absence of any plan.

ORGANIZATION OF THE BOOK

In a sense the main goal of this book is to explain the empirics and the theories that underlie Figures 1.1 and 1.2. We will also devote much space to a discussion of the more recent experiences with austerity plans implemented after the financial crisis, especially in Europe, including the events in Greece.

In Chapter 2 we review the basic "theory" of fiscal policy. We start with the simple Keynesian theory and then add a number of elements including supply-side effects, expectations, and tax distortions. In Chapter 3 we review several examples of austerity plans implemented before the financial crisis. We compare more or less costly plans, including examples of expansionary austerity. Chapter 4 reviews previous econometric evidence on the effects of austerity and the related empirical evidence on "fiscal multipliers." Chapter 5 presents our main methodological innovation, the notion of fiscal plans. Chapter 6 describes the construction of our data: a link to these is available to other researchers at https://press.princeton.edu/titles/13244.html along with all the replication packages that allow the reader to reproduce the results presented in the book. Chapter 7 presents our main results on the effects of expenditure-based and tax-based austerity plans. We discuss effects on GDP and its components—consumption, investment and net exports—but also on consumers' and business confidence and on interest rates. We also study the role of accompanying policies: devaluations, monetary policy, and structural reforms in the goods and labor markets. We also examine the effects of austerity on the debt over GDP ratio. Chapter 8 focuses on the recent round of austerity plans implemented after the financial crisis. We discuss whether they look different from previous cases and whether they have been more costly in terms of output losses. One of the reasons why the postcrisis austerity in Europe might have been especially costly is that it was started when the economies were still in a deep recession. Motivated by this observation in Chapter 9, we examine what difference it makes if an austerity plan is introduced at a time when the economy is growing rather than during a recession. Chapter 10 asks the political economy question of whether austerity is the kiss of death for the government that implements it, concluding that the answer is much less obvious than the popular debate would seem to suggest. The last chapter concludes.

The main body of the book is non-technical. We illustrate the more technical aspects in Chapter 12.

How to Read This Book

We hope with this book to satisfy both the technical and the non-technical reader, a reader interested mostly in recent events and a graduate student looking for a review of the literature on fiscal multipliers. The technical reader principally interested in the econometric and measurement methodology that underlies our results can jump to Chapter 5, continue from there and focus also on Chapter 12. The non-technical reader can start from Chapters 2 and 3, skim over chapters 5 and 6, and concentrate on Chapters 7, 8, and 10, which contain all the basic results, skipping Chapter 9. The reader looking for a broader connection of this book with recent research in fiscal policy will find Chapter 4 especially valuable. The reader interested only in events following the financial crisis can skip Chapters 3 to 6 and focus on Chapters 7 to 10. The reader interested in case studies, rather than in econometrics can focus on Chapters 2, 3 , 8, and 10.

What This Book Does Not Do

We want to be clear about what we do not cover in this book. First, we focus only on OECD countries, and in fact not even on all of them. Our sample includes mostly European and North American countries (plus Japan and Australia). The effects of different types of austerity may be different in developing countries, which, among other things, have much smaller governments than richer countries. Second, we are concerned only about what the effects of austerity are in the short run: namely, within five years from the introduction of a plan. Of course there are many important fiscal issues that go well beyond the short run. For instance, the aging of populations in many countries implies serious problems for pension systems; any austerity plan that reduces the deficit in the short run may not have a permanent effect on public debt if pension reform is not addressed. We do not investigate these long-run intergenerational issues in this book. Furthermore, the flip side of austerity is discretionary fiscal expansion, that is, increases in government spending or tax cuts implemented to stimulate the economy: this is another topic we do not address. Finally, we study only the effects of austerity on aggregate macroeconomic variables: we do not study the consequences on income distribution or on sectoral reallocations.

CHAPTER TWO

Theory

INTRODUCTION

The popular anti-austerity argument is that tax increases, and especially expenditure cuts, reduce aggregate demand and cause deep and long-lasting recessions. Therefore austerity should be avoided at all costs.

Much is missing from this argument. First, the effects of fiscal policy are not limited to the demand side of the economy. Changes in taxes and government spending also have incentive effects that influence the supply side. Second, current economic decisions of consumers, investors, workers, and savers depend on the future, not only the present. This matters, because decisions regarding taxes and spending made today affect the future.

Third, and related to the second point, austerity plans are not one-shot: fiscal policy decisions do not come in the form of isolated shifts in this or that tax rate, or this or that spending item. When governments implement a major fiscal correction to reduce a deficit, they typically propose to the legislature a budget that includes the announcement of multiyear measures affecting both the revenue and the spending sides of the budget. Given that expectations matter, the multiyear nature of these announcements should not be ignored. In addition, if one thinks about the future, one has to consider uncertainty about what may come. Austerity plans are often implemented in moments of crisis, associated with a fall in confidence and an increase in uncertainty about the sustainability of the public debt. Thus, austerity may affect both expectations and confidence. On the other hand, when austerity is delayed the perception of a prolonged crisis may worsen confidence and increase uncertainty.

Fourth, fiscal austerity plans are often part of a package, adopted along with other policies. Clearly monetary policy matters, with implications for interest rates and exchange rates. But there is more. Often austerity plans are accompanied by structural reforms in the labor, goods, and service markets.

Finally, and this a major theme in our analysis, spending cuts and tax increases have different effects on the economy. The basic Keynesian message is that spending cuts are more recessionary than tax increases. As we shall see, this is not the case.

The empirical rejection of some conclusions of the Keynesian model in its simplest form should not be viewed as undermining the fundamental importance of Keynes's work in the 1920s and 1930s during the Great Depression. However, when John Maynard Keynes was writing, the size of government, measured by the share of government spending in GDP, and therefore the level of taxation, were a fraction of what they are today. Currently in the United States the government (state, local, and federal) represents close to 40% of GDP, in Europe it is close to 50% on average, and in some countries (such as France) close to 60%. In the 1920s, before the Great Depression, the US government was around 12% of GDP; in France that figure was 27% (see Tanzi and Schuknecht [2000], p. 6). The effects of changes in taxes and expenditures may be quite different when the starting point in the size of government is so different.

The late Rüdiger Dornbusch used to say that the beauty of the Keynesian model was that a Treasury Secretary could use it to answer most of the macroeconomic questions she or he might be asked. Unfortunately, the world today is not as simple and sometimes those answers today are not right.

THE SIMPLE KEYNESIAN MODEL

The basic Keynesian model, as it is presented in introductory macroeconomics classes, is the framework still underlying most popular discussions. The basic version of this model deals only with the demand side of the economy, and it is static; thus it is not concerned with the future consequences of current policies. In the closed economy version of the model, current income, set equal to production, is the sum of current private consumption, investment, and government expenditure. The open economy version adds net exports (exports–imports). Prices are fixed.

Within this framework, the effects of austerity are clear and stark. A cut in government spending reduces demand and thus triggers a decline in output, which in turn reduces GDP and private income, generating a multiplier effect. This is because the direct recessionary effects of a cut in public spending reduce private consumption, which translates into an additional fall in output, and thus in GDP and income. The higher the propensity to consume out of current income, the larger the multiplier effect. The reduction in aggregate demand also deters investments by hitting firms' sales.

An increase in taxes has a smaller negative impact on output. Higher taxes decrease disposable income and translate into lower consumption. The reduction in consumption lowers production, and in turn income. But consumers spend just a fraction of their disposable income, while government expenditure affects national income in a one-to-one relation: thus the reduction in GDP in the case of a tax hike is less than in the case of spending cuts. This means that austerity implemented by raising taxes should be less painful in terms of output losses compared to austerity via spending cuts. The results presented in this book are a striking rejection of this key implication of the model.

The reduction in GDP that accompanies an austerity plan—so continues the simple Keynesian story—will reduce the demand for credit, pushing interest rates down. Lower interest rates will help the economy recover, but not enough to offset the reduction in output, unless the central bank intervenes with a monetary expansion. However, this channel is frozen when nominal interest rates have reached zero and cannot fall further, that is, when the economy has fallen in a "liquidity trap."

This is the investment–saving (IS)–liquidity preference–money supply (LM) model, a framework developed in the 1930s by Roy Harrod, James Meade, and John Hicks to explain Keynes's main intuition. The principal limitation of this model is that it does not include any supply-side and incentive effects, which are a basic force driving neoclassical economic models. In addition, as already mentioned, the IS–LM model assumes prices are fixed and it is static, that is, it does not consider the future and expectations that may affect both the demand and the supply side of the economy.

Of course, most Keynesian economists today do not take the IS–LM model at face value. A "new-Keynesian" approach has been developed since the 1980s. It extends the original model by incorporating a supply side and allowing prices to adjust, although with frictions, by recognizing various imperfections in the way labor and financial markets work, and by taking into account expectations about the future. However, these extensions have not altered the main message, at least in the short run: austerity is costly, especially if implemented on the expenditure side. Thus the fog is still deep. Clearing it is crucial because popular discussions—and often even policy decisions—continue to be based on the conclusions of the overly simple Keynesian model. Many aspects are missing in that model: we explore them in the text that follows, beginning with what is missing on the demand side.

THE FUTURE

Modern macroeconomics emphasizes that people's decisions about what to do today are influenced by their expectations of what will happen in the future. Evaluating tax and spending programs taking the future into account can substantially affect our conclusions about how they work.

Future Taxes and Future Spending

Many spending programs have a life of their own, becoming bigger and bigger over time. Think of pensions or health care expenditure in aging societies; Medicare in the United States is an eminent example of the latter. A revision in the rules driving a particular entitlement program thus signals a long-run reduction in the government's fiscal needs. If these changes are credible, they indicate that taxes in the future will also be lower. The same effect applies, though to a lesser extent, to cuts in discretionary spending perceived as long lasting, namely, not reversed after the austerity plan is over. If instead the dynamics of spending programs are left unchanged, then an increase in taxes today—introduced to finance a widening spending program—will be followed by more tax increases in the future.

Thus spending cuts, unlike tax increases, signal that future taxes will be lower, perhaps permanently. Consumers will feel richer, as lower taxes make their expected future income higher. If instead taxes are expected to be higher for a long time, consumers will feel poorer. To the extent that consumers look at their long-term income rather than only at their current income, as Milton Friedman and Franco Modigliani taught us seventy years ago, private consumption may react immediately to the announcement of a permanent cut in government spending. However, for some consumers, the poorest, it may not be possible to internalize the effects of lower taxes in the future. They often consume all their current income and have no savings that they can reduce anticipating higher income tomorrow, nor can they borrow against future income. In economic jargon, they are "liquidity constrained," "hand-to-mouth" consumers. This may be true also for some wealthy consumers who hold little or no liquid wealth, either in cash or in checking or savings accounts, despite owning sizable amounts of illiquid assets (that cannot be sold without incurring a transaction cost) such as housing or retirement accounts, as in Kaplan and Violante (2014). For the simplest Keynesian model described in the foregoing to hold, you would need most individuals to consume only out of their current income. If at least a fraction of consumers has some savings, then the future matters.

Investment plans are forward looking. If entrepreneurs and investors expect taxes to go up in the future, they will invest less today for two reasons. First, their profits may be taxed more in the future. Second, higher taxes on consumers in the future will depress sales. On the contrary, if a spending cut signals a reduction in future taxes, this may stimulate investment today. In fact, we will show how the reaction of investment is especially sensitive to different types of austerity plans.

Future Austerity

Imagine a country with a high and growing level of public debt. To avoid the risk of a default the growth of debt needs to be stopped. If that does not happen, investors, including foreign ones, might become concerned about debt sustainability and run away from the country's bonds, thus preventing the government from rolling over its expiring debt. This might lead to a default, or some other form of renegotiation of the government's obligations. If this has to be avoided, consumers and investors know that sooner or later austerity will be needed. The longer the government waits, the more costly the stabilization will be, because the debt will become higher and higher. Delays (i.e., postponing austerity) worsen expectations and may drag down growth if everybody expects even harsher policies in the future. Implementing an austerity plan today signals that in the future, once stabilization is achieved, draconian austerity policies may no longer be needed. The preoccupation about an unsustainable fiscal situation leads to high interest rates on government bonds, which in turn may affect the overall level of interest rates in credit markets. The implementation of a successful austerity plan that stops the growth of debt would then lead to a sizeable reduction in interest rates. This in turn would help to sustain growth in the economy, in particular the growth in private investment. The net effects of current austerity on the one side, and the avoidance of draconian austerity measures in the future on the other, may therefore have a positive effect on aggregate demand, both on consumption and investments.[1]

CONFIDENCE AND UNCERTAINTY

Austerity measures often occur in periods of crisis, caused by a combination of policy mistakes and unfortunate economic developments, which worry consumers and (especially) investors. As their confidence in the future declines, they become pessimistic and cut consumption and investment. The announcement and implementation of an austerity plan designed to stabilize the debt may boost investors' confidence, leading to a surge in investment. Indeed, we will find strong evidence of this effect when austerity is based on spending cuts. Instead business confidence does not improve when austerity is mostly tax-based, probably because consumers and firms realize that increases in taxes cannot stop the growth of spending and thus cannot stabilize the debt.

Confidence and uncertainty are related. If consumers and firms do not know whether and when a fiscal stabilization will take place—but they are aware that it is unavoidable—then this will increase the uncertainty, possibly reducing consumption and investment. In a period of runaway debt, economic actors know that something sooner or later needs to happen. They may wait until the uncertainty is resolved before spending. The announcement of a credible austerity policy may eliminate the uncertainty, boosting investors' confidence. Bloom (2009) has emphasized the important role of uncertainty in affecting aggregate demand and supply.

AUSTERITY AND THE BUSINESS CYCLE

When unemployment is high, the share of hand-to-mouth consumers is relatively high, thus making the Keynesian outcome more likely. This means that in an economy already in a recession, the negative shock to aggregate demand produced by austerity policies is more likely to have a bigger negative effect on growth. On the other hand, when the economy is expanding, the cost of austerity could be lower.

The argument about timing is subtle, however. Suppose an economy is in the depth of a recession. At that point it might be already self-correcting, embarking on an upward trend. If an austerity plan is initiated (especially one that is well designed on the spending side) then by the time it has an effect on the economy the latter might already have recovered. On the contrary, suppose an economy is in a boom and austerity begins then. By the time the fiscal contraction has an effect, the economy could already be slowing down and the austerity plan, especially if it is on the tax side, may have large negative consequences. In other words, the timing of policies is a complicated matter: as Milton Friedman used to say, there are "long and variable lags" between the decision about a policy, its implementation, and its effects on the economy. In addition, governments often do not have the luxury to wait and choose the best moment to begin an austerity plan. The turn of a crisis may force decisions.

MULTIYEAR PLANS

Large fiscal consolidations typically are multiyear processes in which a government announces and then implements, more or less as promised, a sequence of deficit reduction policies. These plans often are revised and adjusted during the course of their implementation, generating a complex interaction of expected, revised, and unexpected policy actions. This has been largely ignored in the economic analysis of austerity programs. Most studies have looked at year-by-year policy changes without considering whether such changes were anticipated or not and without much attention to announcements of future policies. This is a remarkable omission, because macroeconomic theory and empirical analysis have emphasized the importance of expectations for decades.

As we shall see, different countries have different "styles" in the sense that they implement different types of plans. In some cases, multiyear plans are announced in advance and then executed with small changes. For instance, this was the case of the Canadian austerity plans in the 1990s. In other cases, policies are announced and then reversed: this has sometimes happened in Italy, where deficit reductions were implemented through temporary measures, such as tax amnesties. These different styles have different effects because of the distinct ways in which they affect expectations. Suppose, for example, that a government announces a temporary increase in the value-added tax (VAT) this year, to be reversed next year. Consumers will postpone their consumption for a year, so consumption today will fall and next year will rise. If a government instead announces a permanent VAT increase, then consumption will fall both today and tomorrow. Or, suppose a government announces that as of next year investment will be taxed more. Then investment will increase this year and fall the next as firms rearrange their plans.

INCENTIVES AND THE SUPPLY SIDE

Fiscal policy changes the incentives of workers and firms, thus affecting the supply side of the economy. The most obvious example are labor taxes that reduce the incentive to work. There is a wide discussion among economists about the size of this effect[2]: most labor economists would agree that it is small for prime-age male workers, but much larger for women and elderly workers. Second earners in a family, most often women, are relatively more sensitive to the cost–benefit analysis of whether to work in the market or at home: an increase in labor taxation may shift their cost–benefit analysis against work in the market. Elderly workers may choose to retire earlier if their take-home salary while they work falls. Youngsters may delay entering the labor market, weighing on the family budget. Income taxes can be raised in many different ways, for instance, lifting tax rates or increasing the tax base upon which tax rates are applied. The incentive effects of these different types of tax hikes can be quite different. The latter have stronger disincentive effects and this is why optimal taxation theory suggests widening the tax base by closing loopholes and deductions rather than increasing tax rates.

Capital taxation discourages investment. Payroll taxes also increase firms' cost of labor. In unionized economies, for a given pretax wage if the take-home wage falls, then unions will demand higher pretax wages as discussed in Daveri, Tabellini, Bentolila, and Huizinga (2000) and Alesina and Perotti (1997a). This increases costs for firms, reducing their competitiveness. Thus, an increase in labor taxes may lower exports.

There might also be other, more subtle effects. Imagine that some of the spending cuts come in the form of a reduction in the rate of growth of the total amount of salaries of public employees, either because the number of public employees falls or their per capita salaries do not rise as expected. This will put downward pressure on private sector wages. This effect may be especially strong in highly unionized economies where union policies often link public and private contracts. Wage moderation in the private sector will increase profits and investment, although it may reduce consumption of workers. Similar effects may also occur in nonunionized economies if public sector wages are a competitive benchmark for private salaries.

Thus, incentive effects may explain why expenditure-based austerity plans are so different from tax-based plans in their effects on macroeconomic variables. Tax-based plans, by raising tax revenues, especially when they involve increasing tax rates, reduce incentives to work and invest. Among expenditure-based austerity plans, we need to distinguish the three types of government expenditures: current spending; capital spending; and transfers to the private sector, such as social security and unemployment benefits. Current spending does not, at least not directly, affect private incentives—except for the links between public and private sector wages. A reduction in public investment in infrastructures, though, may affect the productivity of an economy, especially in the long run. We will not enter into this discussion because our emphasis is on the short-run effects of austerity. Finally, reductions in transfers to citizens have two effects. On the one hand, they operate like a tax increase that lowers disposable income. On the other hand, the incentive effects go in the opposite direction: lower transfers increase work effort because people feel poorer.

ACCOMPANYING POLICIES

Many austerity plans are multifaceted. Often governments announce other policies beyond expenditure cuts and tax increases. These may include tax reforms, measures to fight tax evasion, social security reforms, and reforms of the labor or goods markets. And, of course, we need to consider the reaction of monetary policy to austerity plans and the possibility of exchange rate devaluations.

Austerity measures on the tax side often include not only tax hikes but also tax reforms designed to increase the tax base for given tax rates. Thus, ideally one would want to distinguish the effects of austerity based upon hikes in tax rates and the effects of plans accompanied by tax reforms that make the system less distortionary by expanding the base and not the rates. In many countries tax evasion is epidemic: progress sometimes occurs, normally slowly. However, announcements of changes in tax enforcement rules may have an immediate effect. Some tax policies, including reforms of the social security system, may affect people's expectations about their retirement. Yet their immediate effects may be small. An example is the Italian austerity plan initiated in 2011. Probably the most important provision of that plan was an acceleration of the implementation of a pension reform that had been introduced years earlier. If the reform is not reversed it will lead to substantial savings in future decades, but only small savings in the short run.

Many OECD countries adopted stringent regulations in the goods, services, and labor markets in the 1970s and 1980s. These regulations prevent competition, especially in the service sector. Tight labor market regulations, such as high minimum wages and high firing costs, have decreased employment. Long paid vacation periods have reduced the number of hours worked in Europe when compared with the United

States.[3] In the last few decades, though, the tightness of labor and goods market regulation has decreased. In many cases the feeling of being in a "serious crisis," which leads a government to implement exceptional fiscal measures, may also provide the political capital to accompany austerity with market liberalizations. In some cases, labor market reforms have accompanied austerity programs. One case we will discuss is Spain during the 1990s. The significant labor market reform launched in Germany in 2003—which cut long-term unemployment benefits and reinforced the mechanisms for job matchings penalizing workers who do not accept subsequent job offers—was accompanied by a period of fiscal consolidation, including a mixture of tax increases and spending cuts.

The exchange rate is not independent of fiscal policy. An austerity program may affect interest rates. A reduction in the latter (for instance, due to lower government borrowing) may lead to a depreciation of the nominal exchange rate, which helps exports. An austerity plan thus can induce a change in the exchange rate that in turn helps to make the plan more successful and less harmful. On the other hand, an austerity program could reduce the chances that the country might resort to the inflation tax: this would strengthen the exchange rate instead.

Last but not least, the way monetary policy responds to the adoption of an austerity plan plays an important role—even in the simplest IS-LM Keynesian model. Monetary policy could help an austerity plan by reducing interest rates beyond the effect of lower government borrowing, favoring investment and depreciating the exchange rate. Central banks may be more willing to accommodate when they perceive the government as being "serious" about a change in the fiscal stance. The recent rounds of austerity plans after 2010, however, have occurred when monetary policy could do relatively little in terms of reducing interest rates that had already reached the zero lower bound. When interest rates have reached the zero lower boud unconventional monetary policies, for instance, "quantitative easing," could also help with a fiscal adjustment. This is not the place to discuss the pros and cons, the successes and the failures, of nonconventional monetary policies. The only point we are making is that the recent rounds of austerity occurred in an exceptional period in terms of the potential accompanying role of monetary policy.

28 | Chapter Two

CONCLUSIONS

Studying the effects of austerity is complicated. The popular debate has been long on ideology and short on facts and details. The tendency has been to talk about "austerity" as a unique set of policies. Moreover, the discussion about austerity to date has vastly downplayed the role of expectations and of policy announcements and the incentive effects of various tax and spending policies. The crucial difference between austerity plans based mostly on raising taxes versus plans based mostly on reductions in government spending is often overlooked, as is the role of various possible accompanying policies, such as labor and product market reforms. Their complex interaction with fiscal measures may make an austerity plan more or less costly and successful.

CHAPTER THREE

Expansionary and Recessionary Austerity up to the Financial Crisis of 2008

INTRODUCTION

Austerity policies, in our sample, occurred in several countries in the 1980s as a response to the debt accumulated in the previous decade and to a sharply rising cost of financing the debt because of rising world interest rates. In the 1990s a handful of countries in Europe adopted austerity policies to early satisfy the requirements on debts and deficits needed to join the European economic and monetary union. Canada entered the 1990s with a very high level of debt and put in place policies to reduce it. The first decade of the new millennium witnessed few austerity plans, even though some countries, such as Italy and Greece, should have taken advantage of this relatively calm period to stop the growth of their debts. In Ireland and Spain debt problems were hidden by a housing bubble that was generating unsustainable levels of tax revenue. After the financial crisis of 2008, there were many adjustment programs throughout Europe, a few of them draconian. Some of these programs did not entail significant output losses, while others were deeply recessionary.

In this chapter we illustrate several of these episodes of austerity, some successful, meaning that they did not entail large output losses and resulted in reductions in deficits, and other that were not as successful. Broadly speaking, the former are expenditure based plans, the latter tax based ones. As examples of "expansionary austerity" we review Austria and Belgium in the 1980s, and Spain and Canada in the 1990s. These are not the only examples: there are other cases, for instance Ireland in the late 1980s, Denmark in 1983–4, Sweden in the mid-1980s and Australia in the late 1980s. Some of these cases have been discussed before: see, for instance, Giavazzi and Pagano (1990) on Ireland and Denmark, and Alesina and Ardagna (1998) and Perotti (2014) for several others. Other austerity programs were associated with recessions: as an example we illustrate the cases of Ireland and Portugal in the 1980s. We defer to Chapter 8 the illustration of the austerity episodes that occurred after the start of the Great Recession of 2008–9 including the Greek disaster.

The point of the case studies described in this chapter is to provide a few concrete examples of our main results, namely the different effects of tax-based and expenditure-based austerity and the possibility of austerity at very low or no cost (at least in terms of output losses). In doing so we shall also highlight that many moving parts are involved in determining the effects of austerity and that simple conclusions should be considered cautiously. These case studies should serve as a motivation to go more deeply into the data.

To describe these episodes and make them comparable we use a uniform set of tables. The tables that report changes in fiscal variables report only shifts in tax revenues or spending that were motivated only by the desire of reducing deficits, not by the state of the economy. All of these measures are scaled by GDP of the year prior to the consolidation episode, to avoid using a measure of GDP that might be affected by the shift in fiscal policy. We exclude austerity episodes that were motivated by the current state of the economy: for example, we exclude episodes of reductions in spending explained by a fall in unemployment benefits made possible because the economy was growing and unemployment falling. Including them we would run into a "reverse causality" problem as already described at the beginning of Chapter 1. The columns in these tables are labeled "Exp" for expected, namely measures implemented in a given year but that had been previously unannounced, "Unexp" for unexpected, and "Ann" for announced, namely announced in advance. This is because within an austerity plan some shifts in fiscal variables are the implementation of measures adopted in previous years and thus were expected; others were implemented immediately, that is, within the year in which they were announced: we consider them to be unexpected; other measures, instead, were announced when the plan was introduced, but implemented one or more years later.[1] While a plan is being implemented, expected and announced measures can be modified: when this happens, the modification is considered unexpected. We shall describe in much more detail in Chapter 6 how these data are constructed for all the countries in our sample.

EXPANSIONARY AUSTERITY

Austria in the 1980s

The Bottom Line

Over a 3-year period, 1980–82, fiscal consolidation measures amounted to 2.5% of GDP. The effect on the Austrian economy was a brief and small slowdown followed by an acceleration. In 1982 and 1983, growth in GDP per capita jumped to 2 and 3% respectively, performing better than the other European countries included in our sample.

Details

In 1980 Austria was perceiving the risk of rising government debt, due to its high interest cost and despite a relatively low deficit. The country thus embarked on an austerity plan: "Introducing the 1980 budget the authorities announced their aim to lower the deficit in the medium term to some 2 1/2 percent of GDP. Therefore, in the budget proposals for 1980, restrictive measures were incorporated" (IMF, "1979 Recent Economic Developments," p. 28). The 1980–81 adjustment consisted mostly of expenditure cuts, which accounted for 74% of all the measures adopted. Cuts fell mainly on social transfers (reductions in the federal contribution to the social security system, mostly affecting pensions), cuts in price subsidies for agricultural products, and reduced contributions to savings promotion schemes. Table 3.1 shows the size of the measures adopted.

The effect on the Austrian economy was an initial slowdown followed by an acceleration. Income per capita, which had grown exceptionally fast in 1979 (+5.4%), slowed to +1.7% in 1980 and −0.4% in 1981. In 1982 and 1983, growth in GDP per capita jumped to 2 and 3% respectively, performing better than the average of our European sample. In 1984, when a new consolidation plan was adopted, this time mostly based on revenue increases, growth slowed. The exchange rate doesn't appear to have played a role: on the contrary, in 1979, the year preceding the fiscal correction, Austria's nominal effective exchange rate appreciated slightly. Monetary policy was also not accommodative: in fact interest rates were quite high in this period, around 10%,

TABLE 3.1. Austria: Spending-Based Fiscal Consolidation

		1979	1980	1981	1982	1983
		Unexp.	Unexp.	Unexp.	Unexp.	Unexp.
Expenditure	Cons&Inv	0.00	0.00	0.00	0.00	0.00
	Transfers	0.00	0.72	1.13	0.00	0.00
	n.c.	0.00	0.00	0.00	0.00	0.00
	Other	0.00	0.00	0.00	0.00	0.00
	Total	0.00	0.72	1.13	0.00	0.00
Revenues	Direct	0.00	0.00	0.00	0.00	0.00
	Indirect	0.00	0.00	0.00	0.00	0.00
	Other	0.00	0.00	0.00	0.00	0.00
	n.c.	0.00	0.12	0.53	0.00	0.00
	Total	0.00	0.12	0.53	0.00	0.00

Source: Elaboration on the authors' dataset.

Note: "Cons&Inv" denotes cuts to government current and capital spending. "n.c." denotes measures that it was not possible to classify. "Unexp." denotes measures immediately implemented, or, in any case, implemented in the same year in which they were introduced. In the following tables two other types of measures will also appear: "Exp."refers to measures adopted in a given year but announced in previous years; "Ann." refers to measures voted for in a given year but planned for adoption in subsequent years. All measures are scaled by GDP of the year before the plan introduction.

declining after the adjustment. With an inflation rate around 5% the real cost of debt was high, and this explains why the debt over GDP ratio did not fall during the fiscal adjustment. It remained, however, below 50%.

Belgium in the 1980s

The Bottom Line

Over a 6-year period, fiscal consolidation measures amounted to more than 8% of GDP, three-fourths of them on the spending side. Per capita GDP grew on average 1.5% per year throughout the program. Accompanying policies have not played a role; in fact monetary policy was not accommodative.

TABLE 3.2. Austria: Macroeconomic Variables

(First four variables per capita)	1979	1980	1981	1982	1983	1984	1985
Output (growth rate in %)	5.39	1.72	−0.40	1.92	3.09	0.06	2.42
Output, European average (growth rate in %)	3.36	1.74	0.08	1.53	1.43	1.91	2.35
Consumption (growth rate in %)	4.81	2.49	1.01	1.83	5.45	−2.14	1.75
Capital formation (growth rate in %)	7.81	5.15	0.15	−9.11	−0.14	−0.20	7.06
Primary deficit (as % of GDP)	1.57	0.78	0.66	1.91	2.81	0.82	0.89
Total deficit (as % of GDP)	2.91	2.19	2.20	3.83	4.73	3.08	3.22
Short-term interest rate (%)	5.87	10.79	11.91	9.19	5.62	6.86	6.46
Long-term interest rate (%)	7.95	9.31	10.59	9.91	8.16	8.00	7.76
Cost of debt (%)	4.13	4.08	4.27	5.07	4.77	5.15	5.03
CPI (% variation, index is 100 in 2010)	3.64	6.13	6.59	5.30	3.28	5.51	3.14
Nominal effective exchange rate (growth rate in %)	1.74	3.15	−0.61	3.27	2.43	0.28	1.23
Real effective exchange rate (growth rate in %)	−1.14	0.47	−3.45	1.32	0.21	0.77	−0.02
Exports volume (growth rate in %)	10.73	3.62	4.77	−0.08	1.57	7.99	8.58
Gross debt over GDP ratio (%)	33.94	35.40	37.27	39.50	43.41	45.75	47.51

Sources: OECD Economic Outlook No 97 and 102, BIS Effective exchange rate indices, IMF Working Paper No. 10/255, ECOFIN AMECO, OECD Historical population data and projections. IMF Global Debt Database.

Note: The countries included in the sample used to compute average European growth are Austria, Belgium, Denmark, Finland, France, Germany, Ireland, Italy, Portugal, Spain, and the UK.

Details

Belgium had a staggering deficit of 16.4% of GDP in 1981. Following the November 1981 elections, the new government stated in early 1982 that the fiscal deficit would be cut in half by 1985. The announced measures almost exclusively targeted the expenditure side of the budget, mostly transfers. Table 3.3 describes the size and the composition of the fiscal adjustment from 1982 to 1987. Over this 6-year period (1982–7) the measures on the spending side amounted to about 6.5% of GDP; on the revenue side, they were 1.8%. In 1982 spending cuts of about 1.8% of GDP affected the education sector; public employment and salaries; and pensions, transfers to social security funds, and subsidies to public enterprises. In 1983, spending cuts amounted to about 1% of GDP; this time taxes also were increased but by much less (amounting to just 38% of the overall adjustment). Value-added tax (VAT) rates were increased from 17% to 19% and the tax on petrol products increased; direct taxes also went up with an increase in social security contributions.

In March 1984 the government introduced additional measures, some with immediate effects and others for implementation in the future. On the spending side, these were cuts in government consumption (operating costs in the public sector and some de-indexation of public sector wages) and in transfers (de-indexation of social security benefits with the exception of minimum guaranteed transfers). On the revenue side, there were increases in corporate and personal taxation and an adjustment of tax deductibility for both individuals and corporations. The size of tax increases was about the same as that of spending cuts, but the bulk of both measures (about two-thirds) was announced but postponed to future years. In 1986 a new corrective program was adopted. It was based mostly on cuts in social expenditures (education, pensions, and health) in government transfers to local authorities and in various items of government consumption and investment. This plan also included a special levy on the income of public sector employees designed to act as compensation for their job security.

As Table 3.4 shows, per capita output growth was negative in 1981; turned positive in 1982, the first year of the plan; and remained positive (+1.5% on average) throughout the 6 years of consolidation, peaking at

TABLE 3.3.   Belgium: Fiscal Consolidation

		1982			1983			1984		
		Exp.	Unexp.	Ann.	Exp.	Unexp.	Ann.	Exp.	Unexp.	Ann.
Revenues	Direct	0.00	0.00	0.00	0.00	0.14	0.00	0.00	0.30	0.82
	Indirect	0.00	0.00	0.00	0.00	0.47	0.00	0.00	0.00	0.00
	Total	0.00	0.00	0.00	0.00	0.61	0.00	0.00	0.30	0.82
Expenditures	Cons&Inv	0.00	0.41	0.00	0.00	0.32	0.00	0.00	0.16	0.34
	Transfers	0.00	1.16	0.00	0.00	0.65	0.00	0.00	0.28	0.70
	n.c.	0.00	0.00	0.00	0.00	0.00	0.00	0.00	0.00	0.00
	Other	0.00	0.20	0.00	0.00	0.00	0.00	0.00	0.00	0.00
	Total	0.00	1.77	0.00	0.00	0.97	0.00	0.00	0.44	1.04

		1985			1986			1987		
		Exp.	Unexp.	Ann.	Exp.	Unexp.	Ann.	Exp.	Unexp.	Ann.
Revenues	Direct	0.82	0.00	0.00	0.00	0.00	0.00	0.11	0.00	0.11
	Indirect	0.00	0.00	0.00	0.00	0.00	0.00	0.00	0.00	0.00
	Total	0.82	0.00	0.00	0.00	0.00	0.00	0.11	0.00	0.11
Expenditures	Cons&Inv	0.34	0.00	0.00	0.00	0.00	0.00	0.34	0.00	0.34
	Transfers	0.70	0.00	0.00	0.00	0.00	0.00	1.64	0.00	1.64
	n.c.	0.00	0.00	0.00	0.00	0.00	0.00	0.00	0.28	0.00
	Other	0.00	0.00	0.00	0.00	0.00	0.00	0.00	0.00	0.00
	Total	1.04	0.00	0.00	0.00	0.00	0.00	1.98	0.28	1.98

Source: Elaboration on the authors' dataset.
Note: see Note to Table 3.1.

TABLE 3.4. Belgium: Macroeconomic Variables

(First four variables per capita)	1980	1981	1982	1983	1984	1985	1986	1987	1988	1989
Output (growth rate in %)	4.27	−0.28	0.62	0.32	2.44	1.61	1.77	2.20	4.30	3.05
Output, European average (growth rate in %)	1.74	0.08	1.53	1.43	1.93	2.35	2.58	3.16	3.92	3.66
Consumption (growth rate in %)	2.23	−0.29	1.84	−0.87	0.65	1.94	1.99	2.15	2.87	3.26
Capital formation (growth rate in %)	11.24	−21.43	−2.33	−4.19	7.53	6.18	4.76	7.21	15.77	15.36
Primary deficit (as % of GDP)	5.23	9.37	4.69	6.33	1.62	0.62	0.14	−1.63	−2.00	−3.11
Total deficit (as % of GDP)	10.67	16.45	12.70	14.76	10.17	10.09	9.91	7.78	7.27	7.44
Short-term interest rate (%)	14.03	15.27	13.97	10.40	11.42	9.52	8.08	7.05	6.73	8.80
Long-term interest rate (%)	11.90	13.44	13.43	11.94	12.24	10.97	8.63	8.18	8.01	8.59
Cost of debt (%)	8.12	9.78	9.47	8.97	8.22	8.76	8.67	8.00	7.60	8.61
CPI (% variation, index is 100 in 2010)	6.44	7.35	8.37	7.38	6.15	4.75	1.29	1.54	1.16	3.06
Nominal effective exchange rate (growth rate in %)	−0.57	−4.76	−9.47	−2.33	−1.11	1.61	6.16	4.31	−0.34	0.31
Real effective exchange rate (growth rate in %)	−3.94	−6.76	−9.07	−0.83	−0.39	1.56	3.59	2.68	−2.64	−1.45
Exports volume (growth rate in %)	−0.15	3.34	2.74	2.59	6.27	0.33	2.70	4.85	9.20	7.84
Gross debt over GDP ratio (%)	74.25	86.71	96.33	106.63	110.81	115.43	120.53	124.94	125.39	122.22

Sources: See Table 3.2.
Note: See Note to Table 3.2.

2.4% in 1984. The expansion continued, reaching 4.3% per capita growth in 1988. Relative to the European average, growth was lower in 1982 and 1983, higher in 1984, and oscillating around that average in the following years. Consumption growth took a bit longer to recover, but eventually reached 2.2% in the last year of consolidation and continued along an increasing trend up to 1989. The investment growth rate started rising almost immediately, averaging 6.4% between 1984 and 1987. The debt over GDP ratio started to slow down its growth, peaking at 125% of GDP in 1988 but then stabilized. The initial increase in the debt over GDP ratio is due to very high cost of financing it: mostly above 8% in the years of austerity.

Canada in the 1990s

The Bottom Line

A policy package of large cuts in government spending, accompanied by an accommodating monetary policy and structural reforms, was expansionary. The growth rate of output per capita remained positive throughout, rising from 1.5% in 1993 to 3.4% in 1994, then slowing in 1995–6 and increasing again to 3.2% in 1997. The debt over GDP ratio peaked to just above 100% in 1996, then started to decrease. The devaluation of the exchange rate helped.

Details

In the early nineties the debt over GDP ratio of Canada was above 80% and the deficit above 8% of GDP. Canada implemented fiscal consolidation policies for a large part of the 1990s. Prime Minister Brian Mulroney, of the Progressive Conservative Party, introduced two "Expenditure Control Acts," designed to stop the growth of expenditure, in 1990 and later in 1992. The latter limited spending up to fiscal year 1995–96 to the levels estimated in the 1991 budget. The following year, 1993, Mulroney introduced additional spending cuts, some of which went into effect immediately, while others were planned for future years. In 1993, the Liberals, led by Jean Chrétien, defeated the Progressive Conservatives, who ended up in fifth place with just two seats, their worst result ever. The two parties that eroded the Progressive Conservatives were the nationalist Bloc Québécois and the Reform Party. All major parties running in this election, but especially the winners, explicitly favored austerity. Cairns (1994) observes that the 1993 election marked a paradigmatic shift in favor of "the retreat of the Federal Spending State": the issue of reducing debts and deficits was accepted by almost all the contending parties.

In 1994, the new government announced many spending cuts, to be implemented in the following 3 years and to be reviewed in 1995. Business subsidies were cut by about 60% and public employment reduced by 15% over a period of 4 years. Transfers from the federal government to the provinces also were cut. The peak of the consolidation process was reached in 1995, with measures amounting to over 2.3% of GDP. This figure includes both new measures included in the 1995 Programme Review and measures that had been announced previously, that is, in 1992, 1993, and 1994. In addition, from 1995 to 1997 Canada accompanied its fiscal consolidation with a series of structural reforms aimed at enhancing productivity: deregulation, privatization, plans for small business and for boosting research and development.

Table 3.5 shows the amount of fiscal measures implemented or announced in Canada between 1993 and 1997. Over this 5-year period expenditures were cut at the rate of nearly 0.5% of GDP per year, while revenues remained virtually flat, increasing by less than 0.5% of GDP in the entire 5-year period. Increases in direct and indirect taxes were small. In terms of direct taxation changes concerned the taxation of employer-paid life insurance premia, income-tested age credits, the elimination of some preferential tax rates for large corporations, taxation on securities held by financial institutions and on the reserves of insurance companies, the introduction of an additional tax on investment income of private corporations, a special tax for large corporations, and a capital tax for large banks. As to indirect taxation, the measures increased excise taxes on tobacco and gasoline. Overall, spending cuts were more than two-thirds of the overall adjustment.

Table 3.6 shows the macroeconomic outcomes. The growth rate of output per capita in Canada remained positive throughout, even though it oscillated, rising from 1.5% in 1993 to 3.4% in 1994, then slowing in 1995–6 and increasing again to 3.2% in 1997. The growth rate of per

TABLE 3.5. Canada: Fiscal Consolidation

		1993			1994			1995			1996			1997		
		Exp.	Unexp.	Ann.	Exp.	Unexp.	Ann.	Exp.	Unexp.	Ann.	Exp.	Unexp.	Ann.	Exp.	Unexp.	Ann.
Revenues	Direct	-0.02	0.00	0.00	0.04	0.06	0.15	0.12	0.04	0.08	0.08	-0.09	0.06	0.07	-0.04	-0.04
	Indirect	0.06	0.00	0.00	0.00	0.00	0.00	0.00	0.05	0.02	0.02	0.00	0.00	0.00	0.01	0.00
	Other	0.00	0.00	0.00	0.00	0.00	0.00	0.00	0.00	0.00	0.00	0.00	0.00	0.00	0.00	0.00
	Total	0.05	0.00	0.00	0.04	0.06	0.15	0.12	0.09	0.9	0.10	-0.08	0.06	0.07	-0.04	-0.04
Expenditures	Cons&Inv	0.03	0.11	0.20	0.07	0.12	0.28	0.22	0.11	0.19	0.21	0.00	0.03	0.17	0.00	0.00
	Transfers	0.00	0.11	0.20	0.09	0.09	0.27	0.27	0.20	0.29	0.26	0.00	0.01	0.13	-0.01	-0.03
	Other	0.12	0.02	0.04	0.04	0.01	0.22	0.06	0.07	0.06	0.19	0.00	0.00	0.06	0.00	0.00
	Total	0.15	0.24	0.44	0.20	0.22	0.77	0.55	0.37	0.55	0.65	0.01	0.04	0.36	-0.01	-0.03

Source: Elaboration on the authors' dataset.

Note: See *Note* to Table 3.1.

The estimate includes the implementations of past announcements by 0.7% of GDP, unexpected and immediately implemented measures by 0.5%, new announcements by 0.6%, and past announcements to be implemented in future years by 0.5%. The first three objects are the totals respectively of the columns Unexp. Exp. and Ann. for 1995 in Table 3.3. The last one is the component of the column Ann. of the previous years that was expected to be implemented after 1995.

TABLE 3.6. Canada: Macroeconomic Variables

(First four variables per capita)	1991	1992	1993	1994	1995	1996	1997	1998	1999
Output (growth rate in %)	-3.39	-0.33	1.48	3.36	1.67	0.62	3.17	3.22	4.06
Output, G7 average (growth rate in %)	-0.24	0.69	0.23	2.39	1.88	1.49	2.22	1.95	2.27
Consumption (growth rate in %)	-2.38	0.34	0.67	1.75	1.20	1.85	3.84	1.94	2.95
Capital formation (growth rate in %)	-7.25	-4.53	-2.89	6.06	-2.61	6.34	13.22	2.69	3.09
Primary deficit (as % of GDP)	2.97	3.74	3.37	1.52	-0.38	-2.47	-4.93	-4.87	-5.90
Total deficit (as % of GDP)	8.18	8.98	8.59	6.60	5.20	2.73	-0.25	-0.22	-1.79
Short-term interest rate (%)	8.98	6.58	5.01	5.47	7.10	4.46	3.53	5.05	4.90
Long-term interest rate (%)	9.50	8.07	7.27	8.31	8.16	7.23	6.14	5.28	5.54
Cost of debt (%)	6.99	6.43	5.86	5.35	5.72	5.19	4.67	4.89	4.40
CPI (% variation, index is 100 in 2010)	5.46	1.49	1.82	0.19	2.15	1.56	1.61	0.99	1.72
Nominal effective exchange rate (growth rate in %)	2.94	-5.16	-4.71	-4.66	-0.78	1.84	1.38	-2.52	-0.10
Real effective exchange rate (growth rate in %)	2.63	-7.91	-7.10	-5.86	-2.46	0.29	-0.44	-5.14	-1.03
Exports volume (growth rate in %)	1.57	7.16	10.28	12.08	8.50	5.57	8.25	9.09	10.29
Gross debt over GDP ratio (%)	81.53	89.18	95.04	97.78	100.40	100.57	95.59	93.61	89.27

Sources: See Table 3.2.
Note: See *Note* to Table 3.2.

capita consumption improved significantly in the period of fiscal consolidation, while the growth rate of capital formation had a trough at −2.6% in 1995, but then recovered to a buoyant 13% in 1997. The debt over GDP ratio peaked to just above 100% in 1996, but then started to decrease rapidly. The real effective exchange rate of the Canadian dollar (measured by the Bank for International Settlements [BIS] Real, Consumer Price Index (CPI)-based, Narrow Index) fell by 23% between January 1990 and January 1995 (see also Ong [2006], pp. 41–6). This clearly helped, as the growth rate of net exports stayed at near double digits throughout the intervention period.

Spain in the 1990s
The Bottom Line

Spain started introducing austerity measures in 1992–3. The first plan, in 1992–3, was based mostly on revenue increases, but consolidation shifted to expenditure cuts in 1994. By 1998 the deficit was reduced from close to 7% of GDP to below 3%. After falling in 1993, output growth per capita recovered, increasing from 2% in 1994 to almost 4% in 1998. There was a 12% devaluation of the nominal effective exchange rate during this period.

Details

In 1993 Spain had a deficit of about 8% of GDP and a debt over GDP ratio of almost 55%. In 1993 revenue increases constituted the largest share of the adjustment and the growth rate of income per capita fell below that of the European countries in our sample, a deviation of −0.8% in 1993 (see Table 3.8). After the 1993 election, won by the Socialists, the nature of the adjustment changed. Between 1994 and 1998 fiscal consolidation measures were mostly spending cuts totaling about 5% of GDP over 4 years. Revenues increased by only 0.3% of GDP. Reductions in government consumption constituted the largest share of the spending cuts, amounting to 1.6% of GDP in 1994 and another 1% in 1996. Public investment and military spending also were reduced. In 1997 there was a freeze in public sector wages and reductions in unemployment benefits. A mixture of "unexpected" and "announced" measures policies were introduced in 1992, as can be seen in Table 3.7.

After falling by 1.6% in 1993 (and 0.8% relative to the European sample mean), output growth per capita recovered when the consolidation shifted from taxes to spending, growing from 2% in 1994 to almost 4% in 1998. Relative to the other European countries in the sample, growth in Spain gradually recovered from a 1% negative gap in 1994 to 0.2% in 1997, becoming positive in 1998 (0.4%). Capital formation collapsed in 1993 and then reversed immediately. Consumption growth was negative in 1993 and turned positive starting in 1994. The effective exchange rate of the peseta devalued by about 12% in 1992–3 during the European Monetary System crisis, followed by a much less significant devaluation in the subsequent years.

RECESSIONARY AUSTERITY

Ireland in the Mid-1980s

The Bottom Line

In 5 years, 1982–86, Ireland introduced new consolidation measures amounting to more than 6% of GNP, almost entirely on the revenue side.[2] The economy entered a recession. Slow growth and high real interest rates pushed up the debt ratio.

Details

Between 1982 and 1986 Ireland embarked on a sizable fiscal consolidation. As the International Monetary Fund (IMF) explained: "The authorities introduced strong measures to arrest and gradually reverse the deterioration in the public finances. The objective is to eliminate the current budget deficit by 1987" (Recent Economic Developments, 1983, p. 7). Reflecting on that experience 10 years later, Patrick Honohan wrote: "The decision to target the deficit for elimination had unfortunate consequences. By setting an effectively unattainable goal, the government set the scene for public disillusionment as the failure to reach

TABLE 3.7. Spain: Spending-Based Fiscal Consolidation

		1992			1993			1994			1995		
		Exp.	Unexp.	Ann.	Exp.	Unexp.	Ann.	Exp.	Unexp.	Ann.	Exp.	Unexp.	Ann.
Expenditure	Cons&Inv	0.00	0.00	0.00	0.00	0.00	0.00	0.00	1.55	0.00	0.00	0.56	0.00
	Transfers	0.00	0.37	0.29	0.29	0.00	0.00	0.00	0.00	0.00	0.00	0.00	0.00
	n.c.	0.00	0.00	0.00	0.00	0.00	0.00	0.00	0.00	0.00	0.00	0.00	0.00
	Other	0.00	0.00	0.00	0.00	0.00	0.00	0.00	0.00	0.00	0.00	0.21	0.00
	Total	0.00	0.37	0.29	0.29	0.00	0.00	0.00	1.55	0.00	0.00	0.78	0.00
Revenues	Direct	−0.60	0.27	0.27	0.27	0.18	0.00	0.00	0.00	0.00	0.00	0.00	0.00
	Indirect	0.00	0.55	0.18	0.18	0.00	0.00	0.00	0.00	0.00	0.00	0.00	0.00
	Other	0.00	0.00	0.00	0.00	0.00	0.00	0.00	0.00	0.00	0.00	0.00	0.00
	n.c.	0.00	0.00	0.00	0.00	0.09	0.00	0.00	0.00	0.00	0.00	0.00	0.00
	Total	−0.60	0.82	0.46	0.46	0.27	0.00	0.00	0.00	0.00	0.00	0.00	0.00

		1996			1997			1998			1999		
		Exp.	Unexp.	Ann.	Exp.	Unexp.	Ann.	Exp.	Unexp.	Ann.	Exp.	Unexp.	Ann.
Expenditure	Cons&Inv	0.00	1.06	0.00	0.00	1.09	0.00	0.00	0.00	0.00	0.00	0.00	0.00
	Transfers	0.00	0.00	0.00	0.00	0.27	0.00	0.00	0.00	0.00	0.00	0.00	0.00
	n.c.	0.00	0.00	0.00	0.00	0.00	0.00	0.00	0.00	0.00	0.00	0.00	0.00
	Other	0.00	0.00	0.00	0.00	0.00	0.00	0.00	0.00	0.00	0.00	0.00	0.00
	Total	0.00	1.06	0.00	0.00	1.36	0.00	0.00	0.00	0.00	0.00	0.00	0.00
Revenues	Direct	0.00	0.00	0.00	0.00	0.00	0.00	0.00	0.00	0.00	0.00	0.00	0.00
	Indirect	0.00	0.19	0.00	0.00	0.09	0.00	0.00	0.00	0.00	0.00	0.00	0.00
	Other	0.00	0.00	0.00	0.00	0.00	0.00	0.00	0.00	0.00	0.00	0.00	0.00
	n.c.	0.00	0.00	0.00	0.00	0.00	0.00	0.00	0.00	0.00	0.00	0.00	0.00
	Total	0.00	0.19	0.00	0.00	0.09	0.00	0.00	0.00	0.00	0.00	0.00	0.00

Source: Elaboration on the authors' dataset.
Note: See *Note* for Table 3.1.

TABLE 3.8. Spain: Macroeconomic Variables

(First four variables per capita)	1990	1991	1992	1993	1994	1995	1996	1997	1998	1999	2000	2001
Output (growth rate in %)	3.61	2.30	0.40	−1.57	1.87	2.29	2.22	3.21	3.81	4.00	4.70	3.40
Output, European average (growth rate in %)	2.46	0.43	0.41	−0.77	2.87	3.15	2.39	3.44	3.38	3.52	4.08	1.71
Consumption (growth rate in %)	3.35	2.64	1.62	−2.45	0.59	1.27	2.01	2.41	3.94	4.38	4.00	3.14
Capital formation (growth rate in %)	4.24	0.99	−2.76	−11.70	2.02	9.54	5.54	5.13	9.98	10.17	8.25	3.89
Primary deficit (as % of GDP)	2.86	3.22	1.79	4.02	3.62	2.67	0.94	−0.10	−0.70	−1.78	−1.83	−2.00
Total deficit (as % of GDP)	5.34	6.01	4.94	8.19	7.71	7.04	5.37	3.91	2.95	1.32	1.02	0.55
Short-term interest rate (%)	15.15	13.23	13.34	11.69	8.01	9.36	7.50	5.37	4.24	2.96	4.39	4.26
Long-term interest rate (%)	14.68	12.36	11.70	10.21	10.00	11.27	8.74	6.40	4.83	4.73	5.53	5.12
Cost of debt (%)	6.21	6.73	7.51	9.41	7.45	7.63	7.17	6.09	5.65	4.96	4.69	4.39
CPI (% variation, index is 100 in 2010)	6.50	5.77	5.76	4.47	4.61	4.57	3.50	1.95	1.82	2.28	3.38	3.53
Nominal effective exchange rate (growth rate in %)	6.42	1.17	−1.07	−11.25	−4.87	0.31	0.98	−4.49	2.32	0.16	−3.50	1.34
Real effective exchange rate (growth rate in %)	5.27	1.14	−0.65	−11.36	−0.56	1.30	1.56	−4.85	1.10	−0.20	−2.42	1.96
Exports volume (growth rate in %)	4.59	7.93	7.24	7.55	15.42	8.98	9.47	13.62	7.73	7.70	9.97	3.61
Gross debt over GDP ratio (%)	41.46	42.02	44.30	54.77	57.23	61.81	65.86	64.57	62.62	60.91	57.96	54.16

Sources: See Table 3.2.
Note: See *Note* for Table 3.2.

TABLE 3.9. Ireland, Tax-based Fiscal Consolidation

		1981	1982	1983	1984	1985	1986
		Unexp.	*Unexp.*	*Unexp.*	*Unexp.*	*Unexp.*	*Unexp.*
Expenditure	Cons&Inv	0.00	0.20	0.07	0.00	0.00	0.00
	Transfers	0.00	0.10	0.00	0.00	0.00	0.00
	Total	0.00	0.30	0.07	0.00	0.00	0.00
Revenues	Direct	0.00	0.05	0.47	−0.12	−0.08	0.09
	Indirect	0.00	2.67	2.10	0.44	0.22	0.51
	Other	0.00	0.22	0.14	0.00	0.00	0.00
	Total	0.00	2.95	2.71	0.32	0.14	0.60

Source: Elaboration on the authors' dataset.
Note: See *Note* for Table 3.1.

that goal became apparent. Significant tax increases in the succeeding years were barely sufficient to prevent the deficit from growing, let alone reduce or eliminate it. Not only did this have an adverse political effect on the government itself, but by increasing public anxiety about the nature and scale of an eventual crunch, it may have contributed to the high savings ratio and depressed private investment demand of the mid-1980s."(Honohan, 1992). In 5 years, 1982–86, new measures worth 6.7% of GNP were introduced, almost entirely on the revenue side, as shown in Table 3.9. Spending was reduced by a total of less than a half percent of GNP, mostly thanks to an embargo on the filling of vacancies in the public service. No sector of the economy was spared the increase in tax burden: households, firms, and the financial sector all were affected. Both indirect and direct taxes were increased, among the latter: VAT, tobacco, alcohol, table water, postal charges, etc.

In the 5-year period 1981–86 income per capita grew on average 0.7% per year while the average growth rate in the European countries of our sample was 2% per year. Slow growth, large budget deficits, and high real interest rates pushed up the debt over GDP ratio, from 74% in 1982 to 107% in 1986. The exchange rate did not play a role.[3] After 1987, as a result of the failure of this plan, the Irish government adopted a new plan based fully on spending cuts, and growth immediately picked up. This is the case of expansionary austerity initially studied by Giavazzi and Pagano (1990).

TABLE 3.10. Ireland: Macroeconomic Variables

(First four variables per capita)	1981	1982	1983	1984	1985	1986	1987	1988
Output (growth rate of GNP in %)	1.24	0.43	−1.42	2.44	1.62	0.41	3.41	3.40
Output, European average (growth rate in %)	0.08	1.53	1.43	1.91	2.35	2.58	3.16	3.92
Consumption (growth rate in %)	0.44	−8.22	0.15	1.29	4.18	2.80	3.10	4.79
Capital formation (growth rate in %)	7.12	−5.23	−10.48	−1.77	−11.35	1.55	2.46	4.40
CPI (% variation, index is 100 in 2010)	18.52	15.80	9.98	8.23	5.30	3.74	3.07	2.14
Real effective exchange rate (growth rate in %)	−1.21	7.16	0.39	−0.76	1.88	6.57	−1.00	−3.10
Gross debt over GDP ratio (%)	68.87	73.54	86.26	90.35	93.08	107.37	108.40	106.64

Sources: See Table 3.2.
Note: See *Note* for Table 3.2.

TABLE 3.11. Portugal: Fiscal Consolidation

		1982	1983	1984	1985
		Unexp.	Unexp.	Unexp.	Unexp.
Revenues	Direct	0.00	0.69	0.00	0.00
	Indirect	0.00	0.34	0.00	0.00
	Other	0.00	0.00	0.00	0.00
	Total	0.00	1.03	0.00	0.00
Expenditures	Cons&Inv	0.00	0.25	0.00	0.00
	Transfers	0.00	0.00	0.00	0.00
	n.c.	0.00	0.48	0.00	0.00
	Other	0.00	0.00	0.00	0.00
	Total	0.00	0.73	0.00	0.00

Source: Elaboration on the authors' dataset.
Note: See *Note* for Table 3.1.

Portugal in 1983

The Bottom Line

In 1983 Portugal implemented a 1-year austerity program whose size was about 2% of GDP and consisted almost entirely of revenue increases. Output per capita fell, driven by a sharp contraction in consumption and investment. A devaluation of the nominal exchange rate did not help prevent the recession.

Details

In 1981 Portugal's budget deficit was running at around 8% of GDP. In April 1983, after the government led by the conservative Francisco Pinto Balsemão imploded, the Socialists won the elections. In June the new prime minister, Mario Soares, implemented an austerity plan. The overall size of the program, which lasted only 1 year and included no announcements, was about 2% of GDP. As shown in Table 3.11, 60% of the measures were tax increases. A special property tax was introduced along with a tax on wage income. Indirect taxes also were raised, including a stamp duty and a tax on motor vehicles. Expenditures were

TABLE 3.12. Portugal, Macroeconomic variables

(First four variables per capita)	1980	1981	1982	1983	1984	1985	1986	1987
Output (growth rate in %)	3.41	0.74	1.50	−0.64	−2.28	2.50	3.97	6.21
Output, European average (growth rate in %)	1.74	0.08	1.53	1.43	1.91	2.35	2.58	3.16
Consumption (growth rate in %)	2.86	1.86	1.66	−1.71	−3.43	0.37	5.39	5.18
Capital formation (growth rate in %)	−7.28	12.11	2.61	−1.88	−12.53	−1.61	5.23	20.97
Primary deficit (as % of GDP)	4.24	4.60	2.28	−0.78	−0.25	1.10	−0.12	0.95
Total deficit (as % of GDP)	6.28	7.89	5.92	3.61	3.99	6.32	6.39	6.50
Short-term interest rate (%)	16.90	17.08	18.53	22.71	24.90	22.39	15.56	13.87
Long-term interest rate (%)	19.90	20.64	23.16	26.55	29.74	29.03	22.43	19.2
Cost of debt (%)	8.30	9.41	8.43	9.31	8.27	9.18	10.63	9.13
CPI (% variation, index is 100 in 2010)	15.44	18.27	20.48	22.40	25.30	17.94	11.12	8.93
Nominal effective exchange rate (growth rate in %)	−2.84	−1.58	−11.86	−21.81	−17.43	−9.87	−7.56	−7.92
Real effective exchange rate (growth rate in %)	1.88	6.91	−1.69	−7.06	1.50	1.42	−1.24	−1.94
Exports volume (growth rate in %)	2.19	−4.54	4.56	12.76	11.01	6.45	6.54	10.63
Gross debt over GDP ratio (%)	35.00	43.20	47.21	51.29	56.88	61.24	60.80	58.21

Sources: See Table 3.2.
Note: See *Note* for Table 3.2.

only slightly reduced through cuts in investment spending and food subsidies.

Output per capita, which had been growing at the start of the consolidation, declined for 2 years in a row (−1.5% per year on average). Similarly, consumption growth fell, reaching a low of −3.4% in 1984. Investment growth also dropped from 2.6% in 1982 to −12.5% in 1984, recovering only in 1986. These negative effects are also striking because exchange rate policy was accommodating throughout the period: the nominal effective exchange rate decreased by about 20% in both 1983 and 1984. Despite the growth in the volume of exports that accompanied the devaluation (+13% in 1983 and +11% in 1984) the Portuguese GDP fell by 0.6 in 1983 and 2.3% in 1984 , while in the average of the European countries in our sample it grew, over the same period, by more than 1.4% in both years.

CONCLUSIONS

Each episode of austerity is different. There are many moving parts that determine the effects of an asuterity plan on the economy. One is of course the composition of the plan, taxes versus spending; the other is the role of accompanying policies, such as monetary policy and devaluations, the level of interests rates, and structural reforms. But that is not all. As we will see in Chapters 7, 8, and 9, many other factors matter, such as whether the economy is in a recession when the austerity starts, which other trading partners are adopting austerity policies at the same time, and the level of debt when austerity begins. Given the complexity of all of these factors, unqualified statements about the "costs of austerity" are misleading. Exploring these case studies has highlighted that we need to go deeper into the data to uncover more robust correlations. We do so in the next several chapters. We begin, however, in the next chapter with a review of the related literature on estimation of the fiscal multipliers in general and in the case of austerity in particular. This is the "state of the art" upon which our innovations are built.

CHAPTER FOUR

Measuring the Effects of Fiscal Policy

INTRODUCTION

In 2009, when President Obama introduced his "Stimulus program," the American Recovery and Reinvestment Act, worth more than $800 billion (6% of US GDP) to pull the US economy out of the recession, the question he asked his advisers was: "What will this do to the economy?" A lively debate followed. Some economists thought that the additional spending (about $530 billion, two thirds of the package) would do little to help the economy. Others suggested that the increase in spending would add much more than $530 billion to GDP. Similar controversies focused on the effects of tax cuts. By how much GDP increases (decreases) if government expenditure goes up (or down) by one dollar, and similarly if taxes increase or decrease, is the subject of heated debates among economists. Disagreements extend beyond the size of the effects on GDP: some economists even disagree on their sign. So substantial are the disagreements that Eric Leeper (2010) defined this literature as "alchemy." The issue is due not to a lack of trying by economists but to the complexity of the problem.

The arguments center on the value of the "multiplier" that determines by how much output changes in response to a change in government spending or in taxes. A spending multiplier larger than 1 means that a cut in government spending reduces private expenditure, so that total output falls by more than the reduction in government spending. A multiplier smaller than 1 instead means that cuts in government spending are accompanied by an increase in private expenditure so that total output falls by less than the reduction in government spending. If the multiplier is negative, this would mean that a cut in government spending would increase private expenditure so much that total demand would increase, notwithstanding the reduction in government spending. The simplest Keynesian theory, upon which much of the policy discussion is based, implies spending multipliers much greater than 1 and larger in absolute value than tax multipliers.

In what follows we review this debate.

THE EMPIRICAL EVIDENCE

The empirical evidence produces a profusion of different estimates of fiscal multipliers.[1] Tables 4.1, 4.2, and 4.3 are examples of the broad range of estimates. Table 4.1, from the US Congressional Budget Office, reports ranges for a number of multipliers based on the estimated effects of the tax and spending measures contained in the 2009 American Recovery and Reinvestment Act. The multiplier for federal government purchases of goods and services ranges from less than 1 to 2.5. The same is true in the table for increases in government transfers to individuals and firms. On the other hand, tax multipliers seem quite small, ranging from 0 to −0.6, except for the case of a temporary tax cut for lower and middle income individuals. In this case, the multiplier ranged between −0.3 and −1.5.

TABLE 4.1. United States: CBO Estimates of Fiscal Multipliers on Real GDP Growth

	Estimated Multiplier	
Type of activity	Low	High
Federal government purchases of goods and services	0.5	2.5
Transfer payments to state and local governments for infrastructure	0.4	2.2
Transfer payments to state and local governments for other purposes	0.4	1.8
Transfer payments to individuals	0.4	2.1
One-time payments to retirees	0.2	1.0
Two-year tax change for lower and middle-income people	−1.5	−0.3
One-year tax change for higher-income people	−0.6	−0.1
Extension of first-time homebuyer credit	0.8	0.2
Corporate tax provisions primarily affecting cash flow	−0.4	−0.0

Note: The estimates were produced for the Congressional Budget Office (CBO) analysis of the American Recovery and Reinvestment Act of 2009.

TABLE 4.2. Summary of Government Spending Multiplier Estimates for the Aggregate United States

Study	Sample	Identification	Implied spending multiplier
Barro (1981), Hall (1986, 2009), Barro and Redlick (2011)	Annual historical samples	Use military spending as instrument for government spending	0.6–1
Rotemberg and Woodford (1992)	Quarterly, 1947–89	Residuals from regression of military spending on own lags and lags of military employment	1.25
Ramey and Shapiro (1998), Edelberg, Eichenbaum, and Fisher (1999), Cavallo (2005)	Quarterly, 1947–late 1990s or 2000s	Ramey-Shapiro dates, which are based on narrative evidence of anticipated military buildups	0.6–1.2, depending on sample and whether calculated as cumulative or peak
Blanchard and Perotti (2002)	Quarterly, 1960–97	SVARS, Choleski decomposition with G ordered first	0.9 to 1.29, calculated as peak multipliers
Mountford and Uhlig (2009)	Quarterly, 1955–2000	Sign restrictions on a SVAR	0.65 for a deficit-financed increase in spending
Romer and Bernstein (2009)	Quarterly	Average multipliers from FRB/US model and a private forecasting firm model	Rising to 1.57 by the 8th quarter
Cogan, Cwik, Taylor, and Wieland (2010)	Quarterly, 1966–2004	Estimated Smets-Wouters Model	0.64 at peak
Ramey (2011b)	Quarterly, 1939–2008 and subsamples	VAR using shocks to the expected present discounted value of government spending caused by military events, based on narrative evidence	0.6–1.2, depending on sample
Fisher and Peters (2010)	Quarterly, 1960–2007	VAR using shocks to the excess stock returns of military contractors	1.5 based on cumulative effects
Auerbach and Gorodnichenko (2013a)	Quarterly, 1947–2008	SVAR that controls for professional forecasts, Ramey news. Key innovation is regime switching model.	Expansion: −0.3. Recession: 2.2. (−0.4 and 1.7 for defense spending)
Ben Zeev and Pappa (2015)	Quarterly, 1947–2007	Shock that (i) is orthogonal to current defense spending; and (ii) best explains future movements in defense spending over a horizon of 5 years.	2.1 based on integral multipliers at 6 quarters

This table is taken from Ramey (2016).

TABLE 4.3. Summary of Some Tax Multiplier Estimates for the Aggregate United States

Study	Main Sample	Identification	Implied tax multiplier
Evans (1969)	Quarterly, 1966–74	Based on estimates of equations of Wharton, Klein-Goldberger, and Brookings models	−0.5 to −1.7, depending on horizon, type of tax, and model.
Blanchard and Perotti (2002)	Quarterly, 1960–97	Assumed output elasticities in an SVAR. "Taxes" are actually taxes less transfers.	−0.78 to −1.33 (peak to impact)
Mountford and Uhlig (2009)	Quarterly, 1955–2000	Sign restrictions on a VAR. Use same variables as BP.	−5.25 for a tax decrease that is deficit financed
Romer and Romer (2010)	Quarterly, 1947–2007	Legislated tax changes driven by an inherited government budget deficit or to promote future growth, based on narrative evidence.	−3, based on peak effect. Romer and Romer (2009) show that these tax shocks do not raise government spending significantly, so these are close to pure tax shocks.
Barro and Redlick (2011)	Annual, 1917–2006 and subsamples	Average marginal income tax rate	−1.1
Favero, Giavazzi, and Perego (2011)	Quarterly, 1950–2006	Romer-Romer shocks embedded in an SVAR	−0.5
Caldara and Kamps (2017)	Quarterly, 1947–2006	SVAR using outside elasticities	−0.65 (peak to impact)
Mertens and Ravn (2014)	Quarterly, 1950–2006	Proxy SVAR using Romer-Romer unanticipated shocks	−3 at 6 quarters

This table is taken from Ramsey (2016).

Table 4.2 presents a synopsis of studies estimating multipliers for government purchases. Most of the values range between 0.6 and 1.5. When distinguishing between multipliers in periods of expansion and recession, Auerbach and Gorodnichenko (2013a) find negative values during expansions, meaning that an increase in spending will reduce output during an economic expansion. Gechert (2015) has assembled the results from a very large (104) number of studies of multipliers across a variety of countries and using different statistical techniques. With the caveat that both the context and the experiments vary across studies, he finds that government spending multipliers are close to 1.

Considering the multipliers for taxes, Table 4.3 shows that the interval of estimates is even wider, ranging from −0.5 (meaning that an increase in taxes worth 1% of GDP reduces GDP by 0.5%), to a staggering −5.25 in Mountford and Uhlig (2009).[2] Blanchard and Perotti (2002) find a much smaller multiplier at the peak of the response: −1.3, 7 quarters after the increase in taxes. The bottom line is that economists seem to disagree on everything: not only on the size of fiscal multipliers, but sometimes even on their sign.

Why So Much Disagreement?

It is impossible to let the data speak, and simply listen to them. Governments tend to spend more during recessions. So if you looked at the correlation between government spending and GDP you would conclude that the multiplier is negative. This is wrong of course: the recession would have been worse without the spending increase. But by how much? Similarly, during an economic expansion tax revenues typically go up, but that does not imply that raising taxes increases growth. This is the heart of what makes estimates difficult. To assess empirically the response of macroeconomic variables to shifts in taxes or government spending, one needs to *identify* episodes in which taxes and spending didn't change simply because the economy was expanding or contracting.

Economists have looked for changes in spending not related to recessions, such as military spending due to wars. But wars are fortunately rare, and buying tanks and planes might not have the same effect as introducing unemployment insurance. Similarly, some economists have looked at changes in taxes that were motivated by the desire to reduce the size of government. But this points to another difficulty. Much can happen to the economy while taxes are cut and one would need to separate the consequences of the tax cut from all other factors. The central bank could respond to a change in taxes or spending, exchange rate movements may play a role, and so on. Moreover, multipliers will reflect all the different channels through which a shift in fiscal variables can affect output: some working through the effects of fiscal policy on the supply of labor, others working on the demand side. We need an empirical model of the economy to take all these channels into account. The problem is that an empirical model general enough to incorporate all possible interactions between macroeconomic and fiscal policy variables is impossible to estimate because the data available are limited. Thus modeling choices must be made, and they do affect the results.

Alternative Ways of Measuring Multipliers

Two definitions of multipliers are used in the literature. One looks at the effect on output (or some other macroeconomic variable) of a shift in spending (or taxes) that is not related to the state of the economy, such as during a war. In economists' jargon an "exogenous" shift in spending, a change that is not caused by the state of the economy or motivated by the need to stimulate the economy. This impact—measured as the ratio of the *cumulative* change in output to the *initial* shift in government spending—is computed at various horizons. In other words, assume that in year zero government spending is cut by 1% of GDP: the multiplier is defined as the ratio of the cumulative change in output up to some horizon—say 3 years—divided by the size of the shift in government spending in year zero.

The approach has the drawback of overlooking the fact that following the initial shift, government spending (or taxes) will not remain constant: they will typically keep moving. This suggests an alternative measure: defining "multiplier," the ratio of the *cumulative* (discounted) output response to the *cumulative* change in government spending and taxes (also discounted), that is the initial shift, say in spending, plus the shifts in spending that followed the initial exogenous adjustment. This second measure has been advocated by some researchers[3] because it captures the extent to which the size of the multiplier depends on the persistence of fiscal shocks. Although these two measures often produce multipliers of different sizes, when used consistently they rarely result in a different ranking of multipliers. That is, tax multipliers remain larger, in absolute value, compared to spending multipliers, independently of the method used to calculate them. In the results reported and commented in the following chapters of this book we shall adopt, unless specifically indicated, the first definition.

MULTIPLIERS DURING AUSTERITY: THE EARLY LITERATURE

The early literature on the effects of austerity studied episodes of large reductions in the budget deficit. By exploring case studies, researchers tried to get a handle on the various moving parts of austerity episodes and answer several questions. First, what types of fiscal adjustments are less costly in terms of short-run output losses? Tax-based or expenditure-based? "Cold turkey" policy design or gradual approaches? Does the answer depend on the initial level of public debt? Second, which components of private demand (consumption, investment, or net exports) respond, and by how much, to changes in taxes or spending during fiscal adjustments? Third, which accompanying policies— monetary policy, devaluations, structural reforms in labor and goods markets—would make austerity more (or less) successful? Are expansionary fiscal adjustments possible?

Giavazzi and Pagano (1990) analyzed three cases of large fiscal consolidations that occurred in the 1980s. In two, Denmark (1983–7) and Ireland (1987–9), a large reduction in the cyclically adjusted government budget deficit was associated with a vigorous increase in private domestic demand. They attributed this mostly to wealth effects on consumption: reductions in the budget deficit signal that taxes may be lower in the future, with positive effects on net permanent income and thus on consumption. Ireland in 1982–6 (an episode we analyzed in Chapter 3) instead experienced a sharp recession. Later, Alesina and Ardagna (1998), studying the case of the Irish adjustment, emphasized the importance of investment, labor costs, and net exports. They identified five more episodes of large fiscal consolidation (Belgium 1984–6,

Canada 1986–8, Italy 1989–2, Portugal 1984–6, and Sweden 1983–9). These consolidations were "large" in the sense that the cyclically adjusted primary deficit (which is an estimate of what the deficit would be if the economy were at full employment) 2 years after the consolidation was 4 percentage points of GDP smaller than before the adjustment. These episodes were accompanied by growth of private consumption and especially investment in almost every year of the adjustment, sometimes with a year delay or so.[4]

One common finding of this literature was that deficit reductions implemented via spending cuts were much less costly in terms of output losses than those based on tax increases, and that the former type of adjustment sometimes was associated with an expansion of GDP, even immediately after the fiscal adjustment.[5] A related finding (Lane and Perotti [2003]) was that increases in government spending on goods and services raise the real wage and depress profitability in the traded sector, one reason why spending-based adjustments were found to be more successful in terms of decreasing the debt-to-GDP ratio (McDermott and Wescott [1996]).[6] Von Hagen, Hallett, and Strauch (2002) argue that the consolidations whose effects are longer lasting are those obtained through reductions in primary expenditures, especially transfers and wages. With a panel of 19 OECD countries, Perotti (1999) estimates a theoretical model that predicts expansionary adjustments in "bad times"—that is, periods of high indebtedness—and contractionary adjustments in "good times." The intuition is that if debt exceeds a critical level the government is forced to increase taxes by a large amount in order not to default. Then in "bad times," that is, periods when debt growth is particularly rapid and such a critical level is more likely to be reached, an immediate tax hike that rules out an even larger tax hike in the future can induce a positive response of consumption.[7]

In this vein, Alesina and Ardagna (2010), and Alesina, Carloni, and Lecce (2013) studied a panel of OECD countries with yearly observations from 1970 to 2007. They define a period of fiscal adjustment as a year in which the primary cyclically adjusted budget balance improves by at least 1.5% of GDP. An adjustment is defined as "expansionary" if the deviation in average GDP growth from the G-7 weighted average in the current and the two subsequent years is above the 75th percentile of the empirical distribution of the realizations of the same variable in all adjustment periods. In this way, they control for the state of the world business cycle. Imagine that a country implements a fiscal adjustment that would be expansionary, but the world is in a recession. Or, in the opposite case, a country implements a contractionary fiscal adjustment, but the economy grows in spite of it because it is helped by an expansionary world business cycle. In order to take this into account one has to measure how the adjusting country performs relative to the rest of the world. Besides showing that expansionary fiscal adjustments are exclusively spending based, Alesina and Ardagna (2010) find that the fiscal adjustments associated with higher GDP growth are those in which a larger share of the reduction in the primary deficit is due to cuts in current government spending rather than in investment spending. They also document a strong reaction of private investment spending to government spending cuts (a result consistent with Alesina, Ardagna, Perotti, and Schiantarelli [2002]). In some but not all cases, exports also increase as a result of the devaluations associated with a reduction in interest rates that accompanies the fiscal contraction.

The definition of a fiscal adjustment as a year characterized by a large reduction in the budget deficit has been questioned by Perotti (2013): he criticized the choice of treating contiguous adjustment years as separate episodes. In his view, a prolonged deficit reduction of 0.5% of GDP extending over 3 years would not be considered a fiscal adjustment episode (because every year is below the threshold) even though the overall cumulative deficit reduction (1.5%) would be considered such an episode if it occurred in the same year. Thus, he argues, the procedure misses slow moving, multiyear fiscal adjustments. Alesina and Ardagna (2013) make some progress responding to this criticism and show that their earlier results were robust to this extension. But this is indeed a valid criticism and one of the reasons why we shall consider multiyear plans rather than yearly austerity shocks.

This early literature also faced difficult issues of reverse causality. In the attempt to exclude components of taxes and expenditures that were endogenous to the cycle—namely automatic changes in revenues and expenditures that were induced by the business cycle—it identified fiscal consolidations by using a "cyclically adjusted" measure of the deficit. But this variable has an important limitation: it excludes budget changes induced by automatic stabilizers, but not discretionary changes in taxes and spending that might have been motivated by the state of the economy. Nevertheless, as we shall see in the following chapters, the main findings of these early studies—in particular the fact that tax-based fiscal corrections are more costly than spending-based ones—have been confirmed and, if anything strengthened by subsequent analyses that dealt with the endogeneity of some discretionary fiscal actions.

THE NARRATIVE APPROACH

In this book we use a novel approach to identifying episodes of changes in fiscal stance not motivated by the state of the economic cycle: the "narrative" approach, proposed in the context of fiscal policy by Romer and Romer (2010). We have constructed a large dataset of fiscal consolidations that can safely be assumed to have been adopted to reduce the budget deficit, not to cool down the economy. In fact, we will see that many (in fact a majority) of these fiscal adjustments were implemented during recessions, when a countercyclical fiscal policy would have required an expansion, not a contraction, of the budget.

Early Narrative Studies: Wars

Wars and the associated military buildups are episodes of increases in spending not related to recessions—at least most of the time. Barro (1984) studied the effects of US government spending in the run-up to and during World War I, World War II, and the Korean War: he finds a spending multiplier well below 1, around 0.6. Hall (2009) found similar results. In these papers, what produces a multiplier smaller than 1 is some crowding out of private investment, including consumer durables.

However, some military spending occurs before a war, in anticipation of a war and could affect private spending even before the war starts. This cannot be disregarded in estimating multipliers. To address this concern, Ramey (2011a) use information collected from *Business Week* (what has become known as "Ramey's news variable") to isolate political announcements that eventually led to increases in military spending (in Chapter 12 we describe this methodology in detail). Ramey and Shapiro

(1998) identify three episodes of large increases in military spending: the Korean War, the Vietnam War, and the Carter-Reagan military buildup. In each case, military expenditures increased sharply, peaking on average after 2 1/2 years at 36% above trend. At the same time, however, nondefense government purchases fell significantly: the average peak decline is 4% from trend. Both total GDP and private GDP increase in response to the increase in military spending in the first few quarters. Thereafter, while the growth rate of total GDP remains positive for 3 years, the growth rate of private GDP turns negative after 2 years. The implied multiplier is thus above 1 during the first 2 years, then falls way below 1. Using US annual data that include World War II, Barro and Redlick (2011) estimate multipliers for temporary defense spending of 0.4–0.5 contemporaneously, and 0.6–0.7 over 2 years. When they allow for spending multipliers to vary depending on the state of the economy, they do not find robust evidence of heterogeneity across periods of high versus low unemployment.

All of these estimates are derived under the assumption that the increase in expenditure is deficit financed. The results are obviously different in the case of tax-financed increases in spending. Since Barro and Redlick find that a rise in average marginal income tax rates has a significantly negative effect on GDP, with an implied multiplier of 1.1, the balanced budget spending multiplier is negative, contrary to the prediction of the Keynesian model.[8]

These estimates are limited to a particular set of multipliers: those associated with military spending. The "external validity" of these findings, namely the possibility of using them to assess the value of multipliers in situations unrelated to a war or a military buildup, remains an open issue.

Tax Changes in the United States

Romer and Romer (2010) bring the narrative approach to a new level, going beyond the case of wars and analyzing other episodes of exogenous shifts in fiscal variables: changes in US federal taxes. The Romers recover exogenous shifts in taxes from a painstaking analysis of the motivations that US legislatures have offered for each of their tax decisions. This approach has been labeled *narrative identification*, and before its application to fiscal policy it had been used by the same authors to study the effects of monetary policy decisions (Romer and Romer [1989]). The motivations underlying each tax decision are assessed using original sources: budget documents, records of Congressional debates, speeches, and so forth. The authors define as exogenous, that is, not related to the business cycle, all episodes of changes (up and down) in US federal taxes from 1947 to 2007 which were motivated by the aim of either improving "long-run growth" (for tax cuts) or "reducing an inherited deficit" (for tax hikes).

Once a set of narratively identified shifts in fiscal variables is selected, their effects on output can be analyzed by simply running a regression of output growth on the contemporaneous and lagged shifts in taxes because such shifts are, by construction, uncorrelated with the error term of the regression equation. The Romers estimate that in response to an increase in tax liabilities of 1% of GDP, output 10 quarters later is still 3% below its level had no shift in taxes occurred: a very large decline indeed, and a very large tax multiplier. These exogenous shifts in taxes result from the sum of two types of changes in tax revenues: one announced at time *t* and implemented immediately (therefore unanticipated), another announced at time *t* to be implemented in future periods thus anticipated. Not all episodes include both unanticipated and announced tax changes but some do. The estimated multipliers are responses to both unanticipated and announced shifts in taxes, assuming that the two have identical effects on output. This restriction is relaxed in Mertens and Ravn (2013), who find that unanticipated changes in tax rates produce larger short-run effects on aggregate output. Applying this approach to UK data, Cloyne (2013) constructed a narrative time series of legislated tax changes in the United Kingdom, finding that a 1% cut in taxes, as a proportion of GDP, causes a 0.6% increase in GDP on impact, rising to a 2.5% increase after nearly 3 years.[9] Riera Crichton, Vegh, and Vuletin (2016) built a novel value-added tax rate dataset for 1980–2009, applying the narrative approach to tax rates.

The IMF Narrative Dataset

Economists in the research department of the International Monetary Fund (IMF) have used the narrative methodology to construct a time series of exogenous shifts in fiscal variables (both taxes and spending) for 17 OECD countries during 1978–2009 (Devries, Pescatori, Leigh, and Guajardo [2011]). These episodes only include fiscal consolidations: in other words, these adjustments are motivated only by the need to "reduce an inherited deficit," not by a "long-run growth" motive.

These data have been used by Guajardo, Leigh, and Pescatori (2014) to estimate fiscal multipliers for the OECD countries in the sample. In their article, they do not consider announcements but rather add up, year by year, shifts in fiscal variables that were unexpected—that is, implemented immediately—and shifts that were expected, that is, implemented in the same year but that had been legislated in previous years. Thus they assume that the two have identical effects on output growth (we shall discuss this choice carefully in the next chapter). This is not what was done by the Romers, who had added up unexpected and announced shifts in fiscal variables, thus assuming that economic agents react to a shift in taxes when they learn about it, whether its implementation is instantaneous or delayed. Guajardo et al. (2014) instead assume that a measure affects output growth only when it is implemented, while nothing happens at the time it is announced. To explain this difference, one might think about liquidity-constrained agents. The Romers' paper rules out liquidity constraints, assuming that consumers respond to life-time income (present and expected). The Guajardo et al. paper assumes that agents are all liquidity constrained and that consumption only responds to changes in current income.

Guajardo et al. (2014) estimate that a fiscal consolidation of 1% of GDP is contractionary, with a peak effect on the level of GDP of -0.6% after 2 years. This is only about one fifth of the effect estimated by the Romers for the United States, who only considered, however, tax measures. Guajardo et al. (2014) further find that tax-based adjustments are much more recessionary than spending-based ones, a result consistent with Alesina and Ardagna (2010)—although the rhetoric of their paper might suggest otherwise. In fact, Alesina and Ardagna (2013) compare the results obtained using cyclically adjusted and narrative data in the same empirical model—the one used by Guajardo et al. (2014); the differences in results are minor. The latter paper attributes the much smaller (negative) output effect of spending-based adjustments to the role of accompanying monetary policy, that is, to the difference in the response of interest rates to the two types of fiscal adjustment. Alesina and Ardagna (2013) instead find that the results do not qualitatively change if one controls for the response of monetary policy or for competitiveness indicators that try to capture the role of accompanying policies.

The narrative approach is not the only one used in the literature to measure multipliers. In Chapter 12 we describe other approaches and provide some comparative evaluations of their costs and benefits.

CONCLUSIONS

Disagreements among economists on the size and sometimes even the sign of fiscal multipliers persist. The early literature analyzing specific episodes of large deficit reduction policies suffered from the imperfect identification of truly exogenous shifts in fiscal variables, a critical requirement for estimating their effect on the economy. The narrative identification was a watershed in this respect. Both the early and more recent studies considered the effects of year-by-year shifts in taxes or spending. We address this issue in the following chapter, where we introduce our methodological innovation of fiscal plans.

CHAPTER FIVE

Fiscal Plans

INTRODUCTION

Austerity policies are typically not a 1-year, one-shot deal, but occur in multiyear plans, announced in advance and sometimes revised in mid course. When a legislature decides to launch a fiscal consolidation program, normally the first decision is by how much the deficit should be reduced; then, and often after much discussion, which taxes to increase or which expenditure items to cut. Thus, if the goal is to reduce the deficit by a certain amount, spending cuts and tax increases are not independent of each other because they must add up to a defined sum.

In Europe this process takes place in communication with the EU Commission. After a national government has approved a multiyear consolidation plan, with a certain deficit reduction target, and before it is sent to the legislature, the Commission is asked for an opinion about that target. Then a debate takes place in the national legislature and the budget proposal is often amended in a variety of ways, changing the relative contribution of tax hikes and expenditure cuts, under the constraint about the overall deficit reduction target. Eventually, a multiyear plan is voted by the legislature, and during its implementation, the plan is often revised.

The standard approach to evaluating fiscal policy, which consists of assessing the effects of year-by-year isolated shifts in taxes or spending independent from each other, overlooks two important points. One is the multiyear nature of fiscal adjustments, which affects the planning of consumers and investors. The other is the interdependence of the decisions about how much to cut spending and how much to raise taxes, which cannot be assumed to be independent of one another and thus studied in isolation.

In this chapter we first illustrate how we construct fiscal plans starting from raw data on taxes and spending. Next we explain how we use them to estimate fiscal multipliers.

CONSTRUCTING FISCAL PLANS

Consider a legislature that adopts a fiscal plan aimed at reducing the budget deficit. Let us call f the planned change in the primary budget deficit, that is, the budget deficit net of the expenditure for interest payments on the debt. We measure f as a percent of GDP, the latter measured the year before the plan is adopted: the level of GDP while a plan is implemented could reflect the effects of the plan and thus be endogenous. We adopt this procedure for all variables. Thus when we say that a variable increased by x percent (of GDP) we mean the GDP of the year before the start of the plan.

Suppose a new plan is decided on and implemented at the beginning of year t. The plan may include measures that go into effect immediately, that is, the same year the plan is approved by the legislature: we define these as "unexpected" changes in fiscal policy happening in year t. Clearly, even a measure announced and implemented immediately could have been anticipated based on the legislative discussions that preceded its adoption. However, until a measure is implemented, it is close to impossible to evaluate how the expectations of the public move because of these debates. Almost always the composition between tax increases and spending cuts is the result of last-minute political deals that are impossible to predict.

We denote unexpected policy changes e_t^u, where the suffix u stands for unexpected and e stands for the sum of spending cuts and tax increases, to be disentangled later. The plan voted by the legislature in year t may also contain measures to be adopted one or more years later, say in year $t + j$ ($j = 1, 2, 3...$): in other words, announcements of future shifts in taxes or spending. We call them $e_{t,t+j}^a$—that is, policies announced in year t for implementation in year $t+j$. Finally, once year $t+j$ arrives, and the measures announced are implemented, they show up in the national income data: we refer to them as $e_{t-j,t}^a$: policies that had been announced in year $t - j$ and are implemented in year t. Note that here we have replaced $t+j$ with t (and t with $t-j$) because now year $t+j$ has arrived.

f_t the overall (planned) correction to the primary budget deficit introduced by the legislature in year t, can thus be decomposed into the sum of three components $f_t = e_t^u + e_{t,t+j}^a + e_{t-j,t}^a$. Of course, not always will all three terms be different from zero in every year of the plan. For example, if a plan is new and nothing was happening before it, the last term would be zero. e_t^u can be different from zero only in a "new plan" starting in year t. Plans are often amended on the run. When this happens, that is, when a plan is modified either by changing previously announced measures or by introducing new measures, we label this as a "new plan," Thus a period of several years of austerity may consist of several concatenated plans. We could have followed a different convention, labeling the entire period a single plan, with several intervening modifications. With the first convention we would have more numerous and shorter plans; with the latter we would have fewer and longer plans. The choice of labeling is completely irrelevant for our empirical analysis, as will be clear later in the chapter.

Each term e consists of an increase in taxes, τ, and some cuts in expenditures, g. So, for example, in the case of unexpected measures, $e_t^u = \tau_t^u + g_t^u$: the term τ_t^u measures unexpected increases in taxes and g_t^u unexpected cuts in spending. Thus remember that a positive g means a cut, and a positive τ an increase. Of course it is possible that in a fiscal consolidation taxes are reduced and spending is cut even more, or vice versa, but this almost never happens in our data.

We assume that plans are fully credible, namely, that people believe that the legislature will not revoke the measures it has adopted by law. In the event a legislature, voting a new law, revokes or changes some measure that had been adopted through a previous law, we consider these changes to be unexpected. The assumption that plans are fully credible is strong but cannot be removed easily, or its validity tested; for a discussion see Lemoine and Lindé (2016) and Corsetti, Meier, and Müller (2012a).

Because decisions about taxes and spending need to add up to a certain level of deficit reduction, it would be wrong to view them as independent policy actions. If we estimated a model that measures the effect on output growth of shifts in taxes and spending, the coefficients on these two variables would reflect their correlation in the estimation sample, and multipliers based on a simulation carried out giving an impulse to one component of the primary deficit while holding the other constant would be incorrectly measured. We solve this problem by focusing on a distinction between *tax-based* (TB) and *expenditure-based* (EB) plans.

TABLE 5.1. The Portuguese Consolidation of 2010-4

Year	τ_t^u	$\tau_{t,t-j}^a$	$\tau_{t,t+1}^a$	$\tau_{t,t+2}^a$	$\tau_{t,t+3}^a$	g_t^u	$g_{t,t-j}^a$	$g_{t,t+1}^a$	$g_{t,t+2}^a$	$g_{t,t+3}^a$	TB	EB
2010	0.6	0	1.4	0	0	0.5	0	1.4	0	0	1	0
2011	0.5	1.4	1.1	0.4	0	0.6	1.4	2.9	1.4	0	0	1
2012	0.4	1.1	2.1	0	0	0.8	2.9	0.8	0	0	0	1
2013	0.4	2.1	−0.4	0	0	0.1	0.8	0	0	0	1	0
2014	0.5	−0.4	0.1	0	0	1.5	0	0	0	0	0	1

EB plans are fiscal corrections in which the dominant component is a cut in spending. TB plans instead rely mostly on tax hikes. As we will see in the data, very few plans are close to being half and half. In most cases the legislatures have adopted a decisive bend in one direction or the other. In any event, our results are robust to dropping cases that are close to being half and half. To compute the dominant component we add up all fiscal measures entering a plan. These two types of plans, TB and EB—unlike shifts in either taxes or spending—are mutually exclusive, since a plan is either TB or EB. Their effects thus can be simulated assuming that if one type of plan occurs, the other does not. Our results are robust to alternative methodologies, such as considering tax increases and expenditure cuts independently as we will show.

Tax increases are measured by the expected revenue effect of each change in the tax code, due to a change either in tax rates or in the tax base, as a percent of GDP the year before the tax change is introduced. Ideally one would want to distinguish between the two because they may have different economic effects, but classifying them in this way was above what was feasible despite years of data work that is illustrated in the next chapter. Spending cuts are changes in expenditure relative to the level that was expected without the change in policy as normally done. In almost all EB plans government spending did fall also relative to the years before the adjustment.

We illustrate how we construct a plan using the example of the fiscal consolidation implemented by Portugal between 2010 and 2014. Portugal announced a plan at the end of 2009. In 2010, budget measures reduced the deficit by 1.1% of GDP. These measures were unexpected according to our definition: 0.6% of 2009 GDP consisted of revenue increases (τ_{2010}^u in Table 5.1) and 0.5% of 2009 GDP of

spending cuts (g_{2010}^u). The 2010 budget also included two announcements: expenditure cuts amounting to 1.4% of GDP, and tax increases
also of 1.4% of GDP, both to be implemented in 2011 They are denoted
respectively as $\tau_{t,t+1}^a$ and $g_{t,t+1}^a$, where $t+1$ is 2011 since t is 2010.

In 2011 Portugal asked for financial assistance from the European
Union and the International Monetary Fund. As a condition for the
assistance, the two institutions demanded more austerity. Since the new
measures altered the plan adopted at the end of 2009, we label them as
part of a new plan. The measures announced in 2010 for implementation a year later did go through: you can see this in the 2011 row of the
table, in the columns that report the implementation of measures previously announced. For instance, the expenditure reductions, estimated to
be worth 1.4% of 2009 GDP, did happen in 2011 as had been announced
in the previous plan. The new plan agreed on with the EU and the IMF
introduced additional measures. Some went into effect immediately and
are thus classified as unexpected: 0.5% of 2010 GDP on the revenue side
and 0.6% on the spending side. There were also new announcements for
2012 and 2013 (1.1% and 0.4% of GDP respectively on the revenue side
and 2.9% and 1.4% percent of GDP in announced spending cuts).

In 2012 the plan was further reinforced, and thus according to our
labeling a new plan started, but once again the measures that had been
announced the year before were implemented: both the 1.1% of GDP
in additional revenues and the 2.9% in additional cuts. The announcements for 2013 were also changed. The government had announced, in
2011, tax increases worth 0.4% of GDP for 2013: these were increased
to 2.1% of GDP. For spending the announcement for 2013 was scaled
down from cuts worth 1.4% to 0.8% of GDP. We repeat this procedure
for the following years of the consolidation.

The last two columns of the table show the indicator variable classifying the plan as EB or TB. This classification is decided by taking into
account all measures known to agents in any given year, both unexpected measures and announcements. In this particular example it so
happens that the classification would be the same if one considered only
unexpected changes in taxes and spending. But this is not true in general. The nature of a fiscal consolidation, whether EB or TB, can change
over time: for instance, in the Portuguese case we are considering the
consolidation starts as TB and at some point, owing to the introduction

TABLE 5.2.   The Italian Consolidation of 1991–3

Year	τ_t^u	$\tau_{t,t-j}^a$	$\tau_{t,t+1}^a$	$\tau_{t,t+2}^a$	$\tau_{t,t+3}^a$	g_t^u	$g_{t,t-j}^a$	$g_{t,t+1}^a$	$g_{t,t+2}^a$	$g_{t,t+3}^a$	TB	EB
1991	1.7	0	−1.3	0	0	1.1	0	0	0	0	0	1
1992	2.9	−1.3	−1.2	0	0	1.9	0	0	0	0	0	1
1993	3.2	−1.2	−0.6	0	0	3.1	0	0	0	0	0	1

of new spending cuts, turns into EB. We code the various plans using two variables, EB and TB, that take a value of 1 when the relevant adjustment is implemented, and 0 otherwise.

Table 5.2 illustrates a second example: the Italian fiscal consolidation of 1991–3. The consolidation started with a plan voted in the Italian parliament in December 1990. This plan went into effect at the beginning of 1991. In this year consolidation measures amounted to 2.8% of GDP, with tax hikes worth 1.7% of GDP and spending cuts 1.1% of GDP. This is shown in the row of Table 5.2 corresponding to the year 1991. The plan introduced in 1991 was subsequently modified twice, in 1992 and in 1993, with the introduction of further unexpected tax hikes worth 2.9% and 3.2% of GDP respectively, and additional unexpected spending cuts worth 1.9% and 3.1% of GDP.

In its 1992 "Recent Economic Developments—Italy" document (p. 21), the IMF observes that *some of the tax measures introduced in 1991 – worth 19.4 trillion Lira, equivalent to 1.3% of GDP – were of a one-off nature.* Italy is indeed a country that often implemented temporary fiscal measures, in the sense that increases in revenue were accompanied by the announcement that they would vanish, at least in part, a year or two later. These measures were typically temporary tax amnesties. For instance, in 1991 the unexpected tax hike was worth 1.7% of GDP but included an amnesty estimated to produce 1.3% of GDP. It was also announced that the amnesty would expire a year later. We record this announcement as a negative entry (which means a tax reduction) in the fourth column of Table 5.2. Note that in 1992 the amnesty really did expire, thus producing a decline in revenue, relative to 1991, worth 1.3% of GDP. Something similar happened in 1992.

Different consolidation plans feature different correlations between measures announced for future years and measures implemented immediately. Some countries tend to adopt front-loaded plans in the sense that future announced measures reinforce those implemented at the start of an adjustment plan. Other countries start a plan but announce that some measures will be delayed and others will, at least in part, be reversed in the future. If the style of a country is such that the introduction of unexpected measures is typically accompanied by the announcement that more measures will be implemented in the future, then one should not simulate the effects of an unexpected measure assuming that it is not accompanied by announcements about future actions. Doing so would not reflect the way that fiscal policy is implemented in that particular country, nor the data used in estimation.

To take these intertemporal correlations into account one must estimate the parameter φ in the regression $e_{t,t+j}^{a} = \varphi e_t^u + v_j$ that relates announcements to unexpected shifts in fiscal variables. Then, when simulating the effects of an unexpected measure e_t^u, one can accompany this unexpected measure with an "artificial" announcement constructed using the estimated value of φ.

MEASURING THE EFFECTS OF FISCAL PLANS

Having reconstructed fiscal plans, the next step involves estimating their effects on the economy. We proceed in two steps. First, we estimate the parameters of an empirical model that relates macroeconomic variables, such as the growth rate of output or consumption to shifts in taxes or spending. These variables are regressed on the three components of a fiscal plan: the unexpected change in the primary budget deficit; the implementation, each year, of fiscal measures decided in previous years; and announcements of future changes in the primary deficit. Each element of the change in the primary deficit (unexpected, announced, and previously decided) is interacted with an indicator variable, EB or TB, that defines the type of plan in which the change occurs. The next step is the estimation of the correlation between announced and unexpected changes in fiscal variables, that is the parameters φ.

Our empirical model thus contains two blocs: the first is used to estimate the effects of shifts in taxes and spending on macroeconomic variables; the second is used to estimate the correlation between announced and unexpected measures. We could assume that each country has its own style, as reflected in the correlation between announcements and measures immediately implemented or assume that styles depend on the type of plan implemented: for example, TB plans could be front loaded while expenditure based plans rely more on announcements. Our data do not allow us to do both. We choose to allow styles to differ across types of plans.

We use this model to simulate the effect of an EB or TB plan that reduces the primary deficit by 1% of GDP. From these simulations, we construct measures of fiscal multipliers. We do this by simulating the model under two scenarios: a baseline that assumes that the government sticks to the fiscal rule implicit in the estimated model and does not deviate from it; and an alternative simulation that instead assumes that the government implements an adjustment plan. The difference between the two paths measures the dynamic effects on the economy of the introduction of a fiscal plan. Details can be found in Chapter 12.

Monetary or other policies may also react to the introduction of a fiscal plan. If this happens, the overall effect on output growth (or other macro variables) of a shift in taxes or spending will result from a combination of the direct effect, working through the response of consumers and firms, and the indirect effect going through the response of other policies. Decomposing the overall effect into its two components requires a model in which fiscal policy and, for example, monetary policy, are jointly determined. The availability of data will constrain the size of the model and therefore the number of macro variables and policies that we will be able to analyze. We will discuss in Chapter 7 how we deal with these issues.

We use a panel regression, as we do not have a sufficient number of plans for each country.[1] Thus all estimated coefficients in this panel are constrained to be identical across countries, except of course for the presence of country fixed effects, that is, a different constant in the regression for every country. Such a constant allows us to control for any permanent difference between countries affecting the left-hand-side variable of the regression, say GDP growth. The only element that varies across countries is the type of plan, TB or EB. We shall also show some results which allow the φ's to be country specific.

CONCLUSIONS

Our crucial departure from the earlier literature is our use of multi-year plans to study the effects of fiscal policy, as austerity measures are typically implemented through multiyear policy packages, with some policies implemented immediately and others announced for implementation in the future. Some announcements are implemented exactly, other revised. These announcements affect expectations and therefore the current behavior of consumers and firms. Some plans are front-loaded, with measures being immediately implemented, some delay most measures to later in the plan or announce that current measures will later be reversed. Our estimation procedure allows us to take all of these complexities into account.

Our procedure recognizes that plans are generally constructed in sequence. That is, first a decision is taken about the overall size of the fiscal correction. Then the legislature decides how much of that predetermined deficit reduction should come from tax increases and how much from spending cuts, thus generating a correlation between changes in taxes and changes in spending. This is the reason why we analyze the effects of tax based plans and spending based plans rather than those of changes in taxes and spending. TB and EB plans, unlike shifts in either taxes or spending, are mutually exclusive: their effects can thus be simulated assuming that if one type of plan occurs, the other does not.

CHAPTER SIX

The Data

INTRODUCTION: A BROAD LOOK AT OUR DATA

Our annual data are for 16 countries belonging to the OECD and cover the fiscal consolidations they implemented between 1981 and 2014. Figure 6.1 shows the average size of the overall fiscal consolidation effort in our 30-year sample and its distribution across time. This figure is limited to Europe and the United States, and for Europe it plots the average consolidation implemented by the European countries in our sample. For every year reported in the figure, we show the average consolidation measures implemented in that year, which are the sum of unexpected measures and measures that had been announced in previous years but implemented in the current year: in other words, announcements are not included in the data used to build this figure. It is also constructed using only exogenous fiscal measures identified with the narrative approach, that is, measures that were not motivated by the state of the economy.

In both Europe and the United States, fiscal consolidations were concentrated in specific periods. In Europe, the first wave happened in the mid-1980s, when countries with large public debts responded to rising real rates. The United States postponed fiscal adjustment by about a decade when the Omnibus Budget Reconciliation Acts (OBRAs) of 1990 and 1993 were introduced. Large adjustments were further implemented in Europe in the 1990s to meet the criteria required to join the monetary union and in response to the 1992–3 currency crises. Fiscal action was mild in Europe in the early 2000s and nonexistent in the United States. Large exogenous fiscal measures were introduced by most European countries during the 2010–3 European debt crisis, a period of GDP contraction. A peak average adjustment of almost 2% of GDP was reached in 2012; consolidation measures have been declining since then. The United States also implemented a large consolidation during the recovery from the Great Recession of 2007–9.

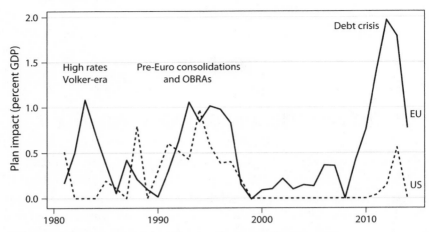

Figure 6.1. Fiscal consolidations in Europe and the United States 1980–2014

For the 16 countries in our sample we have reconstructed a total of 184 austerity plans. Our convention is that whenever a plan is amended we relabel it as new plan. Thus, for example, a 5-year period of austerity in a country that includes an unexpected change in some fiscal variable after 3 years would result in assigning to this 5-year period two austerity plans.

About two thirds of the plans in our sample are expenditure based (EB) and one-third are tax based (TB). Table 6.1. documents the composition of fiscal plans showing the share of their main component, which determines the nature of the plan. As reported in the first column of Table 6.1, in about one half of TB plans taxes account for 75% or more of the total adjustment; the same proportion holds for EB plans. Thus, in most cases a plan is clearly either expenditure-based or tax-based. In rare cases plans have a marginally dominant component (e.g. if the spending share of EB plans or the tax share of TB plans is less than 55%), as shown in the last column of Table 6.1. All our results are robust to dropping these marginal cases.

For our empirics we have used only 170 of these 184 plans because for some of our 16 countries the macro data are not available for the entire sample over which plans were constructed: one example is Germany before unification. We thus consider 170 plans and 216 years of austerity, because a single plan typically extends over more than 1 year, even

TABLE 6.1. Types of plans

| Type of Plan | Share of Main Component | | | |
	≥ 0.75	< 0.75	< 0.65	< 0.55
TB (57 plans)	34	30	19	9
EB (113 plans)	59	61	34	7
Total Plans: 184		*Total Episodes: 234*		

TABLE 6.2. Summary of plans by country

Country	TB	EB	Country	TB	EB
AUS	3	4	FRA	3	7
AUT	1	3	GBR	4	6
BEL	4	11	IRL	6	8
CAN	3	16	ITA	6	12
DEU	3	6	JPN	3	5
DNK	3	5	PRT	4	7
ESP	8	7	SWE	0	5
FIN	2	7	USA	4	4
Total TB:	57		Total EB:	113	

with the convention described earlier. We refer to each year of fiscal adjustment as an "episode" thus a plan includes more than one episode of fiscal adjustment. Table 6.2 documents the characteristics of the plans across countries.

Table 6.3 shows the length of the various plans (in years) and their size, measured by the overall correction to the primary budget as a fraction of GDP: we compute the overall correction adding up unexpected measures and announcements. Plans, whose length is computed at the time of announcement and regardless of subsequent amendments, last on average between 2 and 3 years. This means that if a plan is adopted at the end of year $t-1$, it includes unexpected measures to be implemented right away, that is, in year t, and measures announced for implementation in the years $t+1$ and $t+2$. Sixty-seven plans last 3 or more years, confirming that announcements are relatively frequent. EB plans tend to last a bit longer than TB ones, probably because expenditure cuts, changes in social security legislation in particular, take longer to be

TABLE 6.3. Size and length of plans

Type of Plan	Horizon of plans in years							Size of plans (% GDP)		
	1	2	3	4	5	6	Average	Total	Spending	Taxes
TB	16	20	6	7	7	1	2.51	1.60	0.49	1.10
EB	26	41	7	14	9	16	2.88	1.94	1.46	0.48
All plans	42	61	13	21	16	17	2.76	1.83	1.14	0.69

implemented than tax changes. The last three columns of Table 6.3 document the size of fiscal adjustments. The average dimension of the plans in our sample—meaning the overall correction of the primary deficit over the entire life of a plan—is 1.83% of GDP; EB plans are slightly larger than TB ones.

For most countries we define "government" as "general government." This includes both the central state administration and all levels of local government. For the three federal countries in the sample (Canada, Australia, and the United States) the data refer only to the central government (e.g. the federal government for the United States).

We build exogenous shifts in taxes and spending taking as a starting point the narrative identification procedure introduced by Romer and Romer (2010) and adopted by Devries et al. (2011). Using this approach Romer and Romer identify (for the period from 1947 to 2007) episodes of changes in US tax rates that were not dictated by the state of the economy, but instead were either "long-run growth driven," that is, motivated by the aim of improving growth, or "deficit driven," that is, motivated by the aim of reducing an inherited deficit. Figure 6.2 shows that the deficit-driven tax changes identified by Romer and Romer are all positive, tax increases, while almost all the tax changes motivated by concerns for long-run growth are negative, tax cuts.

Devries et al. used the Romer and Romer methodology to construct a time series of shifts in fiscal variables (in this case both taxes and spending) for 17 OECD countries over the period 1978–2009, concentrating exclusively on fiscal consolidations. In the rare cases in which long-run growth-driven and deficit-driven adjustments happen simultaneously, a period is considered to be an adjustment period only if the deficit-driven adjustment is larger than the long-run growth-

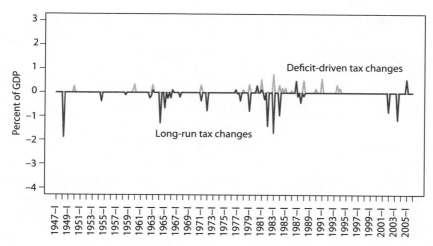

Figure 6.2. Long-run and deficit-driven tax changes (Romer and Romer, 2010)

driven adjustment. For instance, the deficit-driven adjustment implemented in the United States in 1983–4 is dropped from the sample because it was smaller than the contemporaneous long-run growth-driven adjustment.

The historical documents consulted by Devries et al. include Budget Reports and Speeches, Central Bank Reports, Stability and Convergence Programmes submitted by EU governments to the European Commission, IMF Reports, and OECD Economic Surveys. They also relied on country-specific documents, for example, various reports by the Congressional Budget Office and the Economic Reports of the President for the United States; the Journal officiel de la République française for France; etc.

We extend the Devries et al. data in several dimensions. We first extended the sample period, adding the years between 2010 and 2014. Second, we collected additional information on every fiscal measure included in the Devries et al. dataset. This was necessary in order to reconstruct fiscal plans, because given the multiyear nature of plans, we needed to separate unexpected measures from announcements of measures to be implemented in the future, and then to keep track of their implementation when it actually happens. This disaggregation was not in the original Devries et al. data file. Third, we divided government spending separating transfers from other spending, and splitting taxes into direct and indirect ones. While doing this, we double checked the Devries et al. classifications and introduced some modifications, correcting a few errors. These corrections are noted and explained in our online appendix; a link to this is available at `https://press.princeton.edu/titles/13244.html`. This data work was demanding: overall, we analyzed about 3,500 different fiscal measures. Our procedure is described in the online appendix.

In the rest of this chapter we describe in some detail the construction of our data. This information is very useful for anyone who might want to use these data or improve upon our classifications or judgment calls.

THE DATA IN MORE DETAIL

We dropped the Netherlands from our sample, thus reducing it to 16 countries, because fiscal rules in the Netherlands are such that the targets set by the government can be automatically changed ex post depending on the cycle: they are thus not exogenous by our definition. The 16 remaining countries are Australia, Austria, Belgium, Canada, Denmark, Finland, France, Germany, Ireland, Italy, Japan, Portugal, Spain, Sweden, the United Kingdom, and the United States. Each measure is recorded in the year in which it is adopted, if officially voted into law by the legislature before September 30. Measures adopted later in the year are attributed to the following year. For each measure, we collected information on the expected budgetary impact for the current year and for each of the five subsequent years, using the sources listed in the next section. As budget planning is made with regards to the fiscal year, not the calendar year, we followed this rule: if the fiscal and the calendar year do not coincide we split the amount of the fiscal measure among the different calendar years in relative proportion. For example, in Japan the fiscal year starts in April. Thus if a measure was announced for year t, it is split in the following way: 3/4 of the measure is assigned to year t and 1/4 to year $t + 1$.

Sources and Selection of Fiscal Measures
Sources

Our sources vary depending on the country and the period. For members of the European Union the main sources were the Stability and Convergence Programmes and their updates. Additional information came from the National Reform Programmes. For the most recent years in our sample these documents are publicly available on the website of the European Commission.[1] For earlier years, and for non-EU countries, we relied on the sources used by Devries et al.: OECD "Economic Surveys" and IMF documents such as the "IMF Recent Economic Developments" and the "IMF Article IV Staff Reports." In many cases, we also used national budget documents (usually "Budget plans"). If the information in these documents was not clear or was incomplete, we checked the Bulletins issued by the national central bank (this was the case in particular for Finland, France, Italy, and Portugal). When special fiscal packages were launched, we also checked additional documents that were made available, for example, in the case of the Canadian adjustment of 1988. According to Devries et al. the Canadian reform program started in 1987. However, an official document, "White Paper on Tax Reform," published in 1987, reports that the budgetary impact of the reform began in 1988. So we decided not to include 1987 among the years affected by these measures. Tables 6.4 and 6.5 list, country by country, the documents we used as sources.

Selecting Exogenous Measures

We looked for clear sentences in the source documents that attributed measures either to the aim of correcting the dynamics of some budgetary item (such as pension reforms aimed at reducing outlays), or to the aim of addressing the dynamics of the debt over GDP ratio, or the deficit. Because measures often are bundled into a package, we looked for the motivation behind an entire package of measures.

For instance, we decided that the consolidation launched in Finland in 2010 was not motivated by the state of the economy because it is described, in the Stability and Convergence Programme, as a response to the deteriorating long-run sustainability of public finances:

TABLE 6.4. Documents used as sources for each country

Country	Source	Country	Source
IRL	IMF Recent Economic Developments OECD Economic Surveys Supplementary Budget Budget	USA	Treasury Annual Report Social Security Bulletin Budget Romer and Romer (2009)
ITA	Banca d'Italia, Assemblea Generale dei Partecipanti 1991, p. 137 July Emergency Budget		CBO - Update to the Budget and Economic Outlook CBO - Projecting Federal Tax Revenues and the Effect of Changes in tax Law
	Law text IMF Recent Economic Developments 1992, p. 22 OECD Economic Surveys Bollettino Economico di Banca d'Italia Stability Program Update Decree-Law text Documento Economia e Finanza		CBO - The Budget Agreement: An Interim Assessment CBO – An Economic Analysis of the Revenue Provisions of OBRA-93 CBO – Economic and Budget Outlook CBO cost estimate of the budget control act CBO estimates of the American Taxpayer Relief Act
		DEU	IMF Recent Economic Developments IMF Economic Developments and Issues
JPN	IMF; Recent Economic Developments		IMF Staff Report Bundesministerium der Finanzen: Zusammenstellung der Steuerrechtsäderungen seit 1964
	OECD Economic Surveys IMF Staff Reports		OECD Economic Surveys
PRT	OECD Economic Surveys Stability and Growth Programme Banco de Portugal Annual Report IMF Staff Reports Economic Adjustment Program Council Reccomendation on Portugal National Reform Programme Assessment of the national reform programme and stability programme for Portugal Fiscal Consolidation Adjustment Programme	FRA	DIW Berlin, Wochenbericht Financial Stability Programme OECD Economic Surveys IMF Recent Economic Developments Les Echos Le Monde Banque de France, Rapport Annuel
			IMF Staff Report
ESP	IMF Recent Economic Developments OECD Economic Surveys Stability Programme Update Government Budget Medidas Gasto		Rapport social, economique et financier Stability programme Budget supplementaire; Project de loi de finances rectificative Assessment of the national reform programme and stability programme Loi de finances rectificative
GBR	IMF Staff Reports Financial Statement and Budget Report IMF Recent Economic Developments Spending Review Autumn Statement	DNK	IMF Recent Economic Developments OECD Economic Surveys The Danish Budget Quarterly Review Assessment of the 2011 Denmark national reform programme

TABLE 6.5. Documents Used as Sources for Each Country.

Country	Source
AUT	IMF Recent Economic Developments
	OECD Economic Survey
	IMF Staff Reports
	Austrian Stability Programme Update
AUS	IMF Recent Economic Developments
	IMF Staff Reports
	OECD Economic Survey
	Budget
BEL	IMF Recent Economic Developments
	OECD Economic Surveys
	Analysis of the Update of the Stability Programme
	Stability Programme
CAN	Budget
	Expenditure and Programme Review
	The White Paper on Tax Reform
FIN	Bank of Finland Bulletin
	OECD Economic Survey
	IMF Selected Background Issues and Statistical Appendix
	IMF Recent Economic Developments
	Stability Programme
	National Reform Programme
	Decision on spending limits
SWE	Devries et al. (2011)
	IMF Recent Economic Developments
	OECD Economic Survey
	Budget

"General government finances are in a more vulnerable position from which to meet expenditure pressures and the narrowing of the tax base arising from population ageing. Restoring general government finances in Finland will be a particularly challenging task, because the baby boomers are now reaching retirement age."(Stability Program 2011). In Canada in 1995 the government used these words to explain the urgency of reducing the deficit: "Debt and deficits are not inventions of ideology. They are facts of arithmetic. The quicksand of compound interest is real. The last thing Canadians need is another lecture on the dangers of the deficit. The only thing Canadians want is clear action" (1995 Budget Speech by the Minister of Finance).

A few plans include both deficit increasing and deficit reducing policies. To handle these cases, we first verified that the total amount of exogenous deficit increasing measures was smaller than the total of the deficit reducing measures. In doing this we consider all deficit increasing measures, both exogenous and endogenous, to avoid the possibility of labeling as a period of adjustment one in which the exogenous fiscal contractions was more than compensated by other expansionary fiscal measures independently of their motivation. If expansionary measures dominate then the episode is considered as a fiscal expansion and is dropped. If instead the sum of (the budgetary impact) of all expansionary measures (endogenous and exogenous) was smaller than the impact of all exogenous contractionary measures, then we classify it as an exogenous fiscal consolidation. In this case, the size of the contraction is computed as the difference between the size of the exogenous contractionary measures minus the exogenous expansionary measures. This explains why for some years we have recorded measures that were deficit increasing: the reason is that, in previous years, there had been contractionary announcements large enough to overcome the new expansionary measures introduced during the year considered. These cases, however, are very rare.[2] Finally, we also recorded fiscal contractions even if they were announced during a fiscal expansion, according to the following criterion: a subsequent consolidation occurs by the time of their implementation. We consider the impact of these announcements only in the years of consolidation. The US episode of 1983[3] helps understand this classification.

Classification

Categories and aggregation

We identified 27 categories of fiscal measures. The last two columns of Table 6.6 show the label we used for each category and describe some of the measures each category contains. For example, we used the label PIDT, "Personal Income Direct Taxes," for changes in direct taxation on individuals (fifth row). We then aggregated the 27 categories into 15 components, listed in the third column of Table 6.6. Every component contains all of the categories associated with similar areas of fiscal intervention. Thus "Personal Income Direct Taxes" (PIDT) is contained in "Personal Income Tax," which also includes the category "Tax Credit and Deductions—Private" (TCDPT).

TABLE 6.6. Components and Categories

2 Components	8 Components	15 Components	Category	Description
Tax	Indirect	Goods and Services	INDT	Indirect Taxes
			TCDIND	Tax Credits and Deductions—Indirect
		n.c. CvsP	NCPC	Not Classified Corporate vs Private (Direct Taxes)
			TCDNC	Tax Credits and Deductions—n.c. Corporate vs Private
	Direct	Personal Income Tax	PIDT	Personal Income Direct Taxes
			TCDPT	Tax Credits and Deductions—Private
		Property Tax Corporate	PROPCP	Property Taxes—Corporate
		Property Tax n.c.	PROPNC	Property Taxes—n.c. Corporate vs Private
		Property Tax Private	PROPPT	Property Taxes—Private
		Corporate Tax	CDT	Corporate Direct Taxes
			TCDCP	Tax Credits and Deductions—Corporate
	Other Tax	Other Tax	OTHTX	Other Taxes
	n.c. Tax	n.c. Tax	NCTX	Not Classified Taxes
Spending	Cons&Inv	Salaries	SAL	Salaries
		Investment	INV	Investment
		Consumption	CONS	Consumption
	Transfers	Transfers	PENS	Pensions
			FIRSUB	Firm Subsidies
			FCPO	Family and Children Policies
			RD	Research&Development and Firm
			UNEM	Unemployment
			HLT	Health Related
			OTHSS	Other Social Security
			EDU	Education
			OTSUB	Other Subsidies
	Other Spending	Other Spending	OTHEX	Other Spending
	n.c. Spending	n.c. Spending	NCEX	Not Classified Spending

As an example, Table 6.7 presents a sample of the list of measures we obtained for Australia in the years 1993–6.[4] The first two columns and the last column report, respectively, the label of the country, the year, and the source used to identify each measure. Note that every row corresponds to a different measure; hence the years may be repeated across rows if there is more than one measure in the same year. The third and fourth columns instead contain the category and the component under which we have classified the measure. The fifth column briefly describes the measure. For example, the first row of the table reads as follows: using the Budget for 1993/94 and the 1994 OECD Economic Survey (p. 41) we have recorded for Australia in 1993 a measure consisting of a deferral of personal income tax cuts. We classified it into the category Personal Income Direct Taxes (PIDT), a part of the Personal Income Tax component.

The next aggregation step reduces the number of components from 15 to 8. The second column of Table 6.6 lists these eight components: *Indirect, Direct, Other Tax, n.c. Tax* on the taxation side (n.c. meaning *not classified*. These are measures for which the information we found was insufficient, except for the size and timing, to classify them into components) and *Consumption & Investment, Transfers, Other Spending, n.c. Spending* on the expenditure side. The final aggregation step, reported in the first column of Table 6.6, distinguishes between the two components of *Tax* and *Spending*. Proceeding with our initial example, "Personal Income Direct Taxes" (PIDT) is contained in "Personal Income Tax." This belongs to the *Direct* component which also includes "n.c. CvsP (Corporate vs Private)," "Property Tax Corporate," "Property Tax n.c.," "Property Tax Private," "Corporate Tax" and is, in turn, part of *Tax*.

Table 6.8 reports the classification we used for our final dataset, *New_Components1978-2014_final.xlsx* available in the online appendix. In Table 6.9, we show the measures from Table 6.7 aggregated in the 15-components classification.

Different aggregation schemes are possible. For example, we might be interested in distinguishing between taxation on individuals versus firms: this can be done easily, starting from our 15-components classification, and adding up "Personal Income Tax" and "Property Tax Private" to get "Taxes—Personal" and "Corporate Tax" and "Property Tax Corporate," thus obtaining "Taxes—Corporate."

TABLE 6.7. A Sample from the List of Exogenous Measures: Australia, 1993–96

Country	Year	Category	Component	Description	t	$t+1$	$t+2$	$t+3$	$t+4$	$t+5$	Source
AUS	1993	PIDT	Personal Income Tax	Deferral of personal income tax cuts decided in the 1993–94 Budget	0	0.6	0.6	0	0	0	Budget 1993/94. OECD Economic Surveys 1994 (p. 41)
AUS	1993	INDT	Goods and Services	Indirect Taxes: excise duties on petroleum products and tobacco and a 1 percentage point increase in wholesale sales tax for most goods in the base	0	0.55	0.55	0	0	0	Budget 1993/94, OECD Economic Surveys 1994 (p. 41)
AUS	1995	CDT	Corporate Tax	Increase in the company tax rate from 33% to 36%	1.185	1.185	0	0	0	0	Budget 1995/96, IMF Recent Economic Developments 1996 (p. 20)
AUS	1995	NCTX	n.c. Tax	Second round of wholesale sales tax increases and the bringing forward of company tax payments	1.185	1.185	0	0	0	0	Budget 1995/96, IMF Recent Economic Developments 1996 (p. 20)
AUS	1996	HLT	Transfers	Private health insurance incentive	−0.003	−0.2445	−0.244	−0.0025	0	0	Budget 1996/97, OECD Economic Surveys 1997 (p. 59)
AUS	1996	TCDPT	Personal Income Tax	Family tax initiative	−0.124	−0.2415	−0.118	−0.0005	0	0	Budget 1996/97, OECD Economic Surveys 1997 (p. 59)

TABLE 6.8. Different Aggregation Scheme

New_Components1978–2014_final.xlsx aggregation	Components
Taxes—Income	Corporate Tax Personal Income Tax n.c. CvsP
Taxes—Property	Property Tax Private Property Tax Corporate Property Tax n.c.
Taxes—Personal	Personal Income Tax Property Tax Private
Taxes—Corporate	Corporate Tax Property Tax Corporate
Taxes—Goods and Services	Goods and Services
Taxes—n.c. PvsC	n.c. Tax Property Tax n.c. n.c. CvsP
Taxes—n.c.	n.c. Tax
Taxes—Other	Other Tax

(Taxes)

TABLE 6.9. Australia 1993–96 Measures Aggregated in Components for Each Year

Country	Year	Component	t	t + 1	t + 2	t + 3	t + 4	t + 5
AUS	1993	Personal Income Tax	0	0.6	0.6	0	0	0
AUS	1993	Goods and Services	0	0.55	0.55	0	0	0
AUS	1995	Corporate Tax	1.185	1.185	0	0	0	0
AUS	1995	n.c. Tax	1.185	1.185	0	0	0	0
AUS	1996	Transfers	−0.003	−0.245	−0.244	−0.003	0	0
AUS	1996	Personal Income Tax	−0.124	−0.242	−0.118	−0.001	0	0

Similarly, we can construct "Taxes—Income" and "Taxes—Properties." All these different aggregation decisions can be easily and automatically implemented using the Excel files available by clicking the link at https://press.princeton.edu/titles/13244.html.

Not classified (n.c.)

We label three types of measures as *not classified,* which is different from our "*other*" category. The *other* category includes measures that could not possibly belong to any of the remaining specific categories, while the "*not classified*" category includes measures that do belong to some of the specific categories but that we find impossible to credibly and consistently split among those.

For example, the Australian government announced a tax hike of nearly 0.5% of GDP in 1995. Because the Australian fiscal year starts in July, we split the amount of this measure into two components of equal size: an unexpected one (for the current year) and an announced one for the following year. The tax hike itself consisted of two measures: an increase in the corporate tax rate and a second round of wholesale tax increases, along with bringing forward company tax payments. We classified the increase in the corporate tax rate as a direct tax, but the second measure as not classified because its description does not permit us to distinguish between the direct and indirect tax components, nor to properly assign it to the personal or the corporate tax category.

In very few cases, however, we did exercise discretion and classified several ambiguous measures without resorting to the *not classified (n.c.)* labeling. This decision was driven entirely by the need to resolve uncertainty regarding the classification of the fiscal plans into one of four categories: Transfer based (*TRB*), Consumption based (*CB*), Direct tax based (DB), and Indirect tax based (*IB*), the finest classification we have used. These cases, however, are extremely rare. Whenever labeling a plan depends on the assignment of the *not classified* measures, we undertook the following procedure. First, we tried to uncover a credible assignment rule from the official documents describing the fiscal plans. If it was impossible to retrieve such information from the official documents, then we analyzed that country's TRB, CB, DB, or IB plan composition and maintained that structure in splitting the *not classified (n.c.)* measures.

All cases of classification of measures that were initially labeled *n.c.* are presented in Table 6.10.

This table should be read in the following way. If it was possible to split the measured amount on the basis of the description of the consolidation measure in the official documentation, then there is a "YES" in the fourth column of the table. Otherwise, a "NO" indicates that we need the composition of the country's typical plan.

TABLE 6.10. N.C. Resolution Cases

Country	Year	Assignment	Assignment based on the documentation	Dominant type
BEL	1983	Consumption: 1/3, Transfers: 2/3	NO	TRB
BEL	1992	Transfers: 1/3, Consumption: 2/3	YES	–
BEL	1996	Indirect Tax: 1/3, Direct Tax: 2/3	NO	DB
DEU	1997	Salaries: 1/2, Transfers: 1/2	YES	–
DEU	1999	Salaries: 1/3, Transfers: 1/3, Direct Tax: 1/3	YES	–
DNK	1983	Salaries: 1/3, Transfers: 2/3	YES	–
DNK	1984	Salaries: 1/2, Transfers: 1/2	YES	–
DNK	2009	Indirect Tax: 1/3, Direct Tax: 2/3	NO	DB
ESP	1984	Transfers: 1/3, Consumption: 2/3	NO	CB
PRT	1983	Indirect Tax: 1/3, Direct Tax: 2/3	NO	DB

Using Individual Measures to Construct Plans

For each of the 15 fiscal components we classified, we computed, for each year, seven different quantities: e_t is the amount of that component introduced and implemented in year t; $e_{t,t-1}$ is the amount of that component implemented in year t but that had been previously announced (we collapse all previous announcements in year $t - 1$ because, for example, announcements in year $t - 2$ are carried over to year $t - 1$); $e_{t,t+j}$ $(j = 1, \ldots, 5)$ are the five amounts of that component expected to be implemented j years later, according to contemporaneous or previous announcements. Returning to our example of Australia reported in Table 6.9, consider the component "Personal Income Tax," which occurs twice. In 1993, it includes announcements of an increase of 0.6 A\$ bn for the years 1994 and 1995, but in 1996 it includes a reduction of 0.124 A\$ bn, immediately implemented and announcements of further reductions: of 0.242 A\$ bn in 1997, 0.118 A\$ bn in 1998 and of 0.001 A\$ bn in 1999. Now we compute e_t for each year over the period 1993–6 for the component "Personal Income Tax." In 1993, $e_t = 0$ because there is no immediate change in the component that year. In 1994 and 1995 it is the same, because the component does not appear in our records for those years. In 1996, $e_t = -0.124$ A\$ bn: we see in Table 6.9 that an unexpected change (column t) is associated with the component

Personal Income Tax in that year. Next we compute $e_{t,t-1}$ assuming that no announcements were made before 1993. In 1993 $e_{t,t-1} = 0$ because no announcements had been made. In 1994 $e_{t,t-1} = 0.6$ A\$ bn because in 1993 it had been announced that the component would increase the following year (column $t + 1$ of the first entry in Table 6.9). In 1995 $e_{t,t-1} = 0.6$ A\$ bn again because in 1993 it had been announed that the component "Personal Income Tax" would increase 2 years later (column $t + 2$ of the first entry in Table 6.9). In 1996 $e_{t,t-1} = 0$ because no announcements for that component were made to be implemented in that year. Following the same logic we can compute $e_{t,t+1}$ and $e_{t,t+2}$. In 1993 there were two announcements: of an increase of 0.6 A\$ bn 1 year later and of another increase, again of 0.6 A\$ bn, 2 years later. In the row for 1994 we find them in the columns $e_{t,t-1}$ and $e_{t,t+1}$: the first because the measure announced in 1993 for implementation a year later is indeed implemented; the second because the announcement for 1995 is confirmed. In 1995 no new announcements were made concerning a change in "Personal Income Tax" the following year, nor were any previously announced measures expected to be implemented in 1996: as a result $e_{t,t+1} = 0$ for 1995. In 1996, a new announcement of -0.242 A\$ bn to be implemented in 1997 was made, and no previous announcements were recorded: as a result $e_{t,t+1} = -0.242$ A\$ bn in 1996. Table 6.11 shows the results of this exercise for all seven variables of the component "Personal Income Tax," assuming that nothing else happens after 1997.

Finally, we aggregated all measures in the eight components shown in Table 6.6.

TABLE 6.11. Planned Changes for "Private Income Tax" from 1993 to 1999

AUS	e_t	$e_{t,t-1}$	e_{t+1}	e_{t+2}	e_{t+3}	e_{t+4}	e_{t+5}
			Personal Income Tax				
1993	0.000	0.000	0.600	0.600	0.000	0.000	0.000
1994	0.000	0.600	0.600	0.000	0.000	0.000	0.000
1995	0.000	0.600	0.000	0.000	0.000	0.000	0.000
1996	-0.124	0.000	-0.242	-0.118	-0.001	0.000	0.000
1997	0.000	-0.242	-0.118	-0.001	0.000	0.000	0.000
1998	0.000	-0.118	-0.001	0.000	0.000	0.000	0.000
1999	0.000	-0.001	0.000	0.000	0.000	0.000	0.000

Four Different Types of Plans

Exogenous expected and announced measures are aggregated into plans as shown in the document *NewComponents1978–2014_final.xlsx* (to be found in the online appendix). We adopted several approaches. The basic distinction is made between EB (expenditure-based) and TB (tax-based) plans, as mentioned in Chapter 5. However, we also constructed a more detailed classification distinguishing among either three components (plans mostly based on taxes, on consumption and investment, or on transfers), or four components, further distinguishing between direct and indirect taxes.

The rule we followed to classify a plan as EB or TB is the following: if the sum of unexpected and announced measures (in the Excel file *NewComponents1978-2014_final.xlsx* this corresponds to summing up the measures along one row of the database) is equal to zero, then both the EB and TB dummies are set equal to zero. In the opposite case, the choice of the classification depends on whether there was a new fiscal plan introduced in a given year. If no new plan was introduced, then the episode classification remains the same as in the previous year. If a new plan was announced, the episode classification depends on the sum of announced and unexpected measures: if the sum of tax measures outweighs the sum of spending measures, then the episode is labeled as TB, and vice versa.

When we adopt a finer classification, the crucial difference lies in the choice of the decision structure: hierarchical versus nonhierarchical. The hierarchical classification first classifies a plan as EB or TB and then decides on the subcategory (CB/TRB or *DB/IB*). The nonhierchical classification instead directly assigns the fiscal episode to one of the four (or three) components depending on which is dominant.[5] Thus it could happen, as in Austria in 1996, that the hierarchical label is TRB (transfer-based), while the nonhierchical label describes the episode as DB (direct-tax-based), even though the sum of tax measures for that year is less than the sum of spending measures. Keep in mind, though, that we follow this methodology only when a new plan is introduced: otherwise we leave the episode label unchanged. The results of different classification methods are reported in Tables 6.12 and 6.13.

TABLE 6.12. Three-Component Hierarchical Classification

Country	TB	CB	TRB
AUS	4	1	2
AUT	3	0	5
BEL	7	0	8
CAN	8	9	2
DEU	6	0	8
DNK	4	1	3
ESP	8	7	0
FIN	3	1	5
FRA	6	4	1
GBR	6	2	3
IRL	7	6	1
ITA	8	6	4
JPN	5	5	0
PRT	6	5	0
SWE	0	0	5
USA	5	1	1
TOTAL	86	48	48

TABLE 6.13. Four-Component Hierarchical Classification

Country	DB	IB	CB	TRB
AUS	3	0	1	3
AUT	1	1	1	5
BEL	4	0	1	10
CAN	3	0	12	4
DEU	3	2	0	9
DNK	3	0	2	3
ESP	3	5	7	0
FIN	0	2	2	5
FRA	2	2	5	2
GBR	1	3	3	4
IRL	1	5	6	2
ITA	6	0	8	4
JPN	2	3	5	0
PRT	4	0	7	0
SWE	0	0	0	5
USA	5	0	1	1
TOTAL	41	23	61	57

TABLE 6.14. Other Data

GDP scale	Transformation of GDP (rescaled in local currency for EU countries before 2002 and in billions for all countries)
esi con	Consumer confidence indicator
esi ind	Manufacturing industry confidence
ggfl	General government gross financial liabilities, value
gdptr	Potential output of total economy, value
gdp	Gross domestic product, value, market prices
gdpv	Gross domestic product, volume, market prices
r sh	Short-term interest rate
r lo	Long-term interest rate on government bonds
popt	Population, thousands
fbgsd	Trade balances for goods and services
NE	Net Exports (gdpv-fddv)
itv	Gross fixed capital formation, total volume
fddv	Final domestic expenditure, volume
ipv	Private investments, volume
cpv	Private final consumption expenditure, volume
utr	Unemployment rate
totmk	Ds market - tot return index
neer	Nominal effective exchange rate, chain-linked, overall weights
hfce	Household final consumption expenditure, constant prices
pfce new	Household consumption expenditure, incl. NPISHs, nominal
yrg	Current receipts, general government, value
oco	Other current outlays, general government, value
sspg	Social security benefits paid by general government, value
cgv	Government final consumption expenditure, volume
igv	Government gross fixed capital formation, volume
ggdeficit	Government net lending as a percentage of GDP
CPI	Consumer price index–all items
CC	Dummy = 1 if currency crisis
IC	Dummy = 1 if inflation crisis
SMC	Dummy = 1 if stock market crash
BC	Dummy = 1 if banking crisis
rec index	NBER for US and OECD for others indicator of recession (=1 if recession)
EPL	Employment protection index
PMR	Product market regulation - network sectors, all sectors

Although (as shown in the online appendix) we have constructed all four classifications (DB, IB, TRB, and EB), in the results presented in Chapter 7 we use only three (TB, TRB, and EB) because too few plans are based mostly on changes in *Indirect taxes* to allow us to estimate them separately from those based on *Direct taxes*. As new plans will become available, it will be easy to update the information in the online appendix and to estimate DB and IB plans separately. Similarly, though less likely, we could one day have enough data to estimate the effects of plans at a finer level of disaggregation.

OTHER DATA AND SOURCES

Table 6.14 lists the data that were used—beyond the fiscal measures discussed earlier—along with a short description. The data for investment refer to private capital formation for all countries except for Spain and Italy, where, for the early part of the sample, we have data only for total capital formation that includes both private and public capital formation. Our results are unchanged if we drop these two countries. The main source for our fiscal data is the OECD database; unfortunately, series on the debt over GDP ratio consistent with our deficit measures are made available in the OECD database only from 1995 onwards for all countries, with the exception of Italy and Japan (for which the full sample is available). We have therefore complemented the OECD series on debt over GDP with the long-time series on government debt provided by the IMF (https://www.imf.org/external /datamapper/datasets/GDD). The IMF and the OECD series are coherent in the overlapping sample with the exception of a few outliers (which we have removed) and of some systematic difference for Australia (note, however, that we have never used these data in any of the econometric models that are presented in the book). Sources for our data can be found in "MacroData" in the Excel file *New_Components1978-2014_final.xlsx* available at the online appendix, which also contains a detailed description of how the series were constructed and the corresponding data sources.

CONCLUSIONS

Our extensive narrative dataset is one of the most important contributions of this book: these data can be used by other researchers. The documentation we provide is extensive, allowing other researchers to improve on our classification and judgment calls. As the coverage of this dataset is very large, mistakes and imprecisions are possible. Thus, suggestions on how our data could be improved are welcome.

CHAPTER SEVEN

The Effects of Austerity

INTRODUCTION

We are now finally ready to present our results. Tax-based austerity generates the large recessions feared by the critics of austerity. Conversely, austerity based on reductions in government expenditures does not. We also separate transfers from the rest of government spending: transfer cuts have similar effects to cutting government consumption. They do not have similar effects to tax increases. Next we ask to what extent accompanying policies matter: for instance, are the effects of austerity milder when they are preceded by a devaluation, or accompanied by reforms in the labor or product markets, or when monetary policy responds to the shift in fiscal policy? Finally we discuss how to explain our results and consider their underlying mechanisms.

TAXES VERSUS EXPENDITURES

We define output as the growth rate of real GDP per capita;[1] consumption as the growth rate of real final per capita consumption; investment as the per capita growth rate of real gross private capital formation; and net exports as the growth, scaled by real GDP, in net exports. We also use data on inflation, interest rates, public debt, and business and consumer confidence. We evaluate the response over time of all of these variables to a correction to the primary deficit whose size is 1% of GDP. An initial unanticipated correction of 1% of GDP will generate plans of different sizes depending on their intertemporal structure. To make our results comparable across plans, we normalize the size of a plan so that the sum of its unanticipated and announced components is 1% of GDP. The number of plans is not large enough to estimate the effects of fiscal plans country by country. We thus pool the evidence from the various countries in our sample estimating a panel. This means that the fiscal multipliers we estimate vary only across plans, tax-based (TB) or expenditure-based (EB). Technical details on the estimation and simulation of this model are in Chapter 12 along with the estimated coefficients of our models.

Output, Consumption, and Investment

Figure 7.1 shows the response of the level of per capita output to EB and TB plans of the size of 1% of GDP for our entire sample. Austerity plans start in year 0 and responses are cumulated over time, so the points along the impulse response functions measure the deviation of a variable—in this case of the level of real GDP per capita—from what it would have been without the change in fiscal policy. We report the point estimates along with 90% confidence bounds: that is, the reported confidence bounds are such that 90% of the impulse responses lie within them.

TB plans, in red, are much more recessionary than the EB plans, in blue, and particularly within 2 years of the policy shift: EB plans exhaust their very mild recessionary effect 2 years after a plan is introduced. TB plans, on the contrary, have a long-lasting negative, and significantly

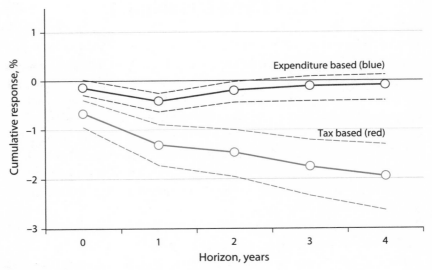

Figure 7.1. Response of GDP to two different plans.

more sizeable, effect on output, estimated to be close to 2 percentage points. This multiplier is smaller than what is reported in Romer and Romer (2010) for the response to a tax hike, but higher than what is reported by Blanchard and Perotti (2002). However, the comparison of results should be interpreted with care, both because those papers use only data from the United States and because the type of policy shift that we analyze is different from theirs.

Our results show that after the introduction of a tax-based adjustment plan of 1% of GDP, with 90% probability GDP has fallen between 1% and 2% within 2 years. And the fall in output does not stop: 4 years after the introduction of a TB plan, with 90% probability GDP has fallen between 1.5% and 2.5%. On the contrary, following a plan of the same size but mostly based on expenditure cuts, within 2 years GDP has fallen (again with a 90% probability) between 0 and 0.5%. Three years after the introduction of such a plan GDP has returned to its pre-austerity level. Moreover, 3 years following the announcement of an EB plan, there is about a 5% probability that output will be above its level before the plan was announced.

Figures 7.2, 7.3, and 7.4 show how households' consumption, business investment, and net exports respond to austerity plans. The different effect on output growth of TB and EB adjustments depends more on the response of private investment than of private consumption and net exports. During EB adjustments, private investment rises within 2 years. The response of net exports is not statistically different between the two types of plans. This fact already sheds serious doubts about movements in the exchange rate being an important factor in explaining the differences in the effects of EB versus TB austerity.

Monetary policy, as measured by the change in the 3-month interest rate, is just slightly more expansionary during EB adjustments (Figure 7.5). However, this difference is much too small to explain the large differences in output responses. Furthermore, the reaction of monetary policy is endogenous: consider the case of EB adjustments, especially those that lead to a correction of expenditures that grow automatically over time, such as entitlements. These plans may be perceived as more permanent and may induce the central bank to be more "relaxed." Guajardo et al. (2014) incorrectly attributed the much larger recessionary effects of tax hikes relative to spending cuts to the reaction

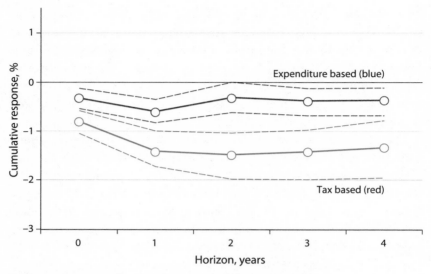

Figure 7.2. Response of consumption to two different plans.

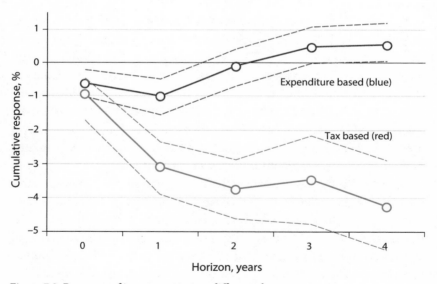

Figure 7.3. Response of investment to two different plans.

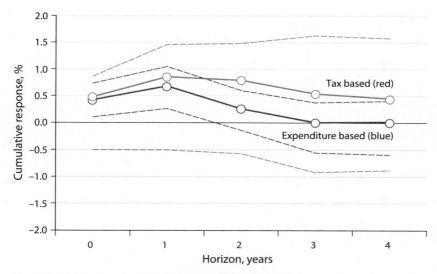

Figure 7.4. Response of net exports to two different plans.

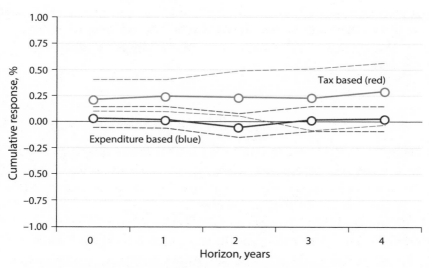

Figure 7.5. Response of short-term interest rates to two different plans.

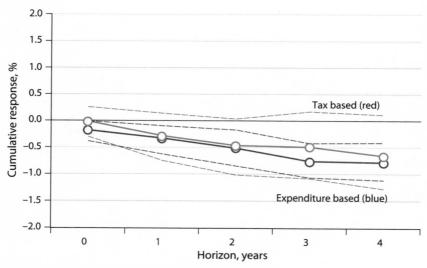

Figure 7.6. Response of inflation to two different plans.

of monetary policy. Their conclusions are not supported by the data, as we will further show below. The pattern of inflation is shown in Figure 7.6. No significant differences emerge on the impact on inflation of TB and EB plans.

Confidence

Figure 7.7 shows how consumer and business confidence reacts to austerity plans. Investors seem to prefer expenditure cuts, probably because they anticipate a future decline, or at least no increase in taxation. Thus they invest more, as we showed earlier.

Business confidence responds more heterogenously than consumer confidence to TB and EB plans. In fact consumption growth does not respond as differently as investment to the two types of adjustments. There may be several reasons for this. First, if some consumers cannot borrow, then they will not respond to a cut in expenditure with improved confidence. They will wait until their taxes fall and income actually increases. Alternatively, if government consumption is complementary to private consumption, then consumers might need to spend less.

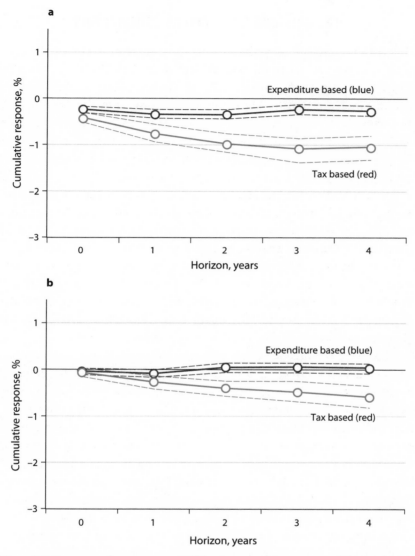

Figure 7.7. Response of consumer and ESI business confidence to two different plans.

Transfers and Government Consumption

We now disaggregate government spending into transfers and all other outlays, as always net of interest payments on the debt. Reductions in transfers to individuals have two effects. On the one hand, they operate as a tax increase that lowers disposable income. On the other hand, the incentive effects go in the opposite direction: lower transfers increase labor supply. It is thus not obvious (assuming you wanted to aggregate them) if they should be aggregated with taxes, as is often done in the literature, or with spending, as we have done so far in this chapter.

We would also like to separate current government consumption from public investment. However, whereas there are a significant number of fiscal stabilization plans whose main component is a cut in government transfers, there are almost none where the main component is a cut in investment. So, we cannot estimate the effects of plans mostly based on cuts in government investment. When aggregating cuts in government consumption and investment, however, the former component represents around 80% of the total correction. Therefore, EB plans mostly consist of cuts in current spending.

Thus we now consider three types of fiscal plans: those based mostly on increases in direct and indirect taxes (TB plans); those based mostly on cuts in transfers (transfer-based [TRB] plans); and those based mostly on reductions in current and capital spending (consumption and investment based [CIB] plans). Figure 7.8 reports the responses of output, consumption, investment, and net exports, while Figure 7.9 shows instead the response of consumer and business confidence to the introduction of these three types of plans. TRB plans are shown in green; CIB plans in blue; TB plans in red. As before, the responses are cumulated over time, so that the points along the impulse response functions measure the deviation of a variable from its level absent the change in fiscal policy.

In terms of output TB plans are significantly more recessionary than CIB and TRB plans, particularly within 2 years after the policy shift. CIB and TRB plans appear to exhaust their mild and statistically insignificant recessionary effect 2 years after a plan is introduced. CIB plans are recessionary for 1 year, then their effect falls to zero. The difference in medium-term output growth between TB and the other two types of

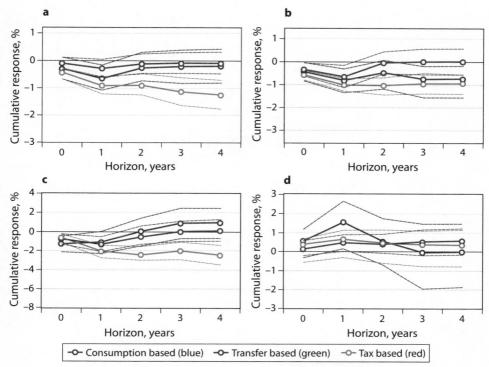

Figure 7.8. Responses to plans under a three-component classification. Panel a shows GDP; panel b, consumption; panel c, investment; and panel d, net exports.

plans is accounted for mostly by the response of investment. After the introduction of a TB plan, investment falls up to 2 percentage points versus a single percentage point in the case of CIB and TRB, where the decline is reversed in 2 years (although the difference is not statistically significant). Three years after the introduction of a CIB plan, output is above its level absent the plan, while output is essentially unaffected by TRB plans. Private consumption falls by 1% after the introduction of a TB plan and slightly less than 1% (although again the difference is not statistically significant) in the case of CIB and TRB plans. Consistent with Romer and Romer (2016) who study the US case only, we find that consumption responds to changes in transfers in the short term but it recovers in 2 years, while in the case of CIB plans it remains slightly negative.

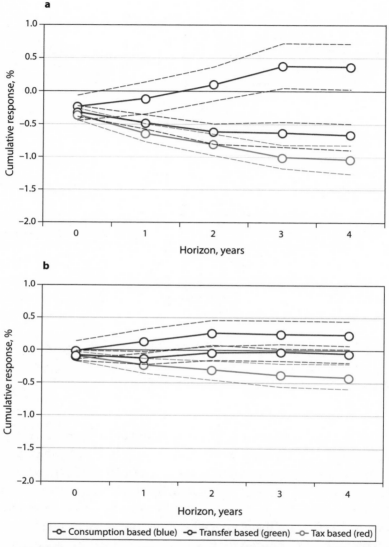

Figure 7.9. Response of consumer and business confidence to three different plans. Panel a shows ESI consumer confidence; panel b, ESI business confidence.

Business confidence responds similarly to the case where we limit the disaggregation to TB and EB plans.[2]

Finally, we have evaluated without reporting the response of short-term interest rates to the various types of plans. The response to CIB and TB plans is positive, and the two are not statistically different from each other. TRB plans generate a drop in the short-term interest rate, as we discussed earlier. See later in the chapter for further analysis of the role of monetary policy.

Disaggregating Taxes

Our extensive data collection also allows us to distinguish between increases in direct and indirect taxes, such as value-added taxes. However, there are so few austerity plans in which indirect taxes were a major player in the policy package, only about 20, that it was impossible to distinguish accurately between the effects of plans relying mostly on direct versus indirect taxes. Thus we could not safely explore this additional distinction.

THE ROLE OF ACCOMPANYING POLICIES

Monetary Policy

One way of assessing the role of monetary policy is to run a counterfactual simulation. We augmented the baseline model by including among the explanatory variables the change in the short-term rate. We then compared the response of output growth to EB and TB plans in a baseline scenario, where monetary policy rates are allowed to respond to fiscal policy, and in a counterfactual scenario in which interest rates are constrained not to respond to shifts in taxes and spending. This comparison allows us to evaluate the importance of monetary policy in determining the output effect of fiscal plans. Figure 7.10 shows that when we do this the heterogeneous effect of TB and EB plans on output is slightly mitigated, but remain large and strongly significant.

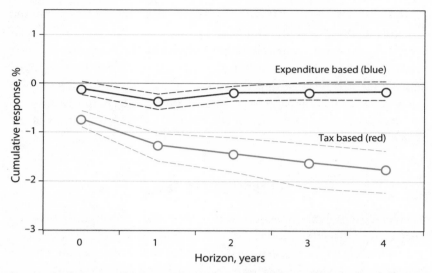

Figure 7.10. Response of GDP to TB and EB plans without a monetary policy response.

This suggests that the conclusions by Guajardo, Leigh, and Pescatori (2014) are not supported by the evidence.[3] We shall further explore the role of monetary policy in Chapter 9.

Exchange Rate Movements

We have already shown that net exports do not explain the differences in the response of output to EB and TB adjustment, suggesting that the exchange rate is not likely to be an explanation of this difference. Now we go deeper.

Imagine that EB adjustments typically happened after an exchange rate devaluation, but that TB adjustments do not follow significant fluctuations in exchange rates. Might devaluations be the reason why EB adjustments have a mild or no recessionary effects on output? Empirical analyses that try to estimate the effects of a devaluation on output, controlling for other drivers of growth, show very mixed results. In some cases, devaluations appear to be contractionary; in other cases, expansionary. For instance, in a sample of 67 countries Barro (2001) finds a negative association between the average rate of devaluation and output growth over the subsequent 5-year period. Edwards (1989) and

Morley (1992) find contractionary effects of real exchange rate devaluations in developing countries by comparing large devaluation episodes with a control group. Gupta, Mishra, and Sahay (2007) show very disparate responses of output growth during currency crises in developing countries: richer countries are less likely to enjoy expansion during such events. Theory suggests that devaluations could be contractionary: for instance, Krugman and Taylor (1978) show that if imports exceed exports, a devaluation will induce a fall in real income—due to price increases in the tradeable sector—depressing demand and inducing a contraction of output. Whether a devaluation could mitigate the possible contractionary effects of a fiscal adjustment thus remains an open question.

We need to distinguish between exchange rate movements that occur during a fiscal adjustment from those that occur before austerity is launched, as the former are endogenous to the adjustment. Imagine an EB correction leading to a reduction in interest rates, which in turn leads to a devaluation: in this case, the devaluation is one of the consequences of the fiscal adjustment. In contrast, a devaluation that occurs before an adjustment is launched could make the former less (or more) contractionary.

To analyze this issue, we ran a binary choice (panel) probit regression of the dummies identifying TB and EB episodes on the growth rate of the nominal effective exchange rate one ($\Delta NEER_{t-1}$) and two years ($\Delta NEER_{t-2}$) before the start of a fiscal plan (results are in Table 7.1). We control for aggregate shocks through year dummies. As shown in the table, an exchange rate depreciation 1 year before the start of the fiscal adjustment increases the likelihood that an EB plan is adopted, while it does not predict the adoption of a TB plan. The coefficient on

TABLE 7.1. Probit Regressions of EB and TB Plan Dummies on Lagged Depreciation

	TB_t	EB_t
$\Delta NEER_{t-1}$	−0.0020041	−0.0240364**
	(0.0137254)	(0.011763)
$\Delta NEER_{t-2}$	0.0070124	−0.0081774
	(0.0138572)	(0.0116028)

TABLE 7.2. Regressions of the Unexpected Component of EB and TB Plans on Lagged Depreciation

	$e_t^u * TB_t$	$e_t^u * EB_t$
$\Delta NEER_{t-1}$	−0.00019	−0.0073141
	(0.003173)	(0.0054783)
$\Delta NEER_{t-2}$	0.0004267	−0.0143565***
	(0.0031796)	(0.0055094)

the change in the effective exchange rate at $t-1$ is −0.02 with a standard error of 0.01; the coefficient on the change in the exchange rate at $t-2$ is not statistically significant and a probit regression of TB on the change in the exchange rate also does not yield significant coefficients. We also checked whether the exchange rate can predict the size of the unexpected component of TB and EB adjustments: we do this by running a regression of the size of the unexpected component of TB and EB plans on the lagged values of the change in the nominal effective exchange rate. Table 7.2 shows that a depreciation occurring at year $t-2$ predicts, though marginally, a larger unexpected EB adjustment in year t. The coefficient on the 2-year lag of the change in the exchange rate is −0.014 with an associated standard error of 0.006. Still, there is no evidence that a larger depreciation predicts a larger TB adjustment.

We then exclude from the sample all episodes of fiscal consolidation that were preceded by a devaluation of at least 3%, which is approximately the first quintile of the distribution of exchange rate changes in our sample. After we dropped these episodes, our results were unchanged. We also tried excluding adjustments that were preceded by a devaluation of at least 10% over the previous 3 years, which is approximately the 10th percentile of the distribution of the 3-year cumulative change in the exchange rate: again the results did not change. All these results are available from the authors.

Finally, we appended to the estimated equation for output growth, in addition to TB and EB corrections, the two lags of the change in the nominal effective exchange rate. The simulated impulse responses based on these new estimates are shown in Figure 7.11. They are very similar to the estimates obtained without conditioning on the exchange rate.

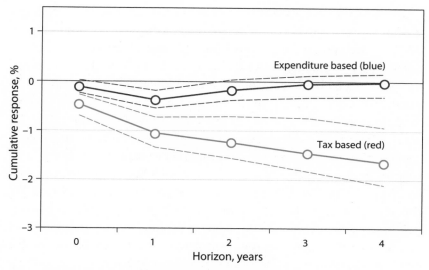

Figure 7.11. Response of GDP, controlling for exchange rate change.

Structural Reforms

The asymmetry might also be explained by the possibility that EB plans, but not TB plans, were accompanied by a set of market-oriented reforms, such as labor and product market liberalizations. For instance, in 1994 Spain introduced a labor market reform in the same year when an EB plan was launched. The reform (Gil Martin [2017]) created incentives for part-time contracts and for setting up private employment agencies to match labor demand and supply more effectively. It also decentralized collective bargaining, with some delay. In 1995 Australia adopted a National Competition Policy (NCP) during a 4-year period of TB austerity. The NCP included (Banks [2004]) measures targeting anti-competitive conduct (by both private and government enterprises), as well as regulation of monopolies, with sector-specific reforms targeting energy, road transport, water, and gas. According to the OECD, the NCP "contributed to the productivity surge that has underpinned 13 years of continuous economic growth, and associated strong growth in household incomes; directly reduced the prices of goods and services such as electricity and milk; stimulated business innovation, customer responsiveness and choice."[4]

We used two indices constructed by the OECD: one covering labor market reforms, the other product market reforms. We then ran a binary choice (panel) probit regression of the dummies identifying the TB and EB episodes on this index. We found no evidence of a relation between the presence of labor or product market reforms and the choice of whether or not to implement a TB or an EB adjustment. That is, labor market reforms are not more or less likely to occur during EB or TB plans. There is also no evidence of a higher likelihood of an EB plan being implemented along with labor market reforms.[5] We obtain similarly insignificant results when we study the choice of whether to adopt an EB or a TB plan and the OECD index of product market reforms. We conclude that the difference between the effects of TB and EB plans is not driven by contemporaneous labor or product market reforms.

Note that this finding is not inconsistent with the evidence and the case studies reported in Perotti (2013) and Alesina and Ardagna (1998, 2013). These papers show that among all fiscal adjustments, the least costly are those that were accompanied by some supply-side reforms and by wage moderation. Our point is different: we checked whether the adoption of EB and TB adjustments can be explained by supply-side reforms, and we found that it cannot.

The Impact on Debt

A relevant question is how the debt over GDP ratio responds to fiscal adjustments. Since our narratively identified fiscal plans are not legislated for cyclical reasons, but for concerns related to the long-term state of the public finances, this is the appropriate setting to assess whether deficit reduction measures are effective at reducing the debt ratio. To answer this question one needs to reconstruct the debt dynamics, which depends on the inherited debt ratio, on the growth rate of GDP and on inflation since these variables, together with government expenditures (including the interest expenses on debt) determine how much revenue is needed to service the debt. Tracking the effects of fiscal plans on the debt ratio thus requires a slightly more articulated simulation model than the one used so far (the model is illustrated in Chapter 12 in the section "Fiscal Adjustments and the Dynamics of Debt over GDP").

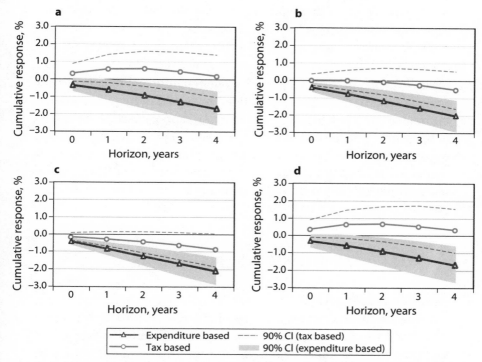

Figure 7.12. Debt dynamics. Panel a shows high debt (to GDP)—high cost of debt; panel b, low debt (to GDP)—low cost of debt; panel c, low debt (to GDP)—high cost of debt; and panel d, high debt (to GDP)—low cost of debt.

The initial level of debt and the interest cost of the debt are crucial in determining how the debt ratio responds to a fiscal adjustment. We study four different situations based on combinations of high and low levels of the debt ratio, and of high and low interest cost. In particular, high and low levels of debt are identified with a debt ratio of around 120% and 60% respectively. High interest cost is that observed in the 1992–3 period; low interest cost that observed in 2013–14. As always, we distinguish between TB and EB plans. The results are in Figure 7.12.

Figure 7.12 reports the difference between the path of the debt ratio in the presence of an austerity plan and the path absent such a plan. The heterogeneity between TB and EB plans appears to be also relevant for the evolution of the debt ratio. EB plans tend to reduce the debt ratio compared to a scenario without adjustment, independently of initial conditions. TB plans are neutral or mildly stabilizing when initial debt is low, but destabilizing when debt is high.

These results can be explained by considering the drivers of debt dynamics. While an increase in revenues may reduce the primary deficit (or increase the primary surplus), the fall in output and inflation that it generates acts in the opposite direction. In the case of EB plans, instead, the milder slowdown in output and inflation cannot offset the reduction in the primary deficit due to the cut in government spending. This is a remarkable result: EB corrections, though moderately costly in terms of output losses, lead to a steady fall in the debt ratio, while TB plans are self-defeating: they slow down the economy and do not reduce the debt ratio.[6]

AN ALTERNATIVE SPECIFICATION

Assume a reader did not buy our argument that one should not estimate the effects of shifts in taxes and expenditure separately because this would be correct only if the two were orthogonal, which in our sample are not. In other words, she did not believe in our plans and wanted to see the results of regressions in which exogenous changes in taxes and spending (all three components—expected, unexpected, and announced) are introduced directly in the equation for output growth.

Table 7.3 shows the results (for output growth) obtained estimating this alternative specification. The model and the estimated coefficients are illustrated in Chapter 12 in the subsection "Alternative specification."

The coefficients in this equation are estimates of the impact on output growth of the different components of exogenous shifts in taxes and expenditure. Note that they cannot—at least in general—be interpreted as partial derivatives, that is, the effect of the variable they are attached to on the dependent variable: they could if the regressors were orthogonal to each other but, within a fiscal adjustment plan, they are not. To simulate the effect on output of one component, for instance taxes, one needs to model the response of the other, in this case spending. We explain in Chapter 12 how this can be done. The impulse responses

TABLE 7.3. An Alternative Specification

Dependent variable: Real GDP per capita growth			
τ_t^u	−0.50	g_t^u	−0.41
	(0.12)		(0.13)
$\tau_{t,0}^a$	−0.86	$g_{t,0}^a$	−0.35
	(0.18)		(0.16)
τ_{t-1}^u	−0.24	g_{t-1}^u	−0.46
	(0.12)		(0.14)
$\tau_{t-1,0}^a$	−0.43	$g_{t-1,0}^a$	0.38
	(0.19)		(0.17)
τ_{t-2}^u	−0.26	$g_{t-2,0}^u$	0.69
	(0.13)		(0.14)
$\tau_{t-2,0}^a$	−0.31	$g_{t-2,0}^a$	0.26
	(0.21)		(0.17)
τ_{t-3}^u	−0.42	g_{t-3}^u	0.28
	(0.13)		(0.13)
$\tau_{t-3,0}^a$	0.10	$g_{t-3,0}^a$	−0.14
	(0.22)		(0.18)
$\tau_{t,t+1}^a + \tau_{t,t+2}^a$	−0.50	$g_{t,t+1}^a + g_{t,t+2}^a$	−0.18
	(0.14)		(0.12)

obtained simulating this alternative specification do not produce any result incoherent with our preferred model.

WHY DO EB AND TB PLANS HAVE DIFFERENT EFFECTS?

Confidence

A successful fiscal consolidation removes uncertainty and stimulates demand by making consumers, and especially investors, more optimistic about the future. Imagine a situation as described in Alesina and Drazen (1991) in which an economy is on an unsustainable path with an exploding public debt due to unresolved political conflict about how to stabilize the debt with austerity policies. Sooner or later a fiscal stabilization has to occur, since default is excluded. The longer one waits, the higher the taxes that will need to be raised (or spending to be cut) in the future. When the stabilization occurs it removes the uncertainty about further delays that would have increased even more the costs of the stabilization;

(see also Blanchard [1990] on this point.) A stabilization that eliminates the uncertainty about higher fiscal costs in the future stimulates demand today—especially, we may add, demand from investors, who are more sensitive to uncertainty about the future given their longer horizons. These beneficial effects associated with the removal of uncertainty are more likely to occur in the presence of EB rather than TB consolidation plans: if the automatic increase of spending is not addressed, taxes will have to be continually increased to cover the increase in outlays. Allowing for default may reinforce these results since the elimination of a default risk may vastly reduce interest rates and eliminate the risk of a major financial collapse.

Investment

The role of confidence is especially relevant for investment spending, which in fact our results suggest is one of the main drivers of the difference between EB and TB plans. In addition, Alesina et al. (2002) found that lower government spending, possibly because it is accompanied by the expectation of lower taxes on capital, results in higher investment. Corsetti et al. (2012a) further show that the size of these effects depends on the transitory or permanent nature of the change in expenditure. An increase in taxation, however, will have an unambiguous contractionary effect on output: this depends on a negative wealth effect on the demand side (affecting both consumption and investment), combined with the negative effect of increased distortions on the supply side.[7]

Persistence

The degree of persistence of changes in taxes and expenditures is very important in determining their effects on output. In Chapter 12 we analyze the difference between TB and EB austerity in a general equilibrium model, finding that EB plans are the least recessionary the longer lived is the reduction in government spending for the simple reason that the longer lasting are the cuts in spending, the larger the wealth effects on consumers arising from future expected tax cuts. Symmetrically, TB plans are more recessionary the longer lasting is the increase in the tax burden and thus in distortions. The intuition is that, when persistence increases, the demand shift due to a cut in government expenditure starts to be dominated by the supply shift due to lower labor supply. The demand effect falls faster than the supply effect, so that the government spending multiplier decreases with persistence. Symmetrically, in the case of an increase in labor taxes, the multiplier increases with persistence. To put it simply, a persistent increase in labor taxes makes the static substitution effect between labor and leisure more permanent and this increases the wage tax multiplier. To the extent that fiscal adjustments are perceived to be permanent, and are on the supply side, a standard neo-keynesian model thus implies that spending cuts are less recessionary than tax hikes.

Erceg and Lindé (2013) studied the effects of expenditure-based versus a labor tax-based fiscal consolidation in a two-country Dynamic Stochastic General Equilibrium (DSGE) model without persistence. They find three key results. First, if the scope for monetary accommodation is limited, TB consolidation tends to have smaller adverse effects on output than EB consolidation in the near term, though it is more costly in the longer run. Second, a large EB consolidation may be counterproductive in the near term if the zero lower bound is binding. Third, a "mixed strategy" that combines a sharp but temporary rise in taxes with gradual spending cuts over time appears to minimize the output costs of fiscal consolidation.

Labor Markets

A reduction in the public sector wage bill also has a depressing effect on aggregate demand, but that may be compensated for by the fact that a reduction in public sector wages could translate into lower private sector wages, thus raising profitability and investment. This could occur because when wages are bargained between firms and unions, a reduction in government employment may affect real wages in both the public and the private sector. In a similar vein, Alesina and Perotti (1997b) show how in unionized economies, such as most of the 16 countries in our sample, increases in income taxes translate into higher wage demands by unions, higher unit labor costs, and a loss of competitiveness for domestic firms.[8]

CONCLUSIONS

EB plans have very small costs in terms of output losses. The average low costs of the former are the result of some of them producing deeper recessions and others being expansionary. TB plans are associated with deep and long-lasting recessions. The component of aggregate demand that responds very distinctly in the two types of plans is private investment. In fact, investors' confidence (which reflects their expectations about the future) reacts positively to EB plans and negatively to TB ones. Consumers' confidence moves in the same general direction but with a smaller difference between types of plans.

These results are very robust: they are not driven by the experience of any particular country, and are not limited to certain time periods. We have also investigated the difference in the effects of various components of government expenditures, in particular separating transfers from government consumption and finding that changes in transfers are not similar to changes in taxes.

Our results cannot be explained by different responses of monetary policy to different type of plans, nor can they be explained by exchange rate movements. Many large fiscal consolidation plans are accompanied by structural reforms, for instance, labor or goods market liberalizations. However, we find no evidence that it is the occurrence of these reforms that explains the different effects of EB and TB plans. This result is not inconsistent with the evidence from the case studies showing that these types of reforms may often make austerity less costly because they sustain growth.

CHAPTER EIGHT

European Austerity during the Great Recession

INTRODUCTION

The discussion of austerity in Europe in 2010 and the following years has been passionate, to say the least. On one side are those who argued that austerity occurred too quickly after the financial crisis, was too draconian, and was the main if not the only cause of the prolonged recession in Europe. The alternative view is that at least for some countries, such as Greece, Italy, Ireland, Spain, Portugal, the markets needed a signal of restraint: in these countries the alternative to no austerity would have been much worse. In fact, Europe in those years suffered for many reasons: fear of debt defaults, banking crises, and bursting real estate bubbles, in different combinations in different countries. Those governments that could still borrow in the market were charged large risk premia. Reassuring financial investors with fiscal stabilization programs was considered essential to avoid contagion, the demise of the euro, and a second even bigger round of financial collapses.

We do not know what would have happened without austerity: debt repudiation? Panic? A second round of banking crises? What we do know is that the certainty with which anti-austerity commentators assure us that everything would have been much better is based on ideology, not facts.

We pose three questions. Does the difference between tax-based (TB) and expenditure-based (EB) adjustments also apply to this latest round of austerity in Europe? How much of the severity of the crisis can be ascribed to the different types of fiscal corrections that were implemented? Have these episodes of austerity been more costly than previous ones, perhaps because they all occurred at the same time and at the zero lower bound with fragile banking sectors? The answers to these three questions are: yes; a lot; and probably no.

We begin with a broad review of the European experience with austerity and analyze in detail a few salient episodes. We then estimate the same model used in Chapter 7, but on a sample that stops in 2007, before the start of the financial crisis. We feed into this estimated model the actual austerity plans implemented by the various countries from 2010 onward and simulate their effects on output. These plans differ in their size, their composition, and in the extent to which they were front loaded. We check whether the simulations are broadly consistent with the actual data: if they are, and with various caveats they indeed are, this means that postcrisis austerity did not display very different effects compared with precrisis austerity. We also explain why our results are different from those of others, in particular, Blanchard and Leigh (2014).

The popular discussion about austerity in Europe sometimes confuses two different issues: whether austerity was too draconian and whether multipliers were larger than we thought, so that for every unit of reduction in deficits the recessions were bigger than anticipated based on precrisis evidence. According to our evidence, it does not seem that multipliers were larger than before the crisis. The smaller the multipliers the sharper can austerity be because the smaller the effects on output.

EUROPE IN THE AFTERMATH OF THE FINANCIAL CRISIS

Many European economies did not enter the financial crisis in 2008 with a clean fiscal slate. In several countries debts and deficits were already high before the crisis, or kept artificially low thanks to booms in tax revenues associated with housing bubbles. One reason of course was the low interest rates of the first decade of the euro, which facilitated large debt build-ups in the European periphery. The countries with the highest ratios of public debt to GDP were Italy and Greece, 102% and 109% respectively. But even some countries with apparently better fiscal positions, such as Spain and Ireland, were running budget deficits, notwithstanding an exceptional and unsustainable level of revenues accruing from a real estate bubble. Still, the interest rates charged on Greek, Spanish, Portuguese, and Italian debt up to the financial crisis were only marginally higher than those charged on German debt. Countries throughout the European Union also faced the challenge

TABLE 8.1. Public Balance

Government net lending (% of GDP)	2007	2008	2009	2010	2011	2012	2013	2014	Change 2010–2014
Euro area (16 countries)	−0.65	−2.16	−6.26	−6.18	−4.21	−3.64	−3.00	−2.57	3.61
OECD - Total	−1.60	−3.76	−8.45	−7.99	−6.60	−5.75	−4.05	−3.47	4.52
France	−2.54	−3.19	−7.16	−6.80	−5.10	−4.81	−4.03	−3.94	2.86
Germany	0.19	−0.18	−3.24	−4.23	−0.96	−0.03	−0.19	0.29	4.52
Greece	−6.70	−10.19	−15.14	−11.17	−10.27	−8.89	−13.16	−3.66	7.51
Ireland	0.27	−6.98	−13.82	−32.13	−12.65	−8.05	−5.72	−3.72	28.41
Italy	−1.53	−2.69	−5.27	−4.25	−3.71	−2.93	−2.92	−3.02	1.23
Portugal	−3.01	−3.77	−9.81	−11.17	−7.38	−5.66	−4.84	−7.17	4.01
Spain	1.92	−4.42	−10.96	−9.38	−9.61	−10.47	−7.00	−5.99	3.39
United Kingdom	−2.89	−4.91	−10.56	−9.57	−7.65	−8.32	−5.72	−5.58	3.98
United States	−3.70	−7.19	−12.83	−12.18	−10.75	−9.00	−5.52	−5.01	7.17

Cyclically adjusted government primary balance (% of potential GDP)	2007	2008	2009	2010	2011	2012	2013	2014	Change 2010–2014
Euro area (16 countries)	0.19	−0.70	−2.06	−2.57	−0.85	0.59	1.50	1.57	4.14
OECD - Total	−1.16	−2.58	−4.83	−4.88	−3.48	−2.43	−0.99	−0.50	4.39
France	−1.51	−1.20	−3.30	−3.42	−2.20	−1.48	−0.74	−0.50	2.92
Germany	1.38	1.27	1.31	−1.21	0.82	1.73	1.58	1.65	2.87
Greece	−5.93	−9.08	−12.26	−5.45	0.21	2.24	−1.42	6.02	11.47
Ireland	−2.51	−6.95	−10.13	−27.81	−8.28	−2.02	0.70	0.02	27.83
Italy	1.77	1.45	1.09	1.18	1.66	4.23	4.55	3.97	2.79
Portugal	−1.40	−1.70	−5.89	−8.13	−2.25	1.69	3.09	0.50	8.63
Spain	0.10	−5.35	−8.07	−5.44	−4.03	−2.02	2.96	3.34	8.78
United Kingdom	−2.67	−3.60	−6.18	−4.72	−2.85	−3.91	−1.84	−2.71	2.00
United States	−2.26	−4.62	−7.67	−7.31	−5.69	−4.27	−1.63	−1.03	6.28

Source: OECD Economic Outlook No. 101, June 2017.

posed by the rapid aging of their populations: social expenditure had increased from an average of 18% of GDP in 1980 to 25% in 2009, with an increase of 5 percentage points of GDP in just the 10 years preceding 2009 (OECD Social Expenditure Database). Total government spending was 43% of GDP in 2007 in the EU on average.[1]

Government budgets, which were already structurally weak, worsened significantly with the start of the financial crisis, in many cases

TABLE 8.2. Public Debt

General government debt (% of GDP)	2007	2008	2009	2010	2011	2012	2013	2014	Change 2010–2014
Euro area (16 countries)	65	69	78	84	87	91	94	94	10
France	64	68	79	82	85	90	92	95	14
Germany	64	65	73	81	79	80	77	75	−6
Greece	103	109	127	146	172	160	178	180	34
Ireland	24	42	62	86	110	120	120	105	19
Italy	100	102	113	115	117	123	129	132	16
Portugal	68	72	84	96	111	126	129	131	34
Spain	36	39	53	60	69	86	95	100	40
United Kingdom	42	50	64	76	82	85	86	88	12
United States*	65	74	87	96	100	103	105	105	10

Source: OECD Economic Outlook No. 101, June 2017.
Source: IMF WEO, April 2017.

because governments had to foot the bill for distressed financial institutions. Ireland was the most striking example: it moved from a budget surplus in 2007 to a 32% of GDP deficit in 2010. The average budget deficit in the EU more than tripled between 2007 and 2008, reaching 6.3% of GDP in 2009 (IMF Fiscal Monitor 2013; see Table 8.1). As a consequence, debt ratios jumped: from 65% to 94% in the euro area (see Table 8.2). Beyond automatic stabilizers and the cost of bailing out banks, discretionary fiscal actions aimed at slowing the rise in unemployment and protecting unemployed workers also played a role, although to a different extent from country to country: the discretionary response was relatively small in Germany and in Italy, while Spain, Portugal, the United Kingdom, France, and Greece show a very large increase in the cyclically adjusted deficit.

These increases in budget deficits implied that many European countries entered the EU Excessive Deficit Procedure around 2009, and as a result their fiscal policies started to be monitored by the European Commission. The UK entered the Excessive Deficit Procedure in 2008, followed in 2009 by Spain, Greece, Ireland, France, Germany, Italy, Portugal, the Netherlands, Belgium, and Austria. Denmark entered in 2010.

After the start of the Greek crisis, in the spring of 2010, there were renewed anxieties about the sustainability of public debt in some

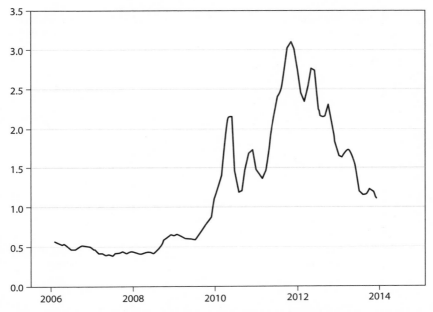

Figure 8.1. Fiscal policy in the media. *Source:* Data gathered from Factiva from January 2006 to January 2014.

European countries. Investors demanded higher interest rates on government bonds: yields spiked throughout the European periphery. The yield spread between 10-year Spanish Treasury bonds and German Bunds increased from less than 1% at the beginning of 2010 to 2% in June of that year. In Ireland the spread rose from 1% to 3% and in Portugal from less than a half percent to 3%.

These pressures also raised concerns among the public. There were few articles discussing fiscal consolidation during the first years of the financial crisis, but they rapidly increased in 2010, typically reaching a peak around the end of 2011 (see Figure 8.1).[2]

Starting in 2010 most European countries, notwithstanding mediocre growth projections for the years to come, began fiscal consolidations, implementing multiyear deficit reduction programs. It is not unusual for austerity plans to begin during recessions, even though the post–financial crisis recessions were especially severe.

Figure 8.2 shows how the fiscal policy of euro area economies changed over time, in relation to the economic cycle. For every year we report

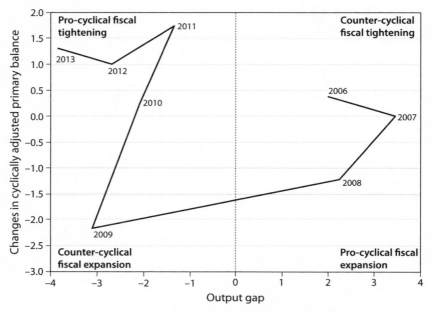

Figure 8.2. Procyclical policies and the financial crisis. We plot the change in the cyclically adjusted primary balance against the output gap registered in the same year. A negative (positive) change in the primary balance means that the cyclically adjusted deficit is increasing (decreasing). As a consequence, years of countercyclical fiscal policy are those in the first and third quadrants, while years of procyclical policies lie in the second and fourth quadrants. *Source:* OECD Forecasting, Analysis and Modeling Environment.

the change in the cyclically-adjusted primary balance—that is the budget deficit net of interest payments as a percent of GDP—and the level of the output gap. The first and third quadrants represent instances of countercyclical fiscal policy where governments squeeze the public budget while the economy is booming, and vice versa. The second and fourth quadrants instead include years in which fiscal policy was procyclical. The majority of the countries in our sample adopted countercyclical (expansionary) fiscal policies at the beginning of the recession (2008–9) but turned to procyclical policies (consolidations) after 2009 since fiscal consolidations indeed started before the recessions were over. Moreover, three additional factors may have made austerity especially difficult: the zero lower bound; the stressful positions of many banks; and the fact that many trading partners engaged in harsh austerity policies at the same time.

EUROPEAN AUSTERITY

About three years after the collapse of Lehman Brothers, when the United States was already emerging from the depths of the recession, Europe, and the eurozone in particular, were entering a second crisis. The "euro crisis," as it is now called, was triggered by the chaos in Greece and by the announcement (by German chancellor Angela Merkel and French president Nicolas Sarkozy) that before the funds of the European Stability Mechanism could be used to bail out a country, there would have been losses for private creditors, the so-called "bail-in," a decision that created turmoil in financial markets because it removed the perception that the debt of euro area countries was risk free. In response to this new crisis, which raised doubts about the sustainability of public debt in some countries, a round of austerity programs was launched. In some countries, for example, the United Kingdom and Ireland, austerity was based mostly on expenditure cuts. As we shall see, it was reasonably successful in terms of a relatively prompt economic recovery despite, in the case of Ireland, a major banking crisis. In other countries—for example Italy, Spain and Portugal—austerity was a combination of tax increases and expenditure cuts (some exceptionally large, as in Portugal and Spain) and, at least in the short run, was associated with deep recessions. In this section we review these episodes in detail. We shall discuss Greece later in this chapter.

UK 2010-14: Expenditure Based

The Conservative government implemented a program of budget cuts. Over a 5-year period exogenous fixed measures amounted to almost 3% of GDP, two-thirds expenditure cuts, and one-third tax hikes. It was harshly criticized by the IMF, which predicted a major recession. The latter did not materialize and the IMF later publicly apologized. The UK grew at respectable rates. In 2009, the year before the consolidation started, growth in output per capita was negative: about −5%. In 2010, during the first year of the program, it was +1.2%; after the 2011 drop of 1.5% (partly as a consequence of the effects on the British economy of the euro area crisis), it was zero in 2012 and peaked at 3.4% in 2013, returning to 0.4% in 2014 and around 1% in 2015, with a 6-year average of 1.6%. The initial devaluation of the pound helped the British economy. The voters eventually rewarded the government that implemented this program.

Details

After the May 2010 elections, when the British Conservative government announced a series of measures mainly targeting public expenditures in order to reduce the deficit, many commentators, and most importantly the IMF, denounced it as too aggressive and predicted it would produce a major and prolonged recession. As it turned out, the UK economy performed quite well after the implementation of the fiscal adjustment.

As shown in Table 8.4, as a result of the measures undertaken to respond to the financial crisis, the UK cyclically adjusted budget deficit had reached almost 10% of GDP by 2009 and public debt had risen from below 50% of GDP before the crisis to 64%. In the March 2010 budget, just before the elections, the Labour government had introduced the first austerity measure: announced tax hikes for approximately 12 £bn. After the elections, the new Conservative government, in a supplementary June budget, launched a consolidation program approximately three times as large as what had been announced by Labour. The government also established an independent authority, the Office for Budget Responsibility, whose main duty was to produce macroeconomic and fiscal forecasts and to assess the consistency of the fiscal measures tabled by the government.

As shown in Table 8.3, consolidation began with a set of measures (including both the tax hikes that had already been announced by Labour and the new measures included in the June budget) amounting to 3.5% of GDP in 2010, then falling to 0.7%, 0.1%, and 0.1% respectively in 2011, 2012, and 2013. The program was mostly spending-based and included both measures immediately implemented and others announced for later implementation. In 2010, the main new components were cuts in government consumption and in public investment. In 2011 the main new measures involved reductions in transfers. In 2010, current and capital spending were cut for a cumulative amount of 20 £bn and 2 £bn respectively. Transfers were reduced, tightening the rules governing access to welfare programs for a total savings of 11 £bn (mainly through announcements for subsequent years). In 2011, transfers were reduced further by some 3 £bn thanks to more restrictive

TABLE 8.3. UK: Fiscal Consolidation

		2010			2011			2012			2013			2014		
		Exp.	Unexp.	Ann.	Exp.	Unexp.	Ann.	Exp.	Unexp.	Ann.	Exp.	Unexp.	Ann.	Exp.	Unexp.	Ann.
Revenues	Direct	0.00	0.00	0.67	0.17	0.14	0.05	0.21	-0.10	0.03	0.22	-0.02	0.14	0.29	0.00	-0.06
	Indirect	0.00	0.14	0.82	0.53	-0.10	0.06	0.18	0.02	0.05	0.10	-0.03	-0.06	0.02	-0.03	-0.05
	Other	0.00	0.00	0.00	0.00	0.00	0.00	0.00	0.00	0.00	0.00	0.00	0.00	0.00	0.00	0.00
	Total	0.00	0.15	1.49	0.70	0.05	0.11	0.39	-0.08	0.08	0.31	-0.05	0.08	0.31	-0.03	-0.10
Expenditures	Cons&Inv	0.00	0.25	0.96	0.22	-0.02	0.06	0.28	0.00	0.07	0.23	0.07	-0.07	0.29	-0.02	0.08
	Transfers	0.00	0.02	0.80	0.07	0.02	0.48	0.25	-0.01	0.04	0.49	-0.01	0.11	0.37	0.01	0.06
	Other	0.00	0.00	0.00	0.00	0.00	0.00	0.00	0.00	0.00	0.01	0.00	-0.01	0.00	0.00	0.00
	Total	0.00	0.26	1.76	0.30	0.00	0.54	0.53	-0.01	0.11	0.72	0.07	0.03	0.67	-0.01	0.13

Source: Elaboration on the authors' dataset.

Note: Exp. measures implemented in the year announced in previous years; Unexp. measures implemented in the year not expected according to past announcements; Ann. measures announced in the year to be implemented in subsequent years.

TABLE 8.4.   UK: Macroeconomic Variables

Growth rates in percent	2008	2009	2010	2011	2012	2013	2014
(First four variables per capita)							
Output (growth rate in %)	−1.00	−5.04	1.21	−1.48	0.00	3.45	0.38
Output, European average (growth rate in %)	−0.78	−5.32	1.64	0.98	−1.11	−0.24	0.82
Consumption (growth rate in %)	−1.14	−3.76	−0.33	−3.03	0.46	3.47	0.08
Capital formation (growth rate in %)	−8.42	−21.18	5.71	1.40	1.20	7.16	5.20
Primary deficit (as % of GDP)	3.29	9.42	7.07	4.75	5.67	2.92	2.86
Total deficit (as % of GDP)	5.02	10.95	9.63	7.60	8.28	5.51	5.32
Short-term interest rate (%)	5.49	1.20	0.69	0.89	0.84	0.49	0.54
Long-term interest rate (%)	4.59	3.65	3.62	3.14	1.92	2.39	2.57
Cost of debt (%)	4.10	3.00	3.99	3.76	3.17	2.99	2.78
CPI (% variation, index is 100 in 2010)	3.55	2.14	3.23	4.39	2.78	2.52	1.45
Nominal effective exchange rate (growth rate in %)	−13.31	−11.12	−0.69	−0.70	4.06	−1.97	7.31
Real effective exchange rate (growth rate in %)	−14.19	−10.24	0.50	0.46	3.94	−1.37	6.74
Exports volume (growth rate in %)	1.62	−8.59	6.05	5.48	0.67	1.47	0.63
Gross debt over GDP ratio (%)	50.18	64.48	75.95	81.61	85.06	86.22	88.06

Source: OECD Economic Outlook No. 97 and 101.

Note: The countries included in the sample used to compute average European growth are Austria, Belgium, Denmark, Finland, France, Germany, Ireland, Italy, Portugal, Spain, and the UK.

policies on employers' contributions, support allowances, and public service pensions. In 2012, there were additional cuts to current and capital spending and again to transfers, as age-related allowances were frozen and restricted, for a total effect of around 2.4 £bn. In 2013, transfers were further reduced by 3 £bn through cuts in working age discretionary benefits, in tax credits, and in social rents. Finally, in 2014, there was a further reduction in public service pensions, for a total of about 1 £bn. In terms of percentages of GDP, as shown in Table 8.3, spending cuts (either announced or immediately implemented) between 2010 and 2014 amounted to 2.9% of GDP: a correction of about 0.6% year on average. Of all these measures, 87% were implemented within this 5-year interval, with the rest deferred to later years.

On the revenue side, most of the measures were announced in 2010: they consisted mainly of an increase in value-added tax (VAT) rates and small increases in direct taxation. There was the introduction of a bank levy, an increase in the rate of the capital gains tax for higher income taxpayers, and an increase in the National Insurance contribution paid by employers and employees, for a total of more than 13 £bn. The main VAT rate was increased to 20% beginning in January 2011 and the tax rates on insurance premia also were raised, for a total estimated increase in revenue of about 14 £bn.[3] Overall, as shown in Table 8.3, between 2010 and 2014 measures on the taxation side (taking into account the small expansionary ones) amounted to 1.7% of GDP, about one-third of the overall adjustment.

Along with fiscal consolidation, the government introduced a number of structural reforms: deregulation in the products and labor markets, and a rise in the age for state pension eligibility, which was also linked to life expectancy. In the 3 years prior to the consolidation, the pound's nominal effective exchange rate had depreciated by around 20%, remaining mostly flat thereafter throughout the austerity period, and appreciating by 9% in 2012–4. This nominal devaluation was accompanied by a rise in exports, which certainly helped in avoiding a slowdown of the economy.

As shown in Table 8.4, growth in the United Kingdom was higher than the average of European countries in our sample. Investment growth recovered from the −21% drop of 2009 to an increase of almost 6% in 2010, remaining positive thereafter. Finally, even though the debt over GDP ratio continued to increase, from 76% in 2010 to almost 90% in 2014, its rate of growth slowed down.

Ireland 2010–14: Expenditure Based

Between 2010 and 2014, government spending cuts amounted to a staggering 11% of GNP.[4] These were accompanied by tax hikes worth almost 4% of GNP, an overall fiscal correction amounting to 15% of GNP, about 3% per year over a 5-year period. GNP growth recovered from below −9% in 2009 to almost 2.5% in 2010, then declined to −4.4% 2011 and −0.9% in 2012, and finally increased to above 4.3% in 2013 and up to 8.9% in 2014. In this period Ireland also experienced a massive banking breakdown.

Details

When the Irish economy was hit by the financial crisis in 2008, it had been growing strongly for two decades, reaching the fourth highest level of GNP per capita in the OECD. Initially, growth was based mostly on productivity gains. At the beginning of the millennium, however, the expansion became increasingly dependent on a housing bubble financed by lax bank lending standards and a buoyant credit expansion. During the latter part of the boom, the acceleration of wages had eroded international competitiveness. The bubble burst in 2008 and banks would have become insolvent without state support. Injections of public funds to help resolve the crisis resulted in a sharp increase in government debt: the debt ratio jumped from 24% in 2006 to 120% in 2012.

Ireland embarked on a fiscal consolidation path with financial support from the IMF and EU. The main bulk of the measures were implemented starting in 2009, with an increase in direct taxes. But from 2010 onwards all of the consolidation measures were expenditure based, with cuts in government consumption from 2010–12 and in transfers in 2013 and 2014. The Irish government noted that

> In framing Budget 2010, the Government focused on curbing spending to adjust expenditure needs to the revenue base which has been reduced as a result of the overall contraction of the economy and the loss of certain income streams. In addition, in formulating policy the Government took on board evidence from international organizations, such as the EU Commission, the OECD and the IMF, as well as the relevant economic literature which indicates that consolidation driven by cuts in expenditure is more successful in reducing deficits than consolidation based on tax increases. Past Irish experience also supports this view and suggests that confidence is more quickly restored when adjustment is achieved by cutting expenditure rather than by tax increases. (Ireland Stability Programme Update, December 2009, p. 15).

In 2010, the cuts in government consumption amounted to 2.45 €bn, mostly implemented in the same year, including cuts in the public sector wage bill for a total amount of around 1 €bn and other savings in education, science, and healthcare and in capital expenditures. On the transfer side, the savings derived from cuts in subsidies to firms and social welfare programs, including a reduction in financial support to families for education and healthcare, totaled around 1.4 €bn. Revenues were increased slightly with several policies regarding personal income taxation announced in 2009 for 2010 and raising indirect taxes with the introduction of a carbon tax. In 2011 the main measures again were on the spending side: further cuts in government consumption totaling 3.4 €bn, of which 80% were implemented the same year, cuts in capital expenditure, the judicial system, transports, defense, and the administrative system in general. Transfers also were trimmed further by more than 2.4 €bn (about 80% immediately) with savings on social welfare and subsidies (e.g., to healthcare, education, and the agricultural sector). On the revenue side measures were minor, mainly concerning personal income taxation, stamp duties, registration taxes, and taxes on oil.

Similarly, in 2012 the main bulk of the measures again concerned government consumption and transfers: healthcare, the judicial system, defense, and education, for a total amount of around 1.6 €bn: 80% of such cuts were implemented immediately. In 2013 the main measures were on the spending side, with around 1 €bn worth of savings from cuts in government consumption and transfers (again healthcare, education, arts, and social welfare) to be implemented mostly in the same year. Personal and corporate taxation were increased for a total of around 0.8 €bn and excise duties also were raised for a total of 0.4 €bn, with two-thirds of the measures being implemented immediately. Finally, in 2014 the government implemented measures similar to those of 2013; again, the main part consisted of spending cuts.

Table 8.5 presents the size of the measures as a percentage of GNP: overall, between 2010 and 2015 spending measures amounted to 11% of GNP, an average reduction in spending of 2.2% per year over 5 years. Because some measures implemented in 2010 had been introduced in previous years, the overall reduction in expenditure was slightly higher, around 12% of GNP. Revenue increases were less than half as large, amounting to 3.8% of GNP over the same period.

In 2010 the nominal effective exchange rate fell by 5%; thereafter, it fluctuated around that level, so it was not a significant factor. Liberalizations in the product market, implemented in 2010, may have had some positive effect as a labor market reform in 2012 (the "Pathways to Work" initiative), although the short-run effects are unclear.[5] Despite the effects of the financial crisis, which entailed a very serious banking crisis, Irish macroeconomic variables recovered quite well after the trough of 2009.

TABLE 8.5. Ireland: Fiscal Consolidation

		2010			2011			2012			2013			2014			
		Exp.	Unexp.	Ann.	Exp.	Unexp.	Ann.	Exp.	Unexp.	Ann.	Exp.	Unexp.	Ann.	Exp.	Unexp.	Ann.	Ann.
Revenues	Direct	0.00	0.88	0.00	0.00	0.00	0.94	0.7	0.7	0.13	0.05	0.05	0.55	0.45	0.45	0.34	0.01
	Indirect	0.04	0.15	0.01	0.04	0.04	0.01	0.04	0.04	0.6	0.11	0.11	0.24	−0.01	−0.01	−0.1	−0.05
	n.c.	0.00	0.00	0.00	0.00	0.00	0.00	0.00	0.00	0.03	0.01	0.01	0.00	0.00	0.00	0.00	0.00
	Other	0.00	0.00	0.00	0.00	0.00	0.00	0.00	0.00	0.00	0.00	0.00	0.00	0.00	0.00	0.00	0.00
	Total	0.04	1.03	0.01	0.04	0.04	0.95	0.75	0.75	0.77	0.16	0.16	0.8	0.44	0.44	0.25	−0.04
Expenditures	Cons&Inv	0.02	0.71	1.73	0.02	0.02	1.93	0.52	0.52	1.07	0.1	0.1	0.5	0.15	0.15	0.34	0.00
	Transsfers	0.11	0.19	0.9	0.11	0.11	1.03	0.17	0.17	0.53	0.35	0.35	0.57	0.17	0.17	0.47	0.00
	Other	0.00	0.02	0.26	0.00	0.00	0.09	0.00	0.00	0.03	0.00	0.00	0.01	0.00	0.00	0.01	0.00
	Total	0.13	0.93	2.89	0.13	0.13	3.05	0.69	0.69	1.63	0.45	0.45	1.08	0.32	0.32	0.81	0.00

Source: Elaboration on the authors' dataset.

Note: Exp. measures implemented in the year announced in prevous years; Unexp. measures implemented in the year not expected according to past announcements; Ann. measures announced in the year to be implemented in subsequent years; n.c.: not classified.

TABLE 8.6. Ireland: Macroeconomic variables

Growth rates in percent	2008	2009	2010	2011	2012	2013	2014
(First five variables per capita)							
Output (growth rate in %)	−5.11	−7.65	−0.75	2.29	−0.54	0.01	4.31
Output, European average (growth rate in %)	−0.78	−5.32	1.64	0.98	−1.11	−0.24	0.82
National product (growth rate in %)	−6.96	−9.79	2.54	−4.41	−0.86	4.21	8.90
Consumption (growth rate in %)	−2.67	−7.08	−0.10	−1.51	−1.68	−0.57	0.78
Capital formation (growth rate in %)	−17.91	−18.81	−22.75	3.50	9.18	−2.07	10.53
Primary deficit (as % of GDP)	6.32	12.50	30.09	10.10	4.92	2.19	0.57
Total deficit (as % of GDP)	7.01	13.95	32.55	12.75	8.15	5.81	4.12
Short-term interest rate (%)	4.63	1.23	0.81	1.39	0.57	0.22	0.21
Long-term interest rate (%)	4.55	5.23	5.99	9.58	5.99	3.83	2.26
Cost of debt (%)	2.87	3.38	3.76	2.94	2.96	2.93	2.84
CPI (% variation, index is 100 in 2010)	3.97	−4.58	−0.95	2.55	1.68	0.50	0.20
Nominal effective exchange rate (growth rate in %)	4.39	1.77	−4.46	0.79	−3.75	2.98	1.02
Real effective exchange rate (growth rate in %)	4.12	−4.81	−7.08	0.16	−4.62	1.54	−0.92
Exports volume (growth rate in %)	−0.89	−4.07	5.97	5.33	4.57	1.11	11.88
Gross debt over GDP ratio (%)	42.42	61.70	86.33	109.67	119.57	119.61	105.42

Source: OECD Economic Outlook No. 97 and 101; IMF WEO, April 2015.
Note: The countries included in the sample used to compute average European growth are Austria, Belgium, Denmark, Finland, France, Germany, Ireland, Italy, Portugal, Spain, and the UK.

As depicted in Table 8.6, growth in output per capita recovered from below −7% in 2009 to almost 2.3% in 2011, then oscillated around zero in 2012 and 2013, and finally increased to above 4.3% in 2014. Growth in consumption per capita recovered less rapidly than output, remaining negative until 2013 and turning positive only in 2014. Except for 2013, investment and exports seem to have been the main drivers of the recovery: the former dropped by 23% in 2010 and then completely recovered by 2014, while the volume of exports kept growing each year, averaging 6% per year. The debt over GDP ratio, after having jumped to 120% in 2012 as a result of the bank bailout, started to decline to around 105% in 2014, a sign that the consolidation was effective in reducing the debt ratio.

Spain 2009-14: a Mix of (Mostly) Taxes and Expenditure

Spain introduced austerity measures in each year from 2010 to 2014, totaling 12% of its GDP, with 7% on the side of taxes. After the real estate bubble burst, the country experienced a deep recession in 2011; it recovered in 2014.

Details

In the decade before the crisis, Spain had grown much faster than the rest of the euro-area, driven in part by a real estate bubble that had led to a construction boom: house prices nearly tripled between 1997 and 2008. The bubble was fed by loans from local banks that had access to cheap funding from euro-area banks, mostly French and German. When the credit crunch hit, real estate prices collapsed. Banks were left with huge losses, as clients struggled to repay mortgages. The country entered a recession in 2011. While the depth of the recession was similar to that of other advanced OECD economies in terms of GDP growth, it led to a much larger increase in unemployment, one of the reasons being that the crisis had wiped out the construction sector, which is very labor intensive, and to a sharper deterioration in government finances. The budget deficit rose to 11% of GDP in 2009. Banks lost the ability to borrow money or raise capital. The savings banks, the "Cajas," were the weakest, and without public support many would have collapsed. Although Spain never lost access to market financing, issuing debt became increasingly expensive. In a bid to calm uncertainty and quickly address the banking issues, Spain requested assistance from the European Stability Mechanism (ESM) in July 2012. The ESM made available up to 100 €bn, but in the end Spain drew only 41.3 €bn. The funds were loaned to the Spanish government, not disbursed directly to Spanish banks. Thus, the loan increased the public debt.

Austerity started in 2009, with a small increase in excise duties, but the main bulk of the program was implemented between 2010 and 2014. As shown in Table 8.7, between 2010 and 2014 spending cuts amounted to more than 5% of GDP, while tax increases totaled more than 7% of GDP. In 2010 the main measures enacted were immediate increases in VAT rates worth 5.2 €bn, public sector wage cuts of 4.5 €bn, restraints in compensation of public employees worth 5.2 €bn, other cuts in government consumption of 1.5 €bn, and in government investments of more than 5.8 €bn. Approximately two-thirds of the measures concerning expenditure cuts were implemented in the same year, and the rest in the following year. In 2011 there was a pensions freeze for a total

TABLE 8.7. Spain: Fiscal Consolidation

		2009			2010			2011		
		Exp.	*Unexp.*	*Ann.*	*Exp.*	*Unexp*	*Ann.*	*Exp.*	*Unexp.*	*Ann.*
Revenues	Direct	0.00	0.00	0.00	0.00	0.00	0.00	0.00	0.00	0.00
	Indirect	0.00	0.29	0.00	0.00	0.49	0.00	0.00	0.00	0.00
	Other	0.00	0.00	0.00	0.00	0.00	0.00	0.00	0.00	0.00
	Total	0.00	0.29	0.00	0.00	0.49	0.00	0.00	0.00	0.00
Expenditures	Cons&Inv	0.00	0.00	0.00	0.00	1.15	0.57	0.57	0.79	0.00
	Transfers	0.00	0.00	0.00	0.00	0.00	−0.01	−0.01	0.14	0.00
	Other	0.00	0.00	0.00	0.00	0.03	0.00	0.00	0.05	0.00
	Total	0.00	0.00	0.00	0.00	1.17	0.56	0.56	0.98	0.00

		2012			2013			2014		
		Exp.	*Unexp.*	*Ann.*	*Exp.*	*Unexp.*	*Ann.*	*Exp.*	*Unexp.*	*Ann.*
Revenues	Direct	0.00	1.31	0.09	0.10	0.49	0.29	0.39	0.43	−0.57
	Indirect	0.00	0.03	0.00	0.00	1.17	0.10	0.00	0.07	0.13
	Other	0.00	0.33	0.74	0.74	0.39	0.49	0.20	0.41	0.51
	Total	0.00	1.67	0.83	0.84	2.05	0.88	0.59	0.91	0.07
Expenditures	Cons&Inv	0.00	1.16	0.67	0.19	0.01	−0.06	0.26	0.23	0.38
	Transfers	0.00	0.34	0.26	0.25	-0.34	−0.08	−0.06	−0.09	0.09
	Other	0.00	0.00	0.00	0.00	0.00	0.00	0.00	−0.17	0.17
	Total	0.00	1.50	0.93	0.45	-0.33	−0.14	0.20	−0.03	0.64

Source: Elaboration on the authors' dataset.

Note: Exp. measures implemented in the year announced in previous years; Unexp. measures implemented in the year not expected according to past announcements; Ann. measures announced in the year to be implemented in subsequent years.

amount of around 1.5 €bn, cuts in current government consumption of 1.2 €bn, further restraints in the compensation of employees, and wage cuts worth around 6.5 €bn. Overall, between 2010 and 2011, the bulk of these measures were implemented immediately. Beginning in 2012, austerity involved a larger share of announcements, that is, measures to be implemented in subsequent years. In 2012, the consolidation included measures around direct taxation (such as a supplementary levy on personal income taxes of 5.1 €bn), government consumption (public sector wages) for a cumulative amount exceeding 13 €bn, health and education expenditures of almost 6 €bn, transfers (through the suspension of wage indexation to inflation) generating savings of more than 1.9 €bn, and cuts in unemployment subsidies of about 1.4 €bn. In 2013, the main part of the fiscal measures fell on the revenue side: increases in excise taxes and the VAT for a cumulative amount of more than 11 €bn; an increase in personal income taxes, taxes on nonresidents, and social security contributions of more than 5 €bn; and in corporate taxation of around 2 €bn. Finally, savings of more than 6.4 €bn were realized in 2014 thanks to cuts in government consumption. Revenues also were increased because of a rise in social security contributions of around 2.1 €bn and in VAT and excise duties of more than 2 €bn.

Between 2009 and 2012 Spain's nominal effective exchange rate fell by 4%, partly recovering thereafter: thus the exchange rate did not play an important role in the way the economy adjusted to the austerity measures. Deregulation of labor and product helped. As shown in Table 8.8, the economy contracted sharply during the consolidation. Until 2014 growth in output per capita remained negative: in 2009 right after the financial crisis, it reached almost −4.5%, then recovered to −0.4% in 2010, only to decline again in 2011 and 2012. It then began to recover, returning to positive values only in 2014 when it grew twice as much as the average of the European countries in our sample. Consumption and investment followed similar trends. In the end, the consolidation was not able to stabilize the debt over GDP ratio: it increased from around 53% in 2009 to more than 100% in 2014.

Portugal 2010–14: A Mix of Taxes and (Mostly)Expenditure

Portugal responded to the sudden stop (a collapse of foreign lending to the private and public sectors) that hit its economy in 2011 with an austerity program amounting to almost 10% of GDP in spending cuts and more than 7% of GDP in revenue increases This was associated with a deep recession. All components of domestic demand recovered in 2014.

Details

The Portuguese fiscal consolidation process began in 2010. "The 2010 Stability and Growth Programme [...] defines [...] the goal of reducing the general government deficit to 2.8% of GDP by 2013 and controlling the growth of public debt [...]. The Portuguese Government makes this commitment aware that a serious and consistent fiscal consolidation

TABLE 8.8. Spain: Macroeconomic variables

Growth rates in percent	2007	2008	2009	2010	2011	2012	2013	2014
(First four variables per capita)								
Output (growth rate in %)	1.75	−0.53	−4.47	−0.41	−0.99	−2.18	−0.87	1.66
Output, European average (growth rate in %)	2.19	−0.78	−5.32	1.64	0.98	−1.11	−0.24	0.82
Consumption (growth rate in %)	1.26	−2.29	−4.51	−0.17	−2.42	−3.03	−1.94	2.67
Capital formation (growth rate in %)	1.37	−6.88	−25.70	−4.59	−3.03	−2.45	−2.69	4.56
Primary deficit (as % of GDP)	−3.09	3.38	9.62	7.84	7.46	7.86	3.98	2.94
Total deficit (as % of GDP)	−2.00	4.42	10.96	9.39	9.42	10.32	6.79	5.80
Short-term interest rate (%)	4.28	4.63	1.23	0.81	1.39	0.57	0.22	0.21
Long-term interest rate (%)	4.31	4.36	3.97	4.25	5.44	5.85	4.56	2.71
Cost of debt (%)	2.81	2.92	3.38	2.93	3.27	3.59	3.43	3.14
CPI (% variation, index is 100 in 2010)	2.75	3.99	−0.29	1.78	3.15	2.42	1.40	−0.15
Nominal effective exchange rate (growth rate in %)	1.24	1.90	1.37	−3.03	0.53	−2.01	2.29	1.77
Real effective exchange rate (growth rate in %)	1.39	1.60	−0.34	−2.97	0.50	−2.29	1.54	−0.53
Exports volume (growth rate in %)	7.93	−0.85	−11.68	9.01	7.13	1.17	4.21	4.07
Gross debt over GDP ratio (%)	35.59	39.47	52.78	60.14	69.54	85.74	95.46	100.44

Source: OECD Economic Outlook No. 97 and 101.

Note: The countries included in the sample used to compute average European growth are Austria, Belgium, Denmark, Finland, France, Germany, Ireland, Italy, Portugal, Spain, and the UK.

process, [...] is a necessary condition for the strengthening of confidence and to sustain economic growth," (Stability and Growth Programme 2010, p. 1). In 2011 Portugal suffered a "sudden stop," meaning the almost impossibility of borrowing. Early that year, Portugal's 2-year bond yields exceeded 10% and 10-year bonds were trading at close to 9%, levels not compatible with public debt sustainability. Portugal's funding costs remained high for more than 2 years, with some episodes of extreme stress. Except for two short windows in January and May 2013, when the Treasury managed to issue a 5- and a 10-year bond, Portugal remained cut off from the sovereign debt markets until late 2013 to early 2014.

In 2011, the Portuguese government added significant additional measures to the 2010 program. These had been asked for by the Ecofin and the IMF in exchange for €78 bn in external financing by the EU, the ESM, and the IMF (more than 40% of Portugal's 2011 GDP).

As shown in Table 8.9, between 2010 and 2014 the Portuguese fiscal consolidation was extremely large, amounting to almost 10% of GDP in spending cuts and more than 7% of GDP in revenue increases. In 2010, the main measures on the side of spending were wage restraints and a freeze in civil servant hiring for a total of 0.6 €bn; the reduction and rationalization of operating expenditure for outsourcing and military equipment for 0.5 €bn; and reductions in capital expenditure, such as stopping road constructions, no infrastructure concessions, and reductions in transfers to local governments and state-owned enterprises for a total of 1.2 €bn. On the revenue side, the main measures were a 1% increase in VAT rates and changes in tax rates for different brackets of personal income, amounting to 1.1 €bn and 0.74 €bn respectively. In 2011, savings again were obtained on the spending side from reductions in public sector wages and hires for a total of 0.69 €bn; capital expenditures for a total of 0.69 €bn; the provision of services and control of general government operating expenditure for 1.2 €bn; public expenditures on healthcare for 1.4 €bn; and finally a suspension of the indexation of pensions worth 0.7 €bn. On the taxation side, the main measures were revisions and limitations of tax allowances and of benefits in personal and corporate taxation for a total of 1 €bn and the rationalization of the VAT tax structure, the latter generating 1.2 €bn in additional revenue. In 2012, savings on the spending side were generated by more wage cuts and by reductions in social transfers and subsidies:

TABLE 8.9. Portugal: Fiscal Consolidation

		2010			2011			2012			2013			2014		
		Exp.	Unexp.	Ann.	Exp.	Unexp.	Ann.	Exp.	Unexp.	Ann.	Exp.	Unexp.	Ann.	Exp.	Unexp.	Ann.
Revenues	Direct	0.00	0.35	0.90	0.90	0.48	0.38	0.00	0.00	1.94	2.33	0.00	0.00	0.00	0.41	0.07
	Indirect	0.00	0.26	0.48	0.48	0.00	0.86	0.77	0.00	0.09	0.19	0.00	0.00	0.00	0.13	0.00
	n.c.	0.00	0.00	0.00	0.00	0.00	0.10	0.10	0.39	0.10	0.10	0.39	-0.39	-0.39	0.00	0.00
	Other	0.00	0.00	0.00	0.00	0.00	0.00	0.00	0.00	0.00	0.00	0.00	0.00	0.00	0.00	0.00
	Total	0.00	0.61	1.38	1.38	1.48	1.34	0.87	0.39	2.13	2.62	0.39	-0.39	-0.39	0.54	0.07
Spending	Cons&Inv	0.00	0.22	0.68	0.68	0.00	3.17	2.02	0.00	-0.19	0.96	0.00	0.00	0.00	1.22	0.29
	Transfers	0.00	0.08	0.23	0.23	0.00	1.06	0.86	0.00	0.97	1.16	0.00	0.00	0.00	0.46	-0.47
	n.c.	0.00	0.00	0.00	0.00	0.54	0.00	0.00	0.78	0.00	0.00	0.10	0.00	0.00	0.00	0.00
	Other	0.00	0.21	0.47	0.47	0.00	0.10	0.10	0.00	0.00	0.00	0.00	0.00	0.00	-0.16	0.16
	Total	0.00	0.51	1.38	1.38	0.54	4.33	2.98	0.78	0.78	2.12	0.10	0.00	0.00	1.52	-0.02

Source: Elaboration on the authors' dataset.

Note: Exp. measures implemented in the year announced in previous years; Unexp. measures implemented in the year not expected according to past announcements; Ann. measures announced in the year to be implemented in subsequent years; n.c.: not classified.

the former totaled 0.68 €bn and the latter 1.7 €bn. On the revenue side, there were more reforms of personal income taxation and increases in property taxes: 1.37 €bn in the former and 0.68 €bn in the latter. Vitor Gaspar, who had been appointed finance minister in 2011 at the beginning of the program, resigned on July 1, 2013. Maria Luís Albuquerque, the Secretary of State of Treasury under him, took the job and essentially pursued the same policies. In 2013, there were no relevant additional measures, only implementation of measures that had been announced in previous years. Finally, in 2014 there were more policies instituted on the spending side, particularly regarding government consumption, with more reductions in the public sector wage bill, personnel costs, and in ministries' expenditure, totaling around 2 €bn. Measures on the taxation side that year were minor. Along with the austerity measures, there were some liberalizations in labor markets in 2010, 2012, and 2013 and in product markets in 2010 and 2013. The EU–ESM–IMF program ended abruptly in April 2014 when Portugal waived its right to draw the last tranche of the funds it had been allocated.[6]

Table 8.10 shows that, after the 2009 crisis, macroeconomic variables in Portugal overall recovered in 2010, but then the situation worsened again in 2011 and 2013, finally improving only in 2014. Output growth per capita recovered from below −3% in 2009 to just above 1.8% in 2010, then turned negative again in 2011 and plummeted to more than −3.7% in 2012, and started to recover, returning to positive in 2014. Per capita consumption growth similarly recovered from around −2.5% in 2009 to above 2.3% in 2010, then declined again, reaching a trough of −5.2% in 2012, when it started to recover, reaching 1.9% in 2014. Investment growth remained negative up to 2014. On average, between 2010 and 2014, output growth per capita was −1.3%, consumption growth per capita was −1.6%, and capital formation growth per capita was around −6.4%. Consolidation efforts were not sufficient to stabilize the debt over GDP ratio: it increased from around 96% in 2010 to more than 130% in 2014.

Italy 2011–12: A Mix of (Mostly) Taxes and Expenditures

In 2011 Italy responded to a sudden stop with a significant austerity program, tilted toward revenue increases. The new measures adopted in 2011

TABLE 8.10. Portugal: Macroeconomic variables

Growth rates in percent	2008	2009	2010	2011	2012	2013	2014
(First four variables per capita)							
Output (growth rate in %)	0.05	−3.12	1.84	−1.70	−3.71	−3.58	0.73
Output, European average (growth rate in %)	−0.78	−5.32	1.64	0.98	−1.11	−0.24	0.82
Consumption (growth rate in %)	1.22	−2.46	2.32	−3.52	−5.24	−3.46	1.90
Capital formation (growth rate in %)	−2.10	−11.79	−9.06	−4.54	−13.75	−7.40	2.91
Primary deficit (as % of GDP)	1.05	7.10	8.47	3.53	1.32	0.60	0.08
Total deficit (as % of GDP)	3.77	9.81	11.17	7.36	5.61	4.83	4.46
Short-term interest rate (%)	4.63	1.23	0.81	1.39	0.57	0.22	0.21
Long-term interest rate (%)	4.52	4.21	5.40	10.24	10.55	6.29	3.75
Cost of debt (%)	3.96	3.77	3.24	3.97	3.84	3.32	3.39
CPI (% variation, index is 100 in 2010)	2.56	−0.84	1.39	3.59	2.74	0.27	−0.28
Nominal effective exchange rate (growth rate in %)	1.54	0.90	−2.24	0.33	−1.43	1.77	1.18
Real effective exchange rate (growth rate in %)	−0.06	−0.65	−2.13	0.86	−1.08	−0.20	−0.71
Exports volume (growth rate in %)	−0.32	−10.77	9.09	6.80	3.35	6.21	3.32
Gross debt over GDP ratio (%)	71.67	83.61	96.18	111.39	126.22	129.04	130.59

Source: OECD Economic Outlook No. 97 and 101.

Note: The countries included in the sample used to compute average European growth are Austria, Belgium, Denmark, Finland, France, Germany, Ireland, Italy, Portugal, Spain, and the UK.

and 2012 were almost exclusively on the revenue side, though the spending cuts that had been previously decided on did go through. Overall, the size of the adjustment was close to 6% of GDP over the course of 2 years with the revenue side accounting for 55% of the total adjustment. Austerity was accompanied by a recession that lasted for about 3 years.

Details

Following the 2007–8 financial crisis, by 2010 Italy was on the right track toward a slow recovery. Between the end of 2010 and August 2011 the center-right government adopted a number of measures that consisted mostly of announcements for 2012 and 2013. These included higher taxes worth 2.4% of GDP and spending cuts worth 1.4% of GDP. During the summer of 2011, in the aftermath of the Greek crisis, and after the announcement in July that the private sector might be involved in the Greek debt restructuring, Italy experienced a sudden stop. Interest rates on 10-year government bonds jumped from less than 5% in June to above 7% in November, and Italian sovereign bonds were downgraded. In November 2011 the government resigned and a new technical executive was appointed, led by former EU competition commissioner Mario Monti, with the goal of restoring confidence in Italian financial markets.

On the expenditure side, retirement rules were changed, leading to expected savings in the pension system, although their immediate effect on the budget was minimal. The government also implemented the spending cuts promised by its predecessor, which included cuts in the budget of individual ministries for a total of 7 €bn in 2012. On the revenue side, the main new measures were an increase in municipal property taxes, a revaluation of the land registry, and an increase in excise taxes. These measures all started to go into effect in 2012. They followed measures of the previous government, including a revision of depreciation rates and the taxation of financial income, measures against tax evasion, regional personal income surcharges, gaming revenues, and stamp duties and an increase in VAT rate. The overall adjustment decided on by the two governments during 2011–12 was almost 6% of GDP, slightly more on the revenue side, which accounted for 55% of the adjustment. The differential between Italian and German government bonds was cut almost in half within 5 months, falling from 5.5% in November 2011 to 3% in March 2012.

Growth in output per capita declined steadily until reaching a trough at −3.2% in the second quarter of 2012. It remained negative until the end of 2013, 2 1/2 years after the introduction of the austerity program. The recovery began only in 2015. Growth rates of consumption and capital formation also fell, reaching a trough of −3.1% and −9.4% respectively in the second quarter of 2012. Italy's debt over GDP ratio kept rising, peaking at 132% in 2014.

Table 8.11 shows the amount of fiscal measures adopted in Italy between 2011 and 2012. The measures both on the spending and revenue sides that actually took place in these 2 years, both unexpected and consequences of previous past announcements, had an impact on the budget of approximately 4.6 percentage points of GDP: 57% was due to tax hikes. Table 8.12 shows the evolution of the main macroeconomic variables during these years.

TABLE 8.11.   Italy: Fiscal Consolidation

		2011			2012		
		Exp.	*Unexp.*	*Ann.*	*Imp.*	*Unexp.*	*Ann.*
Revenues	Direct	0.06	0.01	1.45	0.72	0.6	−0.05
	Indirect	0.07	0.14	0.53	0.43	0.37	0.02
	n.c.	0.00	0.02	0.23	0.16	0.00	0.00
	Other	0.04	0.05	−0.02	−0.03	0.01	−0.10
	Total	0.18	0.22	2.19	1.28	0.96	−0.13
Expenditures	Cons&Inv	0.62	0.25	0.45	0.18	0.39	0.03
	Transfers	0.05	−0.02	0.21	0.20	0.06	0.35
	Other	0.00	0.00	0.50	0.31	−0.07	0.41
	Total	0.67	0.23	1.16	0.69	0.38	0.79

Source: Elaboration on the authors' dataset.

Note: Exp. measures implemented in the year announced in previous years; Unexp. measures implemented in the year not expected according to past announcements; Ann. measures announced in the year to be implemented in subsequent years; n.c.: not classified.

EVALUATING EUROPEAN AUSTERITY IN 2010–14

Did austerity policies in Europe in 2010–14 have different effects on output compared with previous episodes of fiscal retrenchment? We consider this question for 10 EU countries in our sample and the United States for comparison.[7] We did not include Greece in this sample because we do not have sufficiently precise data to reconstruct the plans adopted by Greece before 2010. However, we did reconstruct the Greek plans since 2010: they are reported in the next section, which is dedicated to Greece.

It is important to note here that the austerity plans adopted in Europe—especially in Spain, Portugal, and Ireland, not to mention Greece—were extremely large, and many of them included very large tax increases. As we know from our previous results, tax-based adjustments create deep and long recessions. Thus, the large recessions experienced in some European countries are not prima facie evidence against our previous findings regarding EB and TB adjustments, nor of the fact that they were especially costly, given their size. Obviously this does not imply anything regarding the question of whether austerity in general was too severe. It might have been.

TABLE 8.12.   Italy: Macroeconomic variables

Growth rates in percent	2009	2010	2011	2012	2013	2014
(First four variables per capita)						
Output (growth rate in %)	−6.26	1.19	0.46	−3.34	−2.15	−0.74
Output, European average (growth rate in %)	−5.32	1.64	0.98	−1.11	−0.24	0.82
Consumption (growth rate in %)	−2.11	0.76	−0.25	−4.57	−3.23	−0.06
Capital formation (growth rate in %)	−14.90	2.10	−1.56	−10.06	−6.13	−3.34
Primary deficit (as % of GDP)	1.05	0.12	−0.97	−2.04	−1.71	−1.44
Total deficit (as % of GDP)	5.27	4.25	3.49	2.99	2.95	3.03
Short-term interest rate (%)	1.23	0.81	1.39	0.57	0.22	0.21
Long-term interest rate (%)	4.31	4.04	5.42	5.49	4.32	2.89
Cost of debt (%)	4.13	3.67	3.86	4.29	3.77	3.41
CPI (% variation, index is 100 in 2010)	0.75	1.53	2.70	3.00	1.21	0.24
Nominal effective exchange rate (growth rate in %)	1.92	−3.91	0.49	−2.32	2.62	2.28
Real effective exchange rate (growth rate in %)	0.78	−4.15	−0.05	−1.89	1.48	0.03
Exports volume (growth rate in %)	−19.76	10.75	5.93	1.99	0.74	2.35
Gross debt over GDP ratio (%)	112.62	115.53	116.48	123.36	129.04	131.70

Source: OECD Economic Outlook No. 97 and 101.

Note: The countries included in the sample used to compute average European growth are Austria, Belgium, Denmark, Finland, France, Germany, Ireland, Italy, Portugal, Spain, and the UK.

We divide our sample of countries into three groups. The first includes countries in the core of the euro area; on average they experienced less serious financial trouble (Austria, Belgium, Denmark, Germany, France). The second includes countries in the periphery (Ireland, Italy, Portugal, Spain); the third group includes three countries outside the EMU, with flexible exchange rates (Denmark, United Kingdom, and United States). Using the same model presented in Chapter 7, we start by estimating the effects of plans on a sample that stops in 2007, before the crisis. Then, using the estimated parameters, we simulate what that model would predict for postcrisis austerity, feeding into it the plans actually implemented in 2010–4 in the countries just listed. Then we check (comparing the simulated path of output and the observed one) whether the simulation results are broadly consistent with the actual data.

We present the results of our simulations in Figures 8.3, 8.4, and 8.5. On the left-hand side of each figure we describe, year by year using a histogram, the size and composition of the fiscal plans adopted by each

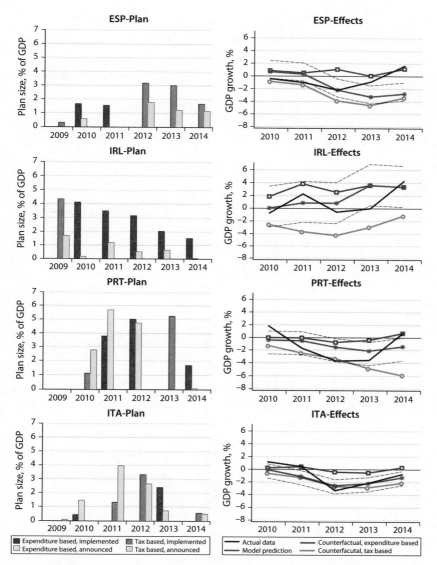

Figure 8.3. Fiscal consolidations in Spain, Ireland, Portugal, and Italy. Histograms on the left-hand side of the graph represent the planned fiscal consolidations in every year. Red columns (light shades for announcements and dark shades for current implementations) represent years of tax-based fiscal consolidation, and blue ones spending-based consolidation. In each histogram we report the yearly impact and all the future announced shifts in fiscal variables, measured as a fraction of GDP. On the right-hand side panels we report the corresponding simulated GDP growth (stars, with 95% confidence bounds) against the actual one (in black). Counterfactual GDP growth paths for totally tax- and expenditure-based plans are, respectively symbolized by red and blue lines.

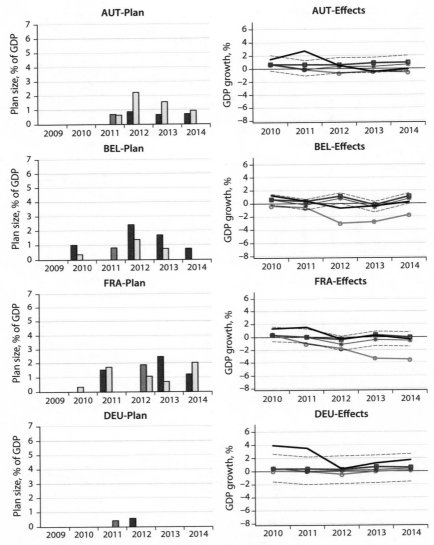

Figure 8.4. Fiscal consolidations in Austria, Belgium, France, and Germany.

country from 2010–14. For each year there are two columns: one in full color, representing the measures implemented that year (either unexpected or previously announced); one cross-hatched in a lighter color showing the total size of the announced measures—that is, including measures adopted in that year but expected to be implemented in later

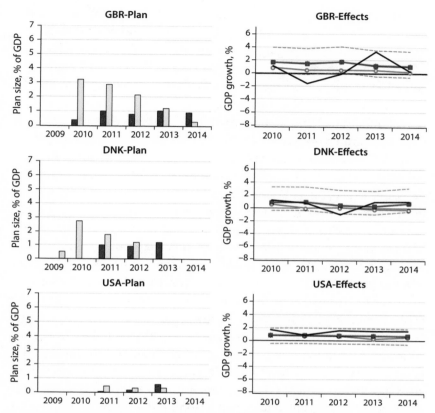

Figure 8.5. Fiscal consolidations in the United Kingdom, Denmark, and the United States.

years. Each year is either a TB or an EB episode. Implementation and announcement columns of TB episodes are in red (dark and light red respectively); the spending-based episodes are in blue. The values indicated in the columns are expressed in percentage of GDP of the previous year. Keep in mind that if a measure is announced in 2010 to be implemented in 2014, it enters the column for announcements in 2010, 2011, 2012, and 2013, while it also contributes to the size of implementations in 2014. However, such long horizons of announcements are rare.

On the right-hand-side panels we report actual GDP growth (in black); simulated GDP growth conditional on the implemented fiscal plan (in green with 95% confidence intervals); what output growth would have been, according to the model, if all the adjustment episodes had been EB (blue line with squared symbols); what output growth would have been, according to the model, had all the episodes been TB (red line with circles). In countries such as the United Kingdom or United States, where all the plans actually implemented were EB, the green and blue lines almost coincide.

Our model matches actual growth reasonably well, although with large standard errors, especially for the countries in the second group: Ireland, Italy, Portugal, and Spain. Several caveats are in order. Because the model projects GDP growth conditional only on fiscal consolidations, one expects a better fit between actual and projected GDP growth in those years when there were no significant economic shocks other than austerity. The evidence from 2012 and 2013 makes clear this point, as those years are more distant from the financial and economic shocks of 2008 and 2009. Also, a few specific nonfinancial shocks could explain why our predictions do not match actual growth. The most relevant ones occurred in Portugal in 2010 and in Germany in the years closer to the crisis. For Portugal, our predicted growth rate for 2010 is considerably lower than realized growth. This may be explained by the EU "Council Recommendation (with a view to bringing an end to the situation of an excessive government deficit in Portugal)" (p. 5): it states that in 2010 "positive growth of 1.4% was largely due to exceptional factors that boosted exports and private consumption." In Germany, our projected growth rate is almost flat, far different from the growth rates realized there right after the crisis. In this instance, the IMF claimed that "the [German] uptick started in the second quarter of 2009, led by exports and aided by policy support and restocking of inventories."

Note too that in some countries, such as Germany and the United States that implemented no or rather small fiscal adjustments, the model's projection differs from actual output growth by almost a fixed quantity each year: for instance, in the United States, projected growth is approximately 1 percentage point below actual growth every year, despite there being no sizeable adjustment measures. This is because when no adjustment takes place, the central forecast produced by our model is the average growth that the country experienced in the 1980–2007 sample.[8] This result is consistent with the broad discussion in the US about the surprisingly slow recovery after the recession. Conversely, as shown in Figure 8.3, for Ireland, Italy, Portugal, and Spain the projected growth shows that the different nature of the fiscal adjustments in each country contributes significantly in explaining growth differentials.

Ireland put in place a draconian adjustment on the expenditure side and experienced a small recession in 2010, 2012, and 2013 following the disastrous banking collapse of 2009. Italy undertook a smaller adjustment, tilted toward the revenue side in 2011–12, and made smaller spending cuts in 2009 and 2013. The result was a deep recession which lasted until 2015. The depth of the recession in Italy was particularly large, even given the size of the tax increase. Probably other factors, such as the uncertainty associated with high debt, played a role there along with endemic political uncertainty.

The predicted path of output in Spain matches the actual data well in the first 3 years of our simulations, given our prediction of a deep recession in 2012 caused by the prevalence of tax measures in that year.[9] However, the Spanish economy slowed its decline in 2013 and recovered in 2014. This path diverges from our projections—which are driven by the tax-based nature of the adjustment in those years and that predict a very severe recession. Portugal's adjustment was significant and mixed, followed by a severe recession, even worse than was projected by our model. The United Kingdom made a moderate EB adjustment and had a small and short-lived recession (Figure 8.5). France's adjustment was also moderate and mixed, and was followed by a moderate recession (Figure 8.4).

Counterfactual Experiments

What if a country had chosen a different composition for its austerity plans? To answer this question we should compare the green line with either the red or the blue lines. The difference in growth rates gives us a sense of how much higher or lower the actual output path would have been if the plans had been entirely spending (blue) or tax (red) based. In countries such as Spain, Italy, Ireland, and Portugal, which implemented the largest fiscal consolidations, the nature of the fiscal plans plays a prominent role in determining their growth experience, as we can see in Figure 8.3. For example, if Spain had implemented exactly the same size and timing of adjustments but had chosen to only cut expenditures—while it instead increased taxes, from 2012 onwards—its GDP growth would have been about 4 percentage points higher in 2014, speeding up its recovery. The same for Italy: had Italy chosen to only cut expenditures, in 2011, 2012, and 2014, its GDP growth would have been 2% higher in every single year since 2011, with a cumulative "additional" 8 percentage points of growth relative to 2011.

THE GREEK TRAGEDY

The Greek economy had done much better than other European countries from the late 1990s up until the crisis, experiencing an extraordinary boom. In terms of GDP per capita, its distance from Spain closed from 85% to 93%; with respect to the euro average, the difference went from 60% to 78%. After 2008, a combination of shocks generated a sharp reduction in GDP per capita that fell to a level lower than when Greece had joined the euro (2002). This remarkable period for the Greek economy is the result of a complex set of events. We discuss them in the text that follows, with special attention to fiscal variables that, however, are only part of the story. Greek data are not available for safely constructing fiscal plans following the methodology adopted in this book, at least up to 2010. We were, however, able to reconstruct the fiscal plans Greece implemented since the crisis, that is, starting from 2010. Overall, in the five years 2010–14, an adjustment of roughly 20% of GDP was implemented, consisting of 12 points in spending cuts and 8 points in tax increases. This is extraordinary.

Up to the Crisis

From the time it joined the euro up to the financial crisis, Greece experienced an extraordinary economic boom that started in the mid-1990s in anticipation of its entry into the monetary union.[10] Average per capita GDP growth was close to 4% per year over 2000–2007, led mainly by a boom in consumption and investment and an extremely loose fiscal policy. Wages were increasing well above productivity so that Greece was losing international competitiveness: poor productivity growth combined with high internal demand severely deteriorated the current account. The same happened in a few other countries of the periphery. Symmetrically the countries providing the funding (mostly Germany) were accumulating large surpluses, whose mirror image was the external lending provided by their banks. The current account balance of the euro area as a whole was close to balance.

Greece had persistently missed its fiscal targets: the budget deficit was never less than 3% of GDP, the threshold required by the Stability and Growth Pact. When it was admitted into the eurozone in 2002, Greece's (later revised) budget numbers showed a budget deficit of 6% of GDP. Systematic waste in spending, tax evasion, and overly optimistic revenue projections were the main causes. General government debt reached 126% of GDP in 2009, up from 97% in 1998, despite the exceptionally high real and nominal GDP growth and low cost of debt.

At the beginning of October 2009, the center-left party PASOK (Pan-hellenic Socialist Movement) won the legislative elections with more than 43% of the votes. On October 6, 2009, George Papandreou was appointed prime minister. He announced that Greek public finances were far worse than what had been stated up to then: in particular, the budget deficit, instead of being between 2% and 3% of GDP, was actually between 12% and 13% of GDP—it was eventually revised to more than 15%, as shown in Table 8.13. This announcement, combined with downgrades by the three major credit rating agencies, led markets to panic. By the spring of 2010 Greece had effectively lost access to financial markets: only 6 months earlier Greece was borrowing at roughly the same rate as Germany. A perfect storm began.

The Crisis

The Greek economy was hit simultaneously by three shocks: a sovereign debt crisis, as investors started to doubt the solvency of the government; a banking crisis, in light of the doubtful solvency position of some Greek banks because of surging nonperforming loans and the large amount of government bonds held on their balance sheets; and a sudden stop. Because the three shocks occurred at the same time, it is not easy to attribute to each of them a share of "responsibility" for the deep recession that followed. Probably the most comprehensive analysis to date of the Greek crisis is by Gourinchas, Philippon, and Vayanos (2017). They

TABLE 8.13. Greece: Macroeconomic variables

Growth rates in percent	2009	2010	2011	2012	2013	2014
(First four variables per capita)						
Output (growth rate in %)	−4.49	−5.31	−9.01	−6.21	−6.65	0.37
Output, European average (growth rate in %)	−5.32	1.64	0.98	−1.11	−0.24	0.82
Consumption (growth rate in %)	−0.57	−6.99	−11.05	−7.76	−4.73	1.38
Capital formation (growth rate in %)	−61.14	−76.27	−287.81	275.15	15.66	−7.84
Primary deficit (as % of GDP)	10.35	5.67	3.44	4.41	9.58	−0.09
Total deficit (as % of GDP)	15.14	11.20	10.28	8.89	13.16	3.59
Short-term interest rate (%)	1.23	0.81	1.39	0.57	0.22	0.21
Long-term interest rate (%)	5.17	9.09	15.75	22.50	10.05	6.93
Cost of debt (%)	4.37	4.35	4.68	2.60	2.25	2.08
CPI (% variation, index is 100 in 2010)	1.20	4.61	3.28	1.49	−0.93	−1.32
Nominal effective exchange rate (growth rate in %)	1.85	−3.56	0.76	−2.48	2.50	3.21
Real effective exchange rate (growth rate in %)	1.41	−0.69	0.59	−3.11	−1.38	−1.64
Exports volume (growth rate in %)	−20.48	4.75	0.03	1.17	1.50	7.46
Gross debt over GDP ratio (%)	126.70	145.90	171.94	159.48	177.57	179.83

Source: OECD Economic Outlook No. 101.

Note: The countries included in the sample used to compute average European growth are Austria, Belgium, Denmark, Finland, France, Germany, Ireland, Italy, Portugal, Spain, and the UK.

conclude that the lion's share of the subsequent severe downturn was the sudden stop, not unlike what happened in a number of developing countries. However, the effect of the sudden stop on Greece was deeper and more persistent than in almost any emerging market economies on record. As these authors observe:

> The reason is that Greece experienced a sudden stop typical of emerging market economies, but with the debt levels of an advanced economy.... Catching the measles as a child is painful, but often relatively short-lived. Catching the measles as an adult can be much more serious and is more likely to lead to complications. Similarly, experiencing a sudden stop as an emerging market economy with moderate levels of debt can be

painful but short lived. Experiencing a sudden stop as an advanced economy with much more elevated debt levels can be much more serious and more likely to lead to complications. Had debt levels been more in line with emerging-market economies, Greece would have experienced a more typical emerging market 'trifecta' crisis.

Extreme Austerity: The Wrong Choice?

When Greece revealed its disastrous fiscal situation, the EU had two options. One was to acknowledge that the country's fiscal stance was unsustainable and immediately move toward an orderly restructuring cum default: in other words, deal with the problem as the IMF would have done in an emerging economy (this was proposed early on by French economist Charles Wyplosz, "And now: a dark scenario," Vox-EU, May 3, 2010). The second was to assume, or, rather, pretend, that extreme austerity would solve the fiscal crisis, despite the enormity of the fiscal problem. Many commentators argued that the first option was the only realistic one. However, debt restructuring was ruled out. Some argue that this was because of the fear that a default on Greek debt might have generated contagion to other countries, such as Italy, Spain, Portugal, and Ireland. An alternative, more cynical, view is that French and German banks (the ones that had provided much of the lending to Greece) would have suffered significant losses that would eventually be passed on to French and German taxpayers. Probably both arguments were at play. In the end, the EU called the IMF, after some hesitation and confusion, and a first austerity plan accompanied by financial support was put in place. A long and complicated series of programs followed, designed by the EU, the ECB, and the IMF, the so-called "Troika," to help Greece financially in exchange for reforms. From the very beginning many observers were skeptical about the success of these plans. The conditions required to disburse a new tranche of financial aid became less and less clear with frequent rewriting of various plans. Confusion was everywhere. A detailed argument against the view that austerity could have worked in Greece is in Ardagna and Caselli (2014), which describes how poor bargaining and poor communications between the parties led to the disaster. Indeed the confusion was often staggering. Zettelmeyer, Kreplin, and Panizza (2017) argue that the assumptions that would have made austerity successful in Greece were unrealistic from the very beginning, and the idea that debt restructuring could be avoided was simply not grounded in good economics but in politics. As was later recognized, even by the IMF, these plans were based on overly optimistic economic scenarios and on unrealistic assessments of what were politically achievable goals.

The Greek Fiscal Plans of 2010–14

In Table 8.14 we have reconstructed the Greek adjustments plans. Building this table was a challenge given the innumerable revisions, discussions, and data adjustments resulting from the exhausting confrontations between Greek authorities and the Troika. This table is our best effort.[11] Given the staggering confusion of this period these data have to be viewed very cautiously.

The Memorandum of Understanding between Greece and the "Troika" of May 2010 reads:

> Following the Greek elections in October, the realization that the fiscal and public debt outturn for 2008 and 2009 were significantly worse than had been reported by the previous government caused confidence to drop, financing costs to increase, and growth and employment to suffer. [...] The deficit of 5.1 percent of GDP in 2007, at the top of the cycle, shows that Greece entered the downturn with a large underlying public deficit. With weak revenue policies and tax administration, especially leading up to the 2009 elections and aggravated by the recession, revenues declined notably. Spending, meanwhile, increased significantly, especially on wages and entitlements, reflecting weak spending discipline and monitoring and control, which also led to new arrears. The deficit jumped to an estimated 13.6 percent of GDP while the public debt rose to over 115 percent of GDP in 2009.

Many reviews occurred in the following months and years, and a second plan was eventually adopted in 2012. The revisions were justified by the failure of the 2010 program to achieve the fiscal surplus initially targeted; the failure was due to the contraction of the economy, but mostly because the forecasts were overoptimistic.[12] The goal of the second program was a primary deficit of 1% of GDP in 2012 and a primary surplus of 4.5% of GDP in 2014. These objectives were entirely outside the realm of good economics.

TABLE 8.14. Greece Fiscal Consolidation

		2010			2011			2012			2013			2014		
		Exp.	Unexp.	Ann.	Exp.	Unexp.	Ann.	Exp.	Unexp.	Ann.	Exp.	Unexp.	Ann.	Exp.	Unexp.	Ann.
Tax	Direct	0.00	0.00	1.10	0.93	0.43	0.00	0.13	0.00	0.00	0.04	0.00	0.00	0.00	0.21	0.00
	Indirect	0.00	0.53	1.52	1.26	−0.33	0.00	0.25	0.00	0.00	0.00	0.71	0.76	0.76	0.10	0.00
	n.c. Tax	0.00	0.00	0.00	0.00	0.25	0.00	0.00	0.00	0.00	0.00	0.00	0.00	0.00	0.00	0.00
	Other Tax	0.00	0.00	1.10	0.53	0.54	1.19	1.46	0.00	0.00	0.31	0.00	0.00	0.00	0.00	0.00
	Total Tax	0.00	0.53	3.71	2.72	0.90	1.19	1.83	0.00	0.00	0.35	0.71	0.76	0.76	0.31	0.00
Spending	Cons&Inv	0.00	0.97	2.23	0.76	0.81	0.55	1.61	0.14	0.00	0.43	1.09	0.66	0.66	0.02	0.00
	Transfers	0.00	0.95	1.05	0.32	0.27	0.44	1.09	0.00	0.00	0.08	2.13	0.28	0.28	0.00	0.00
	Other Spending	0.00	0.00	0.00	0.00	0.05	0.00	0.00	0.00	0.00	0.00	0.00	0.00	0.00	0.00	0.00
	n.c. Spending	0.00	0.00	1.77	0.00	0.00	0.00	0.00	0.00	0.00	1.77	−1.77	0.00	0.00	0.00	0.00
	Total Spending	0.00	1.92	5.05	1.07	1.13	0.99	2.70	0.14	0.00	2.29	1.46	0.94	0.94	0.02	0.00
	Total	0.00	0.00	0.00	0.00	0.00	0.00	0.00	0.00	0.00	0.00	0.00	0.00	0.00	0.00	0.00

Total planned tax	8.10
Total planned spending	11.64

Sources: Authors' dataset.

Note: Exp. measures implemented in the year announced in previous years; Unexp. measures implemented in the year announced in the year not expected according to past announcements; Ann.: measures announced in the year to be implemented in subsequent years.

These austerity plans implied cuts in all items of expenditure and increases in both direct and indirect taxes, with large shares of both unexpected and announced measures. In the years following the adoption of the first and largest consolidation plan in 2010, the plan underwent several adjustments over the course of frequent renegotiations between the Greek authorities and the Troika. In the March 2012 agreement, the government committed to achieving a primary deficit of 1% of GDP in that year. Because the economy was deteriorating more than expected, the target for the 2013 primary deficit was changed to zero. The government reinforced its fiscal effort, with tax increases totaling 5.15 €bn.[13]

The largest plan that we document is the first, introduced in May 2010. It included measures to be implemented immediately (5.8 €bn), measures for 2011 (9 €bn), for 2012 (5.6 €bn), and for 2013 (6.2 €bn). A large share of the 2013 measures consisted mainly of spending cuts yet to be identified (4.2 €bn). The first plan was 59% spending cuts and 41% tax increases. We record increases in VAT rates; in excises on alcohol, cigarettes, fuel, luxury goods; and a special levy on profitable firms. The spending cuts included reductions in pensions and wages achieved by reducing summer, Easter, and Christmas bonuses and by cuts in public investments and in transfers to public entities, and in unemployment benefits. The impact of some of these measures was revised, with further austerity at the end of 2010. In October 2011 several new measures were introduced: a permanent levy on real estate in 2011 (yielding 1.6 €bn), reductions in tax exemptions (2.8 €bn), changes in supplementary pension funds (0.5 €bn), and savings from the introduction of a unified public sector wage grid (0.5 €bn) occurring in 2012. There were also cuts in pharmaceutical procurements.

Table 8.13 shows the disastrous path of the Greek economy. In these years Greece lost all that it had accumulated during the period of very fast growth from the mid-1990s up to the financial crisis. Particularly remarkable is the collapse of investment. Given the collapse of the denominator, no matter how large the efforts to rein in the deficit, and they were large, the debt, as a fraction of GDP, moved from 127% in 2009 to 180% in 2014.

Those who had argued that the stabilization plans for Greece were politically and economically unrealistic were proven right. The Europeans and the IMF knew that their forecasts were too optimistic and were hypocritical about them. The Greek government knew that it could not deliver, but anticipated that the Troika would have accepted a partial delivery on the promises. For a while the Troika and the Greek government tried to instill optimism into the market by pretending that the plans were working, although they were not and they both knew it.

Were Greek Multipliers Underestimated?

Were the effects of austerity in Greece really much more severe than what one would have anticipated based on previous estimates of fiscal multipliers? To answer this question we proceed as earlier in this chapter, using the model estimated in Chapter 7—with the important qualification that Greece was not, for lack of data, in the sample used to estimate that model. We have simulated what that model would predict for post crisis austerity, feeding into it the plans actually implemented in Greece in 2010–14. Then we check (comparing the simulated path of output and the observed one) whether the simulation results are broadly consistent with the actual data. The evidence is in Figure 8.6 which should be interpreted in the same way as the figures shown earlier in this chapter; namely, above are the size and composition of the various plans adopted, below the simulation results.

The black line reports, as in the previous graphs, the actual path of output. The green line is the path obtained by simulating the plans actually implemented, the blue and red lines the paths of output one would have obtained if the plans had been entirely EB (blue) or entirely TB (red). Note first that because the first four plans were EB, the green and blue lines coincide up to 2013. They then diverge because the plan implemented in 2014 was TB. Output fell much more in 2011, which could have been expected based on our simulation, but thereafter the actual and simulated paths of output converge, becoming identical in 2013. Then, in 2014 output growth exceeds its simulated level. Our tentative conclusion is that multipliers estimated on data before the crisis do on average reasonably well: over the sample 2011–14 the error is exactly zero. They do worse in the first and last years: at the beginning of the adjustment probably because in 2011 economic activity in Greece de facto froze, for reasons that go far beyond the fiscal correction and in 2014, symmetrically, because the many structural reforms

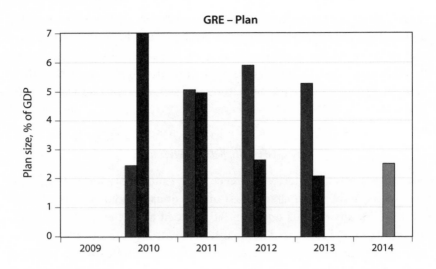

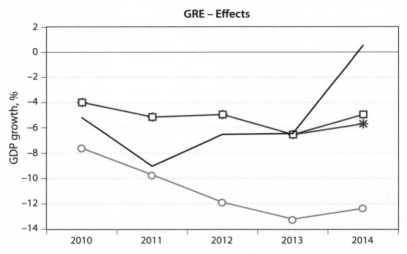

Figure 8.6. Greece: Actual plans vs. model projection.

that accompanied the fiscal plans probably started to exert a positive effect of output.

Based on this evidence we disagree that "actual fiscal multipliers were larger than forecasters assumed" (IMF, WEO October 2012, box 1.1, p. 43). So the answer to the question posed in the title of this section is no: the failure of the Greek plans was not due to a technical problem of underestimation of multipliers, but to a much deeper political and economic failure of the Troika and the Greek authorities to handle the crisis as well as to the size of the plans.

We address more thoroughly the issue of underestimation of multipliers looking beyond Greece in the next section.

DID FISCAL MULTIPLIERS CHANGE AFTER THE CRISIS?

Was austerity in 2010–14 more costly in terms of output losses than previous consolidations had been, as suggested by the IMF document just quoted? In principle there are several reasons why this could be the case. The latest round of European austerity occurred when monetary policy could not help much because economies were at the zero lower bound; many countries implemented fiscal consolidations at the same time, possibly affecting each other's exports. The experience of Europe in 2010–14 seems to be the perfect storm, the worst possible case for austerity, a situation in which it should have been especially costly, a point made by Blanchard and Leigh (2014).

Blanchard and Leigh (2014) attribute the difference between actual output growth and output growth predicted by the IMF to the intensity of austerity. They argue that, in advanced economies, stronger planned fiscal consolidations have been associated with lower growth than expected. They interpret this as suggesting that fiscal multipliers were substantially higher than implicitly assumed by forecasters. Had policymakers known the true value of multipliers they might have implemented less austerity. This result is robust to controlling for the impact of many other economic and financial variables, such as banking crises and panic in financial markets.

An alternative possibility is that austerity programs were the response to the fear of a debt crisis that induced a spike in the cost of financing the debt. This required a heavier dose of austerity than anticipated to shield a country from a confidence crisis. This happened, for instance, in high-debt countries during the Eurozone crisis. In such a situation the degree of austerity is correlated with the spike in long-term interest rates. An unexpected increase in long-term interest rates in Europe could thus be the reason for harsher than expected austerity and thus of forecast errors in growth.[14] One channel through which a spike in the long-term rates, and thus a fall in bond prices, could affect output is the so-called "doom loop"—a phenomenon that arises in the presence of a large amount of government bonds in banks' balance sheets, which erodes the value of bank equity as interest rates spike, thus causing a contraction of lending.

In this case, it would not be a question of multipliers being larger than expected, but of austerity being larger than expected because the degree of austerity, and thus the fall in output, is correlated with the spike in interest rates. We test this hypothesis including in an extended version of the Blanchard–Leigh specification long-term interest rates (at the time of the forecast). We find (the results are shown in Chapter 12) that, on top of the intensity of austerity, unexpected fluctuations in long-term bond yields ahead of the fiscal correction also played as important a role in determining the forecast errors on growth: this makes attributing the result to one channel or the other (underestimated multipliers or the spike in interest rates) impossible.

CONCLUSIONS

In this chapter we studied the European episodes of austerity that occurred after the financial crisis. Once again we find that EB adjustments have been much less costly than TB adjustments in terms of output losses, a result that was not unexpected given the case studies illustrated at the start of the chapter. We do not find convincing evidence that multipliers were significantly larger in recent years. Several, not all, countries did experience deep recessions but the size of the austerity measures implemented, in some cases especially on the tax side, was truly draconian, even outside of Greece. When we use the model estimated in Chapter 7 to simulate these fiscal plans, we find outcomes that are not very distant from those that actually occurred. In addition, one should keep in mind that fiscal policy was not the only player in the field: banking crises, collapse of confidence, and credit crunches also played a role. It would be simplistic to attribute everything that happened in Europe between 2010 and 2014 only to fiscal policy.

One of the reasons why many commentators argued that the austerity choice in Europe was wrong is that it occurred too soon, when the economies had not yet recovered from the Great Recession. Obviously it is not clear what would have happened without austerity. The argument about austerity starting during recessions is, however, an important one, and in the next chapter we examine it more closely.

CHAPTER NINE

When Austerity?

INTRODUCTION

European austerity in 2010–14 started while euro area economies were still in the midst of the Recession at the zero lower bound.

In this chapter we tackle the question of whether the effects of austerity differ depending on when it occurs, in a downturn, during an expansion, and at the ZLB. These issues are often referred to as the question of the "state dependence" of fiscal multipliers, in the sense that multipliers could differ depending on the state of the economy.

Let's begin with the business cycle. When the economy has slack, an increase in government spending is less likely to crowd out private consumption or investment and therefore it may produce a stronger expansionary effect on output.[1] Thus spending cuts could be especially damaging during recessions. Determining the importance of "when" austerity occurs, in recessions or expansions, is tricky and depends on subtle methodological choices. As Milton Friedman reminded us, macroeconomic policies have "long and variable lags," namely, it is very difficult to predict the timing of the delay between implementation of policies and their economic effects. Friedman was referring to monetary policy, but the argument is even stronger for fiscal policy.

According to our preferred methodology, the recessionary effects of austerity are similar regardless of whether the fiscal correction is started during an expansion or a downturn. Using other methodologies, instead, fiscal corrections started in a downturn have larger output costs. In either case, however, tax-based (TB) austerity is more costly than expenditure-based (EB) austerity. Remember that in selecting our austerity episodes, we have excluded episodes of tax increases and expenditure cuts that were motivated by the state of the business cycle, because these would obviously be endogenous, that is, they would *respond* to the state of the economy, not *cause* it. Because policies motivated by the objective of cooling down the economy occur only during expansions, our sample of austerity plans contains, by construction, many more cases of austerity started in a downturn. Thus our estimates of the cost of austerity may overestimate them, in the sense that we over-sample cases of austerity that began during recessions. In particular, an EB plan that does not start in a downturn may have even lower costs than the already small ones we have estimated. Expansionary cases of EB plans would be even more likely.[2]

Assessing, along with the timing of austerity—whether it happens during an expansion or a recession—the role of the ZLB is difficult because our sample contains only a small number of observations at the ZLB. Thus our results are very tentative and fragile. According to some methodologies, we find that differently from what happens in the entire sample, the economic effects of austerity plans adopted during deep economic downturns do not vary much depending on their composition. Different methodological approaches, however, yield different results and the issue thus deserves further research.

Finally we shall show in Chapter 12 that our main result—that is, the difference between TB and EB austerity—is robust to distinguishing between austerity started when the debt over GDP ratio is growing rapidly and when it is stable. Interestingly, we find that the possibility of expansionary austerity based on spending cuts is more likely in cases of austerity starting when debt is increasing rapidly. This is because an austerity plan that removes preoccupations of a fiscal collapse has stronger positive effects on confidence especially for investors. This result is consistent with models by Alesina and Drazen (1991) and Blanchard (1990).

FISCAL POLICY IN BOOMS AND RECESSIONS

Auerbach and Gorodnichenko (2012, 2013a, 2013b) investigated the possibility that multipliers might be related to the state of the business cycle. They addressed the question extending Blanchard and Perotti (2002) allowing the effects of fiscal policy to vary depending upon whether the economy is in a boom or in a recession.[3] Their sample includes both fiscal contractions and expansions. The state of the cycle

TABLE 9.1. Average time in recession

	Avg. time spent in recession (%)		Avg. time spent in recession (%)
AUS	14	FRA	14
AUT	14	GBR	19
BEL	14	IRL	14
CAN	17	ITA	22
DEU	17	JPN	17
DNK	19	PRT	22
ESP	25	SWE	19
FIN	22	USA	17

is measured by an indicator that fluctuates between 0 and 1 and is best interpreted as a measure of the probability that the economy is in a downturn, defined as a year in which the indicator is above 0.8, with "expansion" being a period in which it is below 0.2. We shall use the same measure, so that our result can be more directly compared. Note that the states' "downturn" or "expansion" are not exhaustive, as an economy can be in neither of them for long periods.

Table 9.1 shows the average time spent in a downturn (defined as years of negative growth in output per capital) by each of our 16 OECD economies: it ranges between 14% and 22% of all years in the sample. Figure 9.1 compares the evolution of this indicator—the blue line— with actual downturns (the shaded areas), showing that it does well at identifying them.

Auerbach and Gorodnichenko (2012, 2013a, 2013b) found that expenditure multipliers in the two states are very different and very far from the "average" multiplier (see Figure 9.2).

These authors assume that the state of the economy does not change following a shift in fiscal policy. In other words, if a fiscal adjustment starts during a recession, then the economy is assumed to remain in that state for at least 20 quarters. Ramey and Zubairy (2018) argue that this assumption is problematic: whereas it is reasonable for expansions— which typically last for several years in the United States—it is not for recessions, which have a mean duration of only 3.3 quarters. In our sample, we often observe fiscal consolidations that start in one economic state, for instance, a downturn, but while the fiscal plan is being implemented the economy moves to the other state, of expansion. For example, a large consolidation plan was adopted in Belgium in 1982 following a year of recession, but while it was implemented the economy turned around and resumed positive growth. Ten years later, Belgium's 1992 multiyear consolidation plan began after a period of expansion, but in 1993 the Belgian economy entered a downturn, from which it recovered in 1994.

Ramey and Zubairy (2018) studied spending multipliers during expansions and downturns without imposing this assumption.[4] They found small spending multipliers, ranging from 0.3 to 0.8. When distinguishing between expansions and downturns, they found a statistically significant difference in multipliers in some cases, but this result is not due to particularly high multipliers in recessions, but rather to low multipliers in expansions. In a related paper they used Canadian data (Owyang, Ramey, and Zubairy [2013]) and found higher multipliers in recessions. However, in subsequent investigations these authors found that the difference between the US and Canadian results was probably due to the special circumstances related to Canada's entry into World War II, when output responded to the news long before government spending actually rose.[5]

"HOW" AND "WHEN"

The three top rows of Table 9.2 provide information on the state of the cycle when a fiscal plan is introduced (these are the rows labeled TB and EB respectively) and in the entire sample (in the third row).

The fourth column shows that in 62 out of 99 years of serious economic downturn there was a consolidation, while that occurred in only 13 over the 94 years of vigorous expansion (column 1). However, of all the consolidations implemented during a downturn, two-thirds were EB and one-third TB, the same proportions that hold in the full sample. In other words, it is not the case that EB adjustments occur more frequently than TB ones in a particular state of the economy (recession or expansion). This is important because it means that TB plans do not appear to be more recessionary simply because they are adopted more often during a recession.

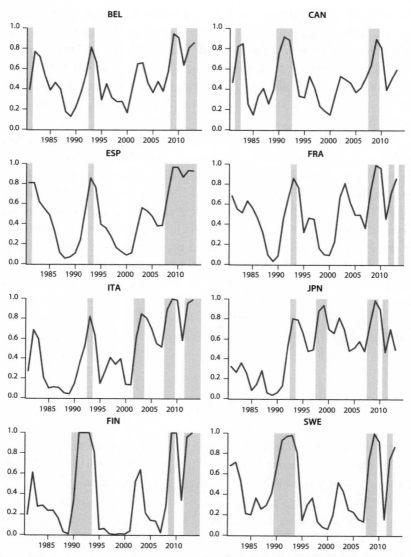

Figure 9.1. Evolution of $F(s)$ and recessions. *Source:* Alesina et al. (2018). *Note:* Evolution of $F(s)$ for the countries in our sample and years of recession (years with negative growth per capita, shaded areas), 1981–2014.

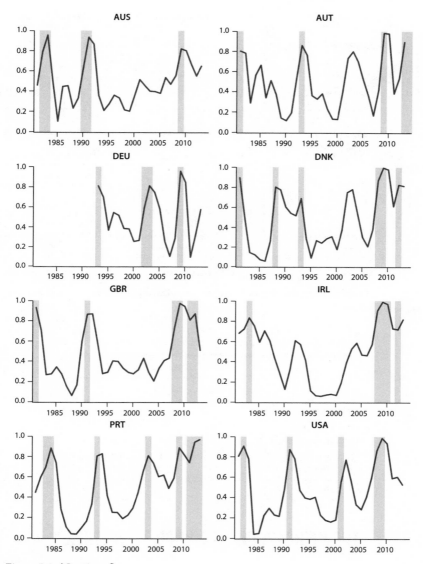

Figure 9.1. (*Continued*)

The last two rows of the table show the same data for fiscal consolidations implemented by the European countries that are members of the eurozone. Out of 52 plans adopted by euro member countries, 47 have been adopted during a downturn—32 during a severe downturn, 15 during a milder one.

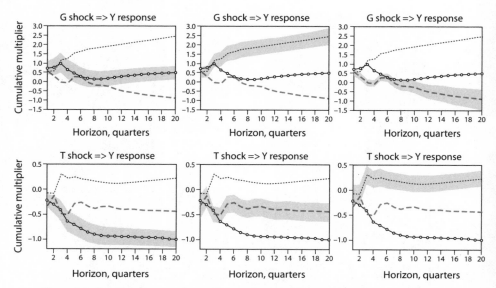

Figure 9.2. Government spending and taxation: Impulse response. *Source:* Auerbach and Gorodnichenko (2012).

TABLE 9.2. Type of plan and probability of recession

	Recession Probability			
Type of Plan	<0.2	<0.5	≥0.5	>0.8
TB (57 plans)	3	17	40	22
EB (113 plans)	10	41	72	40
Years in sample (515)	94	283	232	99
TB: euro area (18 plans)	0	0	18	14
EB: euro area (34 plans)	2	5	29	18

THE "WHEN" AND THE "HOW" TOGETHER

What matters more? The way you implement an austerity plan, rising taxes, or cutting spending,—or the state of the economy when you start the plan, in a recession or an expansion, that is the "when" or the "how"? Alesina, Azzalini, Favero, Giavazzi, and Miano (2018) extend the model estimated in Chapter 7 to answer this question: we describe this extension in the section entitled "The Model of 'How' and 'When' in

Chapter 12" at the end of the book. The main findings are summarized in Figure 9.3.

The four rows of the figure show the impulse responses of output per capita (Y); total tax revenues as a fraction of GDP (T); primary government spending, also as a fraction of GDP (G); and the indicator $F(s)$, the probability of being in a recession regime.[6] Lines with triangles and squares show the responses of the variables in the case, respectively, of an EB and a TB plan introduced at a time when the economy is in an expansionary state (defined as $F(s_t) \simeq 0.2$); the responses of the economy to EB and TB fiscal consolidations starting in a recessionary state (defined as $F(s_t) \simeq 0.8$) are indicated by lines with circles and stars. The state of the economy is affected by fiscal policy and can change as a plan evolves. Instead, the nature of the plan (TB, EB) is known on announcement and does not change throughout the simulation.

The first row of Figure 9.3 shows that the stronger nonlinearity is that between TB and EB plans. In the case of an EB consolidation, the point estimates of the responses of output growth are almost identical across the two states of the economy, whereas in the case of a TB consolidation the point estimates are different, although the difference is not statistically significant. TB plans are always more recessionary than EB plans although the difference is larger when the plan is introduced in an expansion than in a recession.

The second and third rows of Figure 9.3 show the responses of government revenues and government consumption (defined as explained at the top of this section and both measured as a fraction of GDP) to a TB and an EB plan starting from the two initial states. Observe that, on average, revenues increase by a larger amount during a TB consolidation, and spending decreases the most during an EB consolidation. This confirms that our classification of plans is trustworthy. Interestingly, we observe a positive response of revenues also to an EB consolidation, and a negative response of spending to a TB consolidation implemented in recession (while in expansion the response is just above zero). This confirms that spending and tax measures are not taken in isolation and thus supports our choice of analyzing plans rather than individual shifts in taxes and spending.

The fourth row of Figure 9.3 shows the responses of $F(s)$: in all four cases a consolidation increases the recession indicator (the impulse

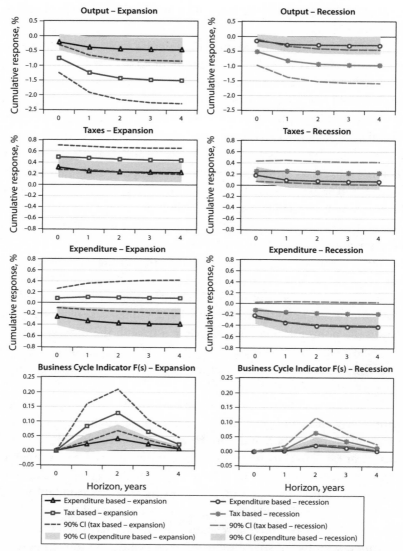

Figure 9.3. Impulse responses of output, taxes, spending, and $F(s)$. *Source:* Alesina et al. (2018). *Note:* Allowing for heterogeneity between EB and TB plans and across states of the cycle.

response is always positive). There is, however, a significant difference between types of plans. During TB consolidations $F(s)$ increases much more than during EB ones, and this holds both in expansions and recessions. Note that when a consolidation starts during a recession the difference in $F(s)$ between TB and EB adjustments initially is not statistically significant. It becomes significant 2 years after the start of the consolidation, indicating that TB consolidations worsen the state of the economy for a more prolonged period of time than EB ones.

The bottom line is that it is not so much the "When" that matters in explaining different effects of fiscal consolidations, but the "How."

Discussion

Auerbach and Gorodnichenko (2012, 2013a, 2013b) investigated the role of the state of the economy when austerity is introduced assuming that the state economy does not change following the shift in fiscal policy. In other words, if a fiscal adjustment starts during a recession, then the economy is assumed to remain in that state for at least 20 quarters. This is different from the assumption we made in the previous section, where we assumed instead that $F(s_t)$, the indicator of the state of the economy, was a function of *lagged* output growth and could be interpreted as the expected probability that the economy is in recession at time t, given the information on GDP growth available at time $t - 1$ and $t - 2$.

The two choices have advantages and costs. The main advantage of assuming a lagged feedback between GDP growth and $F(s_t)$, as we did in the previous section, is that we can treat this indicator as an endogenous variable when the model is simulated, thus allowing the state of the economy to evolve following the introduction of a fiscal plan. In other words, we can track the response of $F(s_t)$ to the introduction of a plan. In this case impulse responses will reflect *both* the difference across states (expansion and downturn) and the evolving probability of an (expected) downturn. If instead s_t were a function of *current* GDP growth (as in Auerbach and Gorodnichenko), then $F(s_t)$ and output growth would be simultaneous: this does not allow the state of the economy to respond to the introduction of a plan and one can only assume that it remains unchanged over the entire horizon of the fiscal adjustment. On the other hand, the cost of assuming a lagged feedback between GDP growth and

$F(s_t)$ is that fiscal corrections could affect the state of the economy contemporaneously. Suppose that a fiscal correction at time t, implemented in a recession, was able to shift the economy out of recession on impact, that is, in the same year in which the plan is introduced. In this case, the plan would be classified—using the lagged indicator—as hitting the economy in a high-probability-of-recession regime although at time t the economy is already out of the recession. This, however, is an unlikely possibility because our narrative identification scheme excludes fiscal corrections driven by the cycle.

In order to assess robustness we investigated the results obtained by making $F(s_t)$ dependent on contemporaneous output growth, while holding the regime constant over the simulation horizon. In Figure 9.4 we report impulse responses obtained adopting this alternative specification. Note that instead of reporting the response of $F(s_t)$ to the fiscal shock, we plot its constant level — fixed either at 0.2 (expansion) or 0.8 (downturn).

These results confirm the findings of Auerbach and Gorodnichenko suggesting an asymmetric response of output to fiscal adjustments. The output cost is higher when austerity is started during a downturn. Austerity started during an expansion has no output cost; in fact it is mildly expansionary. The difference between EB and TB adjustments is confirmed in plans adopted during a downturn, but vanishes when plans are adopted during an expansion. The output effect of EB adjustments in the recession regime is smaller than reported in Auerbach and Gorodnichenko. This is consistent with our identification strategy that, using narrative methods, selects only fiscal stabilization episodes.

The bottom line is that different methodological choices to study the effects of the timing of austerity produce different results. This is an important issue that remains a topic for future research.

AUSTERITY AT THE ZERO LOWER BOUND

We first split the data into two subsamples: the euro area countries (Austria, Belgium, France, Finland, Germany, Ireland, Italy, Portugal, and Spain) from 1999 onwards and the non–euro area countries

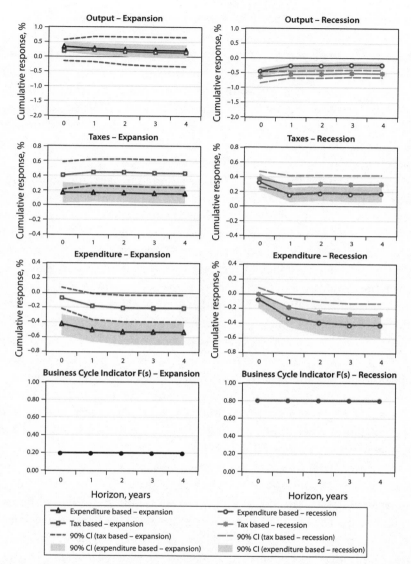

Figure 9.4. Alternative specification: impulse response. *Source:* Alesina et al. (2018). *Note:* Impulse responses with coincident indicator of the state of the economy and constant regime under simulation.

(Australia, Denmark, the United Kingdom, Japan, Sweden, the United States, and Canada) plus the euro area countries before 1999. We do this because the presence of a common currency prevents monetary policy from responding to fiscal developments in the individual member countries. Although it is true that monetary policy cannot respond to country-level fiscal policy, the ECB could still respond if fiscal consolidation was implemented in a large enough number of euro area countries at the same time. To capture this possible common response of monetary policy, these results use year fixed effects.

Table 9.2 shows that out of 52 plans adopted by euro member countries, all the 18 TB plans and 29 of the 34 EB plans have been adopted in a state of the economy where the probability of recession was higher than 0.5. Figure 9.5 shows that in a severe downturn, fortunately a very rare occurrence, austerity has similar effects whether it is EB or TB. But the ability of monetary policy to respond now makes an important difference: the output cost of both types of plans is virtually zero if monetary policy is unconstrained, while both types of plans are equally recessionary if monetary policy is constrained. Remember that when we say "starting in a downturn" or "starting in an expansion" we mean a deep downturn and vigorous expansion: the vast majority of consolidation episodes are not in these two categories but in a situation of "neutral" cycles or mild downturns and mild expansions. In fact, for plans started during an expansion our time-honored result showing that TB plans are much more recessionary than EB plans is confirmed whether or not monetary policy is constrained.

However, when we use the alternative methodology to define the state of the economy—that is, when we assume that the state is constant throughout the consolidation—results are somewhat different (Figure 9.4). The heterogeneity between EB and TB adjustments is there even for consolidations started during deep downturns—although in this case both types of plans seem to be not recessionary when they start during an expansion. Our results should thus be taken with a grain of salt because these comparisons are based on very few observations.

As a further robustness check, one could ask whether the response of the economy to consolidations implemented while interest rates are at the ZLB significantly influences our results. Unfortunately, there are not

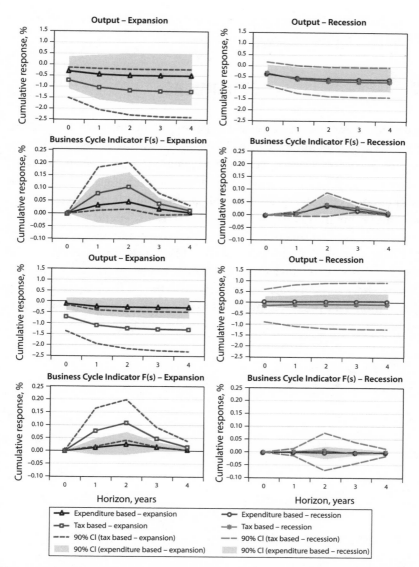

Figure 9.5. Impulse responses with constrained (top two rows) and unconstrained (bottom two rows) monetary policy. *Source:* Alesina et al. (2018) *Note:* Euro area vs. non-euro countries.

enough data to split the sample between years at the ZLB and years out of the ZLB: the former group is too small.[7]

CONCLUSIONS

Both the composition of a fiscal adjustment and the state of the business cycle matter, but the composition effect is stronger and much more robust across different specifications. The effect of "When" austerity occurs is hard to assess and depends on methodological choices. The output costs of austerity are probably higher when it is started during a downturn, but the nature and extent of this result depend on subtle modeling choices. The role of the ZLB is even more difficult to judge given the low number of observations at the ZLB in our sample. However, our (admittedly not conclusive) evidence does not point toward a large difference between episodes at or away from the ZLB, or more generally when monetary policy cannot react to a fiscal adjustment in a monetary union. However, this issue deserves further research.

CHAPTER TEN

Austerity and Elections

INTRODUCTION

The conventional wisdom is that large reductions in budget deficits are the political kiss of death for the governments that implement them. Conversely, governments get reelected when they increase deficits by spending more or taxing less. This is because voters reward short-run benefits without understanding the future costs implied by the government's budget constraints (an idea originally put forward in Buchanan and Wagner [1977]).

However, if one looks at the recent historical evidence on the electoral effects of austerity, the results are much less clear cut than the conventional wisdom would suggest. Sometimes, governments that engaged in even harsh austerity policies were reelected, and many governments were reelected when austerity was a central electoral issue. After a balanced review of the evidence one can conclude that some governments can implement fiscal adjustments and be successful at the polls. In other words, there is no strong correlation between the tightness of fiscal policy and a government's probability of being reelected. Just to be clear: we are not saying that austerity policies always lead to reelection; we are making the much weaker claim that austerity does not systematically lead to an electoral defeat.

Is it possible that governments that are strong and popular for some other reason are reelected despite having implemented austerity policies, not because of them? This would explain the lack of correlation between fiscal adjustments and reelection. Unfortunately, it is not easy to measure the "strength" of a government: often such strength (or weakness) depends on the personalities involved, on the leadership style, and so forth, all of which are close to impossible to measure precisely. For instance, in principle a coalition government should be weaker and more unstable than a single-party government. But certain coalitions may be especially cohesive, and certain single-party governments may hide strong divisions within that party. Another indicator of strength might be the margin of majority of the government in the legislature. But that too could be imperfect, for instance, because of the divisions within the government coalition, even though it may have a large majority of seats. We find no evidence of different behavior, in terms of the electoral effect of fiscal adjustments, of coalition versus single-party governments. And it does seem that single-party governments adjust more often than coalitions.

EXISTING EVIDENCE

There is a vast literature on fiscal policy and electoral results (see Alesina and Passalacqua [2016] for a survey). For example, Brender and Drazen (2008) show that voters are (weakly) likely to punish rather than reward budget deficits accumulated during the leader's term in office. Their results are robust to the distinction among subsamples: developed and less developed countries, new and old democracies, countries with presidential or parliamentary systems, countries with proportional or majoritarian electoral systems, or countries with different histories of democracy.

A related literature directly tests the political consequences of large fiscal adjustments—that is, whether large reductions of the budget deficit have negative political consequences. Alesina, Perotti, and Tavares (1998) consider a sample of OECD countries and find that austerity has a weakly positive, rather than negative, electoral effect: governments that have reduced deficits are more likely (although by very little) to be reelected. Alesina, Carloni, and Lecce (2013) specifically focus on episodes of large fiscal adjustment in OECD countries. Their definition of the latter is simply an observed large reduction in the cyclically adjusted deficit, by more than 1.5 percentage points of gross domestic product (GDP). Tables 10.1 and 10.2 summarize their data sources and data definition. Their sample is 1975–2008 for 19 OECD countries.[1]

These authors begin first presenting some suggestive evidence regarding the 10 largest fiscal adjustments in their sample. These are shown in Table 10.3, reproduced from their article in order of cumulative size.

TABLE 10.1. Cabinet data

Variable name	Description
TERM	Government termination: dummy variable equal to 1 in any year in which a government ends, regardless of the reason. A termination may or may not involve a "change" in cabinet ideology or prime minister.
DURAT	Duration: integer number of years that a cabinet has been in power, up to the current year. A cabinet that falls during its first year in power is counted as 1. Every time there is a government termination (*TERM* = 1), *DURAT* is reset to 1 the year after the termination.
SING	Single party: dummy variable equal to 1 if a single-party cabinet is in power.
COAL	Coalition: dummy variable equal to 1 if a coalition cabinet (including ministers from two or more parties) is in power.
MAJ	Majority: dummy variable equal to 1 if the cabinet has majority support in parliament.
IDEOCH	Change in ideology of cabinet: dummy variable equal to 1 if there is a change in the ideology index between the current year and the next. It is constructed by exploiting the change in the value of variable *EXECRLC* (describing the ideology of the chief executive's party) in the DPI dataset.
ALLCH	Change of ideology or prime minister; dummy variable equal to 1 if either *IDEOCH* or *PMCH* is equal to 1.
SHARE_TENURE	Years left to next election, divided by number of years of regular duration of a government.

Source: Database of Political Institutions (DPI) 2014. Variable names reported as they appear in the dataset.

The 10 episodes are identified as follows: cases in which the cumulative cyclically adjusted deficit reduction, obtained by summing consecutive years of deficit reductions, is the largest. In addition to the size of the adjustments in terms of deficit reduction, the table also reports measures of the composition of the adjustment: spending cuts and tax increases over GDP. Note that the spending share can be greater than 100 if taxes were cut during the adjustment, or can be negative if spending was increased. With "termination", the authors signal that there was an election in the adjustment period and/or in the 2 years following the end of it. Beyond 2 years too much time may have elapsed to attribute

TABLE 10.2. Fiscal categories in Alesina et al. (2013)

Category	Description
All adjustments	All episodes in which the cyclically adjusted deficit is negative.
Large adjustments	Episodes in which the cyclically adjusted deficit is below −1.5% of GDP.
Small adjustments	All adjustments that are not large.
Expenditure-based adjustments	All adjustments in which the cyclically adjusted expenditure decreases more than the increase in cyclically adjusted taxes.
Tax-based adjustments	All adjustments in which the cyclically adjusted taxes increase more than the decrease in cyclically adjusted expenditures.

Source: Database of Political Institutions (DPI) 2014. Variable names reported as they appear in the dataset.

reelection (or defeat) mainly to the fiscal adjustment. The last column, labeled "change in ideology," indicates changes in the political orientation occurring during the fiscal adjustment and in the 2 years following its end.

Table 10.3 shows that out of the 19 government terminations happening during these 10 episodes, government changes occurred in 7 cases, about 37% of the total. But if one looks instead at the five episodes with the largest cumulative adjustment, that ratio decreases considerably, with changes in government occurring in only 1 case out of 10. In contrast, government changes in about 40% of the total number of terminations from 1975 to 2008 in this sample. This indicates that periods of large fiscal adjustments were not associated with systematically higher government turnover. Considering the percentage of the adjustment due to a cut in expenditures, and comparing those five fiscal adjustments for which the value was highest with the other adjustments, these researchers find that the cases in which the expenditure share of the adjustment was higher were associated with less frequent changes in government. This seems to suggest that tax-based adjustments make it more difficult for incumbent governments to be reappointed when they implement large fiscal adjustments—a finding that is consistent with the evidence presented in previous chapters.

TABLE 10.3. Periods with largest cumulative fiscal adjustment (cyclically adjusted variables)

Country	Years	Number of years	Change in cycl. adj. expenditures	Change in cycl. adj. revenues	Fiscal adj. per year	Cumulative fiscal adj.	% of fiscal adj. due to cut in expenditures	Termination	Change in ideology
Denmark	1983–86	4	−0.85	1.58	−2.43	−9.74	35.03	2	0
Greece	1990–94	5	−0.5	1.38	−1.88	−9.39	26.38	2	1
Sweden	1994–2000	7	−0.81	0.38	−1.2	−8.38	67.91	3	0
Belgium	1982–87	6	−0.96	0.3	−1.26	−7.57	76.5	2	0
Canada	1993–97	5	−1.25	0.11	−1.36	−6.8	91.8	1	0
United Kingdom	1994–99	6	−0.66	0.47	−1.12	−6.72	58.45	1	1
Finland	1993–98	6	−0.81	0.23	−1.04	−6.23	78.13	2	1
Portugal	1982–84	3	−1.14	0.75	−1.89	−5.67	60.16	2	2
Italy	1990–93	4	0.13	1.36	−1.24	−4.95	−10.21	2	1
Ireland	1986–89	4	−1.54	−0.33	−1.21	−4.82	127.5	2	1

Source: Alesina, Carloni, and Lecce (2013) calculations on OECD Economic Outlook Database no. 84 and DPI 2009.

The article then proceeds to a more systematic analysis of "large fiscal adjustments"—defined as those in which the cyclically adjusted deficit over GDP ratio fell by more than 1.5% of GDP—versus "fiscal adjustments" in which the cyclically adjusted deficit-over-potential GDP ratio falls by any amount. They find no evidence that either small or large fiscal adjustments are systematically associated with an electoral defeat of the government that implemented them. This result (or "nonresult") is robust to alternative specifications, time periods, and countries. They also explore various definitions of "changes of government"—although that is not always obvious in multi-party systems with switching coalitions, and party members or personnel coming in or exiting coalitions—but find no effect. These results are also confirmed by Passarelli and Tabellini (2017).

These authors also consider whether only "strong" governments can safely engage in fiscal adjustments and then be reappointed "despite" having been fiscally responsible. As mentioned earlier, it is difficult to define what a "strong" government is. One possibility is to consider whether the ruling government is formed by a coalition of parties. A second measure, in this case of of "government stability," is a dummy variable equal to 1 if the party of the executive has an absolute majority in the house(s) with lawmaking powers. This measure seems reasonable, because one would expect a government to last longer if it has the majority in all houses. In fact, it turns out that when this is the case the government lasts on average 4.41 years, while for the rest of the observations the average duration is 4.17 years. There is no convincing evidence that only "strong" governments (defined as above) implemented fiscal adjustments and were reelected.

FISCAL PLANS AND ELECTIONS

We now turn to analyze the effects of austerity measured by the fiscal plans we have constructed in this book. These new results are broadly similar to those described in this chapter thus far. In the statistical analysis presented in Chapter 12 at the end of the book we do uncover a few facts. First, we show that it is more likely that a government implements a fiscal adjustment plan when it is further away from the next scheduled election. By "implementing," we mean introducing a new plan or reinforcing a plan already in existence. One reason for this is that a new government may have been appointed with the specific mandate of reducing budget deficits, as in Canada in 1993. Or, it could be that a government prefers to absorb the possible costs of the adjustment early on in its term, and then run toward the next election with a growing economy. Or perhaps a deficit-prone government is replaced by an "austere" one; in other words, a political battle over the need for austerity is won by the party in favor of it. We also find some evidence that right-of-center governments on average are more likely to implement fiscal adjustment plans. Perhaps surprisingly, we do not find evidence that right-of-center governments are more likely to implement EB plans. We do find that coalition governments are less likely than single-party governments to implement fiscal plans. This is consistent with models in which disagreement within a coalition makes it difficult to implement fiscal changes.[2]

We find no evidence that governments implementing fiscal adjustment plans are more likely to not be reelected; we control for other economic variables that may affect reelection probabilities. We disentangle which types of governments are more or less likely to be reelected after a fiscal adjustment (coalition or single party, right of center, or left of center). In the end, we do not find robust correlations. The truth of the matter may simply be that reelection of governments, especially in multiparty systems with switching coalitions, is a highly complex matter with many moving parts and many factors in place. As a result, isolating the role of fiscal adjustments in any statistical analysis may be difficult. However, our statistical results suggest that the latter are not always the kiss of death for the incumbent.

Figures 10.1, 10.2, and 10.3 refer to fiscal plans as were defined earlier this book. Governments that implement a plan are sometimes more and sometimes less frequently replaced than those that do not, as shown by the comparison between the first two columns of each figure. Those columns represent the share of governments that end one, two, or three years after the event of interest (that is, a new plan, no plan, or a small or large plan). They are either replaced in their cabinet (ALLCH) or in their ideological orientation (IDEOCH). Interestingly, the frequency of both ALLCH (Figure 10.1) and IDEOCH (Figure 10.2) is

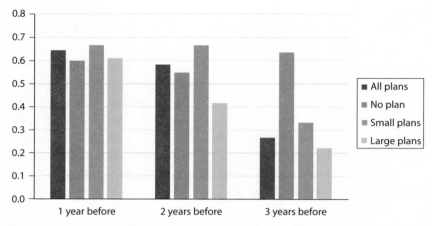

Figure 10.1. Frequency of change in cabinet, given the plan and government termination. *Source:* Authors' calculations on OECD Economic Outlook Database no. 84 and DPI 2009.

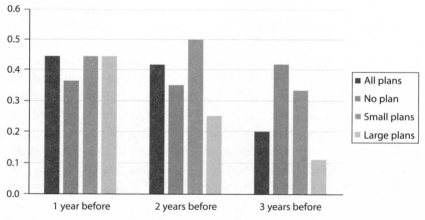

Figure 10.2. Frequency of change in cabinet ideology, given the plan and government termination. *Source:* Authors' calculations on OECD Economic Outlook Database no. 84 and DPI 2009.

much lower for governments implementing a plan than for those that do not, provided the plan is implemented three years before the elections. However, though suggestive, these results are not very robust to more accurate statistical analysis presented in Chapter 12. Figure 10.3 unveils the correlation between government turnover and the composition of a

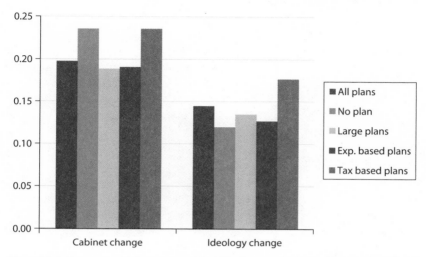

Figure 10.3. Frequency of changes in cabinet ideology and cabinet changes given simultaneous EB or TB plans. *Source:* Authors' calculations on OECD Economic Outlook Database no. 84 and DPI 2009.

plan. Qualitatively, a TB plan seems more likely to lead to a change in ideology in the same year than an EB one. However, this correlation is not statistically robust to the more detailed analysis that we include in Chapter 12.

A FEW EXAMPLES

Table 10.4 provides three examples of governments that implemented large EB plans and were reelected: the reelection of the liberal party with the same leader in Canada after five years of austerity, the reelection of the Social Democrats with the same leader in Finland after three years of austerity, and the reelection of the same leader in Sweden in 1998 after four years of austerity. In these three countries the same parties won again in the following round of elections after the austerity period was concluded.

Table 10.5 summarizes the electoral events that followed the European crisis of 2010–15. We have already discussed the complex Greek case in Chapter 8 and will not repeat it here. In the UK, the conservative government implemented as of 2010 an EB plan, and was successfully

TABLE 10.4. Three cases of reelection after an EB plan

Country	Year	Total measures (% GDP)	Expenditure share (%)	Consolidation (yrs)	Incumbent party	Incumbent prime minister	Coalition	Seats (%)	Change (%) Seats	Change (%) Vote
Canada	1997	2.2	85%	5	Lib.	J. Chretien	Majority	51%	-6	-3
Finland	1999	4.25	118%[1]	3	Soc. Dem.	P. Lipponen	Coalition	26%	-1	-5
Sweden	1998	6.5	63%	4	Soc. Dem.	G. Persson	Minority	38%	-3	-9

Sources: Database of Political Institutions (DPI), 2014.
[1] Since in the same 3-year period some exogenous tax cuts were introduced, the amount of spending cuts is larger than the size of net consolidation.

TABLE 10.5. Elections during European austerity

Country	Election year	Adjustment episodes* Total measures (% of GDP)	EB	TB	Before elections First party in government	Head of executive	Executive type	After elections First party in government	Executive type	Seats (%)	Votes (%)	GDP growth†	Change in ideology
Ireland	2011	8.6	2	1	Fianna Fail	B. Cowen[1]	Coalition	Fine Gael	Coalition	46	36	−3	No
	2016	10	4	0	Fine Gael	E. Kenny	Coalition	Fine Gael	Minority	30	26	8.3	Yes
Italy	2013	2	0	1	People for Freedom	M. Monti[2]	Coalition	Democratic	Coalition	52	29.5	−2.7	Yes[7]
Portugal	2009	5.1	3	0	Socialist	J. Socrates	Single Party	Socialist	Minority	42	38	0.23	No
	2011	3.9	0	1	Socialist	J. Socrates	Minority	Soc. Dem.	Coalition	47	40	0.1	Yes
	2015[3]	13	3	1	Soc. Dem.	P. Passos Coelho	Coalition	Portugal Ahead[4]	Minority	46	38	−0.67	No
Spain	2008	0	0	0	Soc. Workers' Party	J. L. R. Zapatero	Single Party	Soc. Workers' Party	Minority	48	44	1.4	No
	2011	3.5	2	1	Soc. Workers' Party	J. L. R. Zapatero[5]	Minority	People's Party	Single	53	45	−2	Yes
	2015	9	0	3	People's Party	M. Rajoy	Single	People's Party	—[6]	35	29	0	No
	2016	—	—	—	People's Party	M. Rajoy	—	People's Party	Minority	39	33	3.23	No
United Kingdom	2010	0.8	1	0	Labour	G. Brown	Single	Conservative	Coalition	47	36	−0.11	Yes
	2015	3.8	4	0	Conservative	D. Cameron	Coalition	Conservative	Single	51	37	2	No

Source: Database of Political Institutions (DPI).

* Adjustment episodes introduced by the Government before elections.

† GDP growth computed as the percent average of the government period.

[1] Cowen succeeded Bertie Ahern after his resignation in 2008 and did not run in 2011 election, being replaced by Michael Martin.

[2] Monti was appointed as an independent in 2011; the ministries of his government were not politicians and the government was supported by both left- and right-wing parties.

[3] Despite winning the elections, Passos Coelho did not get the majority of votes in the parliament to form a government. A minority government led by the Socialist party was then formed.

[4] Coalition party formed by Social Democratic and the People's party.

[5] Zapatero did not run for 2011 elections. Rubacalba replaced him as leader of PSOE.

[6] The previous executive remained in charge during the period of stall, until new elections were held.

[7] Since the government of Monti was not politically oriented, the ideology change that we register is from an independent government to a left-wing one.

reelected in 2015, winning an absolute majority, well above what polls had predicted. In 2017 the full majority was lost, but because of issues related to Brexit, not to austerity. In Ireland, there were two elections after the financial crisis and during austerity, in 2011 and 2016. In 2011, the easy winner was Fine Gael, led by Enda Kenny. In 2016, Kenny obtained the relative majority of votes but, not having reached absolute majority and not having been able to form a coalition, he resigned. Eventually, after a period during which he served as caretaker, an agreement was finally reached, and he was reelected as prime minister.

In three countries (Italy, Portugal, and Spain) political events were complicated. In Italy, the main austerity push occurred in 2011–13, implemented by a technnocratic government appointed in November 2011 when Italy was on the verge of following a Greek-like path, and this government was supported by almost every party in Parliament. That government could not be "reelected" since it was never "elected." After the 2013 elections, the Democratic Party continued the cautious fiscal policies of the previous government. In Spain in 2008, José Luis Zapatero and the Spanish Socialist Workers' Party (PSOE) won the elections against the People's Party (PP) led by Mariano Rajoy. In 2011, early elections were held because Zapatero resigned. Rajoy won easily. In 2015, after several years of austerity, Rajoy won the elections again, but without having obtained the absolute majority and thus not being able to form a government. Eventually new elections were held in June 2016. Again, Rajoy's PP was the largest party, with 33% of votes and 39% of the seats in Congress. In Portugal there were three elections after the financial crisis, in 2009, 2011, and 2015. In the first round, the incumbent prime minister José Socrates, leader of the Socialist Party, was reelected with 36.5% of votes. The next elections should have been held in 2013, but because the Socialist Party lost the majority in Parliament, they were pulled forward to 2011. The Social Democratic Party, led by Pedro Passos Coelho, prevailed over the Socialist Party and the People's Party, gaining 38.7% of votes. Finally in 2015, Passos Coelho was reelected with the coalition "Portugal Ahead" comprising the Social Democratic Party and the People's Party. But he failed to get Parliament's confidence and a minority government led by the Socialist Party was formed.

The last column of Table 10.5 shows that in these countries, during the austerity period, there have been just as many changes of government as reappointments. This column must be taken with a grain of salt, because in this complicated period what constitutes a reappointment versus a change in government is often quite difficult to define.

DISCUSSION

Not Only Elections

If it is the case that fiscal adjustments do not systematically lead to electoral defeats, then why do they often seem so politically difficult, even when necessary? Two possible explanations come to mind. The first is risk aversion: incumbent governments may be afraid of "rocking the boat" and prefer following a cautious course of action, postponing fiscal reforms until they are truly unavoidable. Second, the political game played around austerity goes beyond the one-person, one-vote counting of votes. For example, Alesina and Drazen (1991) present a model in which organized groups with a strong influence on the polity manage to postpone reforms, even when the latter are necessary and unavoidable, in order to try to switch the costs onto their opponents. The resulting "war of attrition" delays fiscal adjustments.[3] Strikes, contributions from various lobbies, and press campaigns are all means for enforcing (or blocking) policies, above and beyond voting at the polls. Imagine, for example, a public sector union that goes on strike to block cuts in the public wage bill. This may create disruptions with consequences too costly for the citizens and thus for a government to bear. Similar considerations may lead to the postponement of pension reforms. In many countries, pensioners receive strong political support from workers' unions. Thus a government may decide to water down a pension reform to placate this particular lobby, even though a majority of the electorate might have favored the reform.

Ponticelli and Voth (2011) and Passarelli and Tabellini (2017) empirically studied different time periods and different countries; they show that tough fiscal policies have been associated with riots and social protests. So, on the one hand we often observe protests, but on the other hand governments that implemented fiscal consolidations are often reelected. How can one rationalize these two facts? One possible answer is that some groups, feeling that they might lose as a result of a fiscal consolidation, protest in the streets. But the average voter instead sees the consolidation as inevitable and does not punish the incumbent at the polls. To put it differently, voting is not the only channel for political expression. Various groups opposed to austerity—either because it affects them specifically, sometimes by cutting their privileges, or because they see it as an error for the country as a whole—express their protest in the street. These strikes, protests, and so forth are very visible and widely reported, but governments that have suffered this type of protest sometimes are reelected.

Why TB Plans?

If it is true, as shown in previous chapters, that TB fiscal adjustments are much more costly in terms of output losses than EB plans, then why do many governments still raise taxes to reduce deficits? There are at least four reasons.

First, the accumulated evidence at the time of the policy decision was not sufficient to move governments in the direction of spending cuts rather than tax hikes. In fact, as we argued at the very beginning of this book, the presumption from the simplest Keynesian models is that spending multipliers are larger than tax multipliers. Only the Irish government in 2010 referred to the literature on tax multipliers versus spending multipliers to justify its choice of cutting spending rather than raising taxes.

Second, output costs (a short-run downturn in the economy) may not be the only variable considered relevant by an incumbent government. There may be distributional considerations, for example. Normally, recessions increase income inequality; therefore a fiscal plan inducing a recession should increase inequality. But the relationship between fiscal adjustments and income distribution is more complex than that. So the discussion about cutting government spending often turns into a political quarrel about the "negative" redistributive consequences of such cuts. On the other hand, tax increases seem to receive praise because the tacit assumption is that the rich will pay them. The discussion about the redistributive consequences of austerity can get entangled, often in a rather confusing way, with the broader question of the secular increase in inequality in many OECD economies, and especially in the United States. Unfortunately, it is unclear in such cases what kind of redistribution one is talking about, intragenerational or intergenerational. Fiscal decisions about public debt, taxes, and future spending affect both. Future generations are not alive, do not vote, and are only imperfectly cared for by the current generation making fiscal decisions. This is why public debts are left to future generations and social security systems are not well funded. For example, an austerity plan that reduces social security benefits for the current generation redistributes income from today to tomorrow.

As for redistribution across the current generation: is it possible to reduce government spending by a few percentage points of GDP in countries where the share of public spending of GDP is around 50% or more without affecting the welfare of the poor? The implicit answer of the anti-austerity camp is "no." But this may not be correct, especially in countries (and there are many) in which there is much waste and corruption. More importantly, welfare programs often are not well targeted and support the upper middle class instead of the poor and the lower classes. In fact, welfare programs are sometimes so inefficient that the really needy are left unsupported by them. This is especially the case in southern Europe, where such programs are known for being especially misdirected, costly, and wasteful. Table 10.6 documents this fact in a subsample of 12 European countries. These countries (Italy, Portugal, and Spain) have welfare systems that are clearly poorly targeted if compared with the rest of Europe, even though the size of their government sectors is not that much smaller than in other countries in Europe. This suggests that reforms of the welfare state can achieve superior coverage of the really poor even without spending more. Even when welfare programs are not wasteful, simply making some of them means tested would reduce government spending. For example, public health benefits available to all, and tuition-free state universities in Europe, which typically are attended by the upper middle class, might be candidates for means testing. In addition, several European countries do not seem to be in need of much additional spending on physical infrastructure. In fact,

TABLE 10.6. Social expenditures and poverty risk reduction in some EU countries in 2003–5

Country	Poverty rate* Before social transfers and taxes	Poverty rate* After social transfers and taxes	Absolute difference	Social expenditures (% GDP) Gross	Social expenditures (% GDP) Net
Austria	25	13	12	26.1	22.2
Belgium	27	15	12	26.5	26.0
Denmark	28	12	16	27.6	21.6
Finland	29	13	16	22.5	20.6
France	25	13	12	28.7	28.0
Germany	26	13	13	27.3	27.6
Ireland	33	18	15	15.9	14.3
Italy	24	20	4	24.2	22.3
Portugal	25	18	7	23.5	22.1
Spain	24	20	4	20.3	17.7
Sweden	29	12	17	31.3	26.1
United Kingdom	30	19	11	20.6	24.6
Mean	27	16	12	24.5	22.8

Sources: Structural Indicators EU–Social Cohesion (Eurostat: EU-SILC). Table from Caminada and Goudswaard (2009).

*Poverty rate is defined as the share of the population whose income is below 60% of the median income of the country.

some of them (Spain in particular) may have overinvested in the recent (precrisis) past. More generally, the "unfairness" of budget cuts is often an argument used strategically by various groups to protect their specific benefits, if not privileges. An analysis of the redistributive consequences of tax increases and spending cuts clearly would be very complex and would require a separate volume. On the tax side, obviously the redistributive effects of tax hikes depend on how the additional tax burden is shared among income and wealth levels.

The third argument is the difference between concentrated benefits and diffused costs. Coordinated and organized groups (say a business association, a union of workers in the public sector, or a privileged professional association) may be capable of defending their interests by preventing budget cuts that would affect their associates. Taxpayers, on the other hand, are a large, uncoordinated group. An increase in the VAT affects everybody; an increase in the income tax affects many taxpayers proportionally (or progressively). Taxpayers do not have the organizational structure to engage in protests or costly political actions against the government, or to invest in lobbying activities; instead, specific organized groups can do so: employees can strike, creating major problems for the public. Taxpayers cannot. Thus, expenditure cuts that affect specific sectors of society may be more politically costly than other plans. The internal organization of a government also matters. Spending cuts must be assigned to certain ministries. The spending ministers affected by these cuts are always keen on opposing them, defending their turf, because their prestige within the government and their authority within the bureaucracy in their ministry depend on how much they are allowed to spend. Cutting programs means reducing their status. In addition, to maintain their status, bureaucrats in certain ministries may distort information provided to their minister, increasing the importance of this or that program, and protecting themselves from spending cuts. Perhaps less cynically, given their background and interests in a certain topic, say education, defense, and health, spending ministers may be honestly convinced of the importance of their programs but without fully internalizing the government budget constraint. Raising taxes may be a diffuse cost for the entire government while a budget cut is a specific cost for a minister who will try to avoid it at all costs. Thus the internal organization of governments matters. If the treasury minister or the prime minister has sufficient power, de jure or de facto, against spending ministers, he or she can more easily defeat the reluctance to cut. Otherwise spending ministers take over and may even collude.

Similar considerations apply to legislatures. Individual legislators may be especially keen to defend spending programs that affect their constituency, defined geographically or otherwise. Whereas tax increases affect everybody, spending cuts are at least in part localized. Thus a legislator does not fully internalize the costs of taxation that is spread over "everybody," while spending has localized benefits. A vast literature has explored these mechanisms, beginning with the case of the US Congress.[4] Different procedures for approving the budget can make these problems more or less intense.[5] For example, in certain countries the Treasury minister has more power than spending ministers within the government; certain legislative procedures make it easier (or more difficult) for specific groups in the legislature to block fiscal plans. For instance, "closed" versus "open" voting rules give more power to the agenda setter (see Baron and Ferejohn [1989]), namely to the government proposing a budget in parliament, and also limit the possibility of the opposition to introduce amendments. In fact, many believe that reforms of budgetary rules and institutions may lead to better outcomes in the sense that they are less affected by specific groups at the expense of the majority. An important additional factor affecting the implementation of fiscal policy is the bureaucracy, a sector that has not received enough careful attention by economists. A budget cut may pass the parliament but in the process of implementation it may be diluted, changed in often significant ways by the bureaucracy. This is a topic in need of further research.

Fourth, TB plans are easier to design, faster to implement, and can generate immediate revenues for the government. This was especially relevant for the last round of austerity measures undertaken in the immediate aftermath of the financial crisis. For instance, a value-added tax (VAT) rate can be increased with a simple legislative vote and generates additional revenue beginning from the next day. A program of spending cuts requires some time to be developed and some thought as to how to minimize its costs, in terms of operational efficiency, for any given savings on the spending side. In many cases, there is no time for this. In moments of crisis, when markets are losing faith in the ability of a government to fulfill its obligations, a government may want to immediately signal its willingness to reduce deficits. The tax route may appear to be, or indeed may be, the only feasible solution. Thus if a country postpones austerity until when a crisis erupts, it may preclude itself the option of a more carefully designed spending-based plan and it has the only "crisis option": to raise taxes.

CONCLUSIONS

This chapter raises doubts about the conventional wisdom suggesting that austerity always means an electoral defeat for the government that implements it. This does not mean that voters like austerity, but more simply that in some cases they might understand the necessity of it and, when implemented appropriately, they may reward the incumbent for it, or at least not punish him or her. This result is not inconsistent with the observation that some groups may be especially opposed to some austerity measures because they affect them directly, and they may protest against them. It may be the case that only certain types of governments, those more popular to begin with, or that have a more charismatic leader, can be reelected with tight fiscal policies. We could not provide any conclusive evidence on this point, because measuring government popularity or leaders' charisma is not easy. But this hypothesis seems quite plausible. Thus, while not all governments that implement austerity measures get reelected, those who manage to do it well and are relatively popular to start with can be austere and electorally successful. We also find that, in general, governments implement austerity measures early in their term of office; that right-of-center governments are more likely to cut deficits; and that coalition governments are slower in implementing fiscal adjustments.

CHAPTER ELEVEN

Conclusions

Austerity is almost always the correction of past policy mistakes. Starting in the mid-1970s and continuing into the 1980s, many countries accumulated large public debts for no apparent good reason. Some countries tried to stabilize their runaway public debts in the late 1980s and 1990s. The rules required to join the euro forced several other countries to reduce their deficits. Another round of austerity occurred after the Great Recession, in countries facing debt crises. These recent episodes have generated passionate discussions about the costs and benefits of austerity. The debate became fiercely ideological, and hardly based on a careful examination of the data. Vicious attacks became the norm. Aggressive newspapers articles with no data became more common than serious statistical analysis.

On one side of the argument we find commentators and economists who are convinced, above and beyond any reasonable doubt and despite any empirical evidence to the contrary, that spending multipliers are large, tax multipliers are smaller, and therefore spending cuts always produce large recessions and must be avoided at all costs, even if debt reaches 100% of gross domestic product (GDP) or more, and even when markets refuse to lend any more money to indebted countries. These commentators never say what level of public debt would begin to worry them. They argued that even in the middle of the European debt crisis, countries like Italy, Portugal, Spain, Ireland, and possibly even Greece should have allowed their debts to rise rather than trying to reduce them. This argument is debatable, to say the least.

On the opposite side are those, mostly but not only in Germany, who believe that even relatively small budget deficits must be avoided at all costs, anytime, and that any deficit reduction policy is always desirable. This view neglects the basic premise of optimal taxation which implies that deficits, sometimes even large ones, are the necessary buffer during recessions or during periods of temporary and massive spending needs. Those who believe in the antideficit view at all costs seem to rely on a somewhat misplaced "superiority complex," a view that those who run deficits are somewhat "morally" inferior to those who never have any debt. This is just bad economics.

In this book we have shown that both arguments are wrong. We considered models of the economy that take into account effects that go beyond the traditional elementary Keynesian model, allowing for the role of expectations, the supply side, and the multiyear nature of austerity plans. We also devoted much attention to accompanying policies: monetary policy, exchange rate movements, and structural reforms, including labor market reforms and liberalization of goods and services markets. In fact, multiyear plans involving large fiscal consolidations are often part of a "package" of policies, which is one of the reasons why isolating the effect of austerity is hard.

One of the contribution of this book has been the construction of a large dataset of deficit reduction measures taken in 16 countries from the late 1970s to 2014. These fiscal measures were not dictated by the state of the economy, but rather by a desire or necessity to reduce deficits. A link to these data is available at https://press.princeton.edu/titles/13244.html, the web appendix to this book, in a user-friendly form. We also made a methodological contribution with our analysis of fiscal plans. Normally the effects of fiscal policy are studied considering year-to-year or even quarter-to-quarter "shocks" to fiscal variables. In our analysis we recognize and incorporate an important and realistic factor: namely, that austerity is typically implemented with multiyear plans, involving the interaction of announcements, revisions, and implementation of past announcements. In these plans spending cuts and tax hikes cannot be considered independent from each other because a certain level of deficit reduction has to be achieved and typically that total is fixed before deciding on what to cut or which taxes to increase

Our main substantive results can be summarized as follows.

1. We uncovered a very large difference in the output effect of expenditure-based (EB) austerity plans versus tax-based (TB) ones. Spending cuts on average have been associated with very small downturns. A 1% deficit reduction plan based on spending cuts is associated (on average) with less than half of a percentage point deviation of GDP from the country's average growth rate, and this deviation lasts no more

than a couple of years. Average small downturns are the result of episodes of expenditure cuts that were more recessionary and others that were associated with immediate surges in output growth, that is, "expansionary austerity" defined as the case when a fiscal adjustment is accompanied by a growth rate of output higher than the average of the sample used for the estimation. On the contrary, plans based on tax increases are associated with large recessions: output losses of 2% to 3% of GDP, for a 1% of GDP deficit reduction, and these recessions last several years.

2. EB austerity achieves the desired goal of reducing the growth rate of the debt over GDP ratio relative to what would have happened absent the austerity plan. On the contrary, in most cases, owing to the fall in the denominator, TB austerity plans are associated with an acceleration in the growth of the debt over GDP ratio. Obviously the effects of similar austerity plans on the debt over GDP ratio depend on other factors, such as the cost of debt financing, inflation, and the initial level of debt when austerity starts. However, the different effects of EB and TB plans are evident in all cases.

3. The effects of reductions in entitlement programs and other forms of government transfers are different from those of tax increases. They are followed by mild and short downturns, probably because these cuts are perceived as long lasting, leading to a lower tax burden for an extended period. Considering cuts in transfers as analogous to increases in taxes, as sometimes is done, is therefore a mistake. Our dataset could allow for finer analyses, such as distinguishing between increases in direct and indirect taxes, or between cuts in government subsidies and other forms of spending, or in current versus investment spending. However, there were too few austerity plans based on increases in indirect taxes, or based on cuts, for instance in infrastructure spending, to be able to analyze them separately.

4. Among the components of private demand, investment reacts very differently following the two types of austerity plans. It responds positively to spending cuts and negatively to tax hikes. Business confidence behaves consistently with private investment: it increases on the announcement of spending cuts. Private consumption and net exports on average do not differ during the two types of adjustments, though. Thus the exchange rate, which could affect net exports, cannot explain, on average, the different effect of TB versus EB adjustments.

5. We have investigated whether the recent episodes of European austerity that occurred after the financial crisis of 2008, and started during a recession, were different from previous cases—that is, costlier. The popular discussion often confuses two very different issues. One is whether austerity was too draconian. The second one is whether multipliers were larger than we thought, and thus for every unit of reduction in deficits the recessions were bigger than anticipated, based on precrisis evidence. The two questions are different. There are three reasons why austerity might have been more costly, that is, multipliers higher than expected. First, in many countries this round of austerity came in the middle of a deep recession. Second, monetary policy could not help as much as in normal circumstances, because nominal interest rates had reached the "zero lower bound." Third, unlike in previous cases, many countries engaged in austerity all together, leading to negative spillovers via international trade. We studied in detail the austerity episodes that occurred after the financial crisis and compared them with earlier ones. First we documented the sheer size of some of these austerity plans, which was exceptional, not only in Greece but also in Spain, Portugal, Ireland, and to a lesser extent in Italy and the United Kingdom. Then we confirmed the major difference in the effects of spending cuts relative to tax increases. So, we asked whether this recent round of austerity was especially costly. A widespread consensus seems to suggest that this was indeed the case, concluding that the long recession experienced by some European countries was entirely due to austerity programs. This is not so obvious: first there were sharp differences among countries depending on the type of austerity they implemented. Countries that chose TB austerity suffered deeper recessions compared to those that decided to reduce spending. In addition, other factors, such as the bursting of the housing bubble, delays in recapitalizing banks, and credit crunches, also had a much to do with the depth of some recessions.

6. Motivated by postcrisis experience, we investigated the connection between "when austerity is implemented" (in a recession or a boom) and "how it is implemented" with cuts in spending or increase in taxes. Whether fiscal consolidations, both on the tax side and the spending side, are more costly when started during recessions is a difficult point to discern. The answer depends on a variety of issues regarding measurement of the dynamic pattern of the economy before and during the

adjustment. However, for fiscal adjustment started both in recessions and expansions the difference between EB and TB austerity is on average large.

7. The case of Greece is special in a variety of ways. Greece bears a very large responsibility for its own demise, which is the result of irresponsible policies adopted since joining the euro area. After the crisis exploded, the Troika vastly mishandled the situation, creating confusion and uncertainty, and aggravating the problem. In light of what happened, a restructuring of the Greek debt when the extent of the country's fiscal problem was revealed would have been the best option. Given the size of austerity imposed on Greece the Troika should not have been surprised by the size of the Greek recession.

8. We then turned to the electoral consequences of austerity. We show that there is much less support than most people assume for the view that deficit reduction policies have negative electoral consequences. We do not find that governments that aggressively reduce deficits are systematically voted out of office. Maybe the government that implemented austerity was reelected despite austerity, not because of it, but the evidence seems consistent with the view that voters sometimes understand the necessity of deficit reduction policies. At the very least, one can conclude that some governments can, when needed, reduce deficits without suffering at the polls. In certain cases voters elected parties that included austerity measures in their programs.

What could explain these rather remarkable differences between EB and TB fiscal adjustment plans? We explored various alternative explanations. One "theory" is that the difference is due simply to a systematic difference in accompanying policies. The most obvious candidate is monetary policy. In fact, Guajardo et al. (2014) argue that indeed differences in the response of monetary policy are substantially responsible for these findings. This is not correct. In fact, we show that only a small fraction of the heterogeneous effects of the two types of adjustments can be ascribed to monetary policy. A second and related possibility could be that the difference is explained by the behavior of the exchange rate. We show that this is not the case. On average there is no systematic difference in the behavior of the exchange rate before fiscal adjustments based upon tax increases or spending cuts. We also excluded from the sample all episodes of fiscal consolidation that were preceded by a deval-uation. The results were unchanged. In addition, if the exchange rate had been an important explanation of the difference between the two types of austerity, the difference in terms of GDP growth should be associated with a different behavior of net exports. This is not the case. Finally, large fiscal adjustments are often periods of "deep" structural reforms that may include products and/or labor market liberalization. The latter may stimulate growth, and if they were systematically occurring at the time of spending cuts, they could explain the finding. The answer is no: these reforms do not occur systematically during periods of spending cuts.

A second, more promising, explanation has to do with expectations and confidence. With this term we identify situations in which austerity removes uncertainty and stimulates demand by making consumers and especially investors more optimistic about the future. Imagine a situa-tion in which an economy is on an unsustainable path with an exploding public debt. Sooner or later a fiscal stabilization has to occur. The longer one waits, the higher the taxes that will need to be raised (or spend-ing to be cut) in the future. When the stabilization occurs it removes the uncertainty about further delays that would have increased even more the costs of the stabilization. A stabilization that eliminates the uncertainty about higher fiscal costs in the future stimulates demand today—especially, we may add, demand from investors, who are more sensitive to uncertainty about the future given the long-run nature of their plans. It is quite likely that the beneficial effects are more likely to occur in the presence of spending cuts than tax hikes. Because tax hikes do not address the automatic growth of entitlements and other spend-ing programs that grow over time, they are much less likely to produce a long-lasting effect on the budget. If the automatic increase of spending is not addressed, taxes will have to keep rising to cover the increase in outlays. Thus the confidence effect is likely to be much smaller for tax plans, as expectations of future taxes will continue to rise. Expenditure plans produce the opposite effects.

Other explanations relate to the supply side of the economy, which reacts very differently to tax hikes or spending cuts. Spending cuts reduce the demand side directly. However, an expectation of lower taxes tomorrow compensates part of these direct effects. Tax increases affect private demand by reducing after-tax salaries (in the case of income taxes); in addition, they create disincentives to work. These effects are small for prime age men but they are much larger for second earners in a family, for individuals close to retirement, and for youngsters entering the labor market. Indirect tax increases lower the purchasing power of nominal income.

Why has the recent discussion about austerity been so heated? One reason is that this debate gets intertwined with issues such as the role and size of government in society, discussions about the increase in inequality, the fairness of tax systems, and so forth. We think that it is important not to mix different issues. Our results do not have any implications for the "optimal size" of government. If one believes that government spending should be 60% or 70% of GDP, and that taxes should be the same so as to balance the budget, there is nothing in this book to dispute these beliefs. We only claim that if large deficits need to be reduced, then raising taxes creates recessions and cutting spending does not, or does so much less. As for inequality: the effects of tax hikes or spending cuts depend very much on the composition of the two, namely what is cut and which taxes are raised, and this topic goes beyond the scope of this book.

Another line of argument against austerity is that public debt is not really a problem. This argument is especially popular now, given that interest rates are generally very low, so debt is not expensive. We think that this view is problematic for at least three reasons. First, large public debts imply a redistribution between current generations and future ones who cannot vote. This is simply unfair and needs to be taken into consideration by those who seem to advocate more and more debt. If one considers not only measured public debt but also the state of many pension systems, the picture becomes even more troublesome. Second, interest rates will not be low forever. Sooner or later they will return to more "normal" levels. With higher interest rates, more and more taxes will be needed to service the debt, reducing growth and generating a potential vicious cycle: high taxes, low growth, debt over GDP ratio not decreasing, and so forth. Third, in some countries high debt levels may generate default risk, high interest rates, capital outflows (as in Greece), and a debt crisis that may impose austerity when it is particularly costly.

On the other side of the argument are those who are almost "obsessed" with deficits. It is simply bad economics to argue that budgets should be balanced every year. Deficits are a perfectly acceptable tool in the kit of prudent policymakers. Prudent is, however, the key word. It is easy to embrace budget deficits during recessions or in special times, but much more difficult to reverse them when needed. This is why so many countries accumulated large debts before the financial crisis when deficits were not necessary and entered the crisis with little room to maneuver. Countries that had gained a reputation for relatively good fiscal management could run even very large deficits with the trust of markets. But countries that for one reason or another had lost the trust of the market were penalized. Sometimes, austerity policies may be necessary, beyond the needs of the moment, to establish a future reputation that would allow countries to run large deficits in the future when necessary.

Finally, the argument we developed in this book is deeply intertwined with this question: Did many European countries engage in too sharp austerity policies, too soon before the end of the recession? All we can say is that spending cuts were much less costly than tax increases. On the question of whether European austerity could have been postponed, much has been written. We did not observe the alternative. The argument for austerity was that several countries were on the verge of a debt crisis that could have induced banking crises, because many banks held a great deal of domestic sovereign debt. We might have had another round of financial collapses in Europe, possibly the demise of the monetary union, with unpredictable but potentially disastrous effects. Part of the responsibility for the European recessions lies in the delays in recapitalizing banks, unlike in the United States, where a swift intervention in 2008–9 "fixed" the problem relatively quickly. One reason for such delays was the proximity, sometimes the overlap, in many European countries, between politicians and bankers: this created incentives to postpone the recapitalization, because it would have meant wiping out the old shareholders. The other reason was the grudgingness of national banking supervisors who long resisted the establishment of a common banking supervision at the European level.

We find it remarkable that those who opposed any form of austerity seem to be so sure that everything would have worked out, with more government spending and more debt in countries such as Italy,

Ireland, Spain, and Portugal. On the other hand, was Germany right in the attempt to delay the European Central Bank (ECB) from buying government bonds? No, it was not: the ECB should have intervened long before 2012, when President Draghi said: "We'll do everything it takes to save the euro," meaning that the ECB was ready to step in with "unconventional" monetary policy to buy government debt.

CHAPTER TWELVE

The Models in Our Book: A User's Guide

INTRODUCTION

Measuring multipliers requires two steps: (1) identify exogenous shifts in fiscal variables; and (2) analyze their effects on the economy, using an empirical model that allows tracking of the dynamic response of the economy to such exogenous shifts. For this second step, one needs to estimate the parameters of the model and then use the model to generate two alternative paths for the macroeconomic and policy variables, in the presence or absence of the shift in fiscal variables. The difference between these two paths is the "impulse response" that describes the dynamic reaction of the economy to the policy correction (the impulse).[1]

In specifying models for policy simulation there is an important trade-off: the simpler the model the easier it is to calculate the multipliers but the simpler the model the more likely it is that important relations among variables are missed. So the simpler the model the more likely that the model is wrong. To calculate fiscal multipliers a choice is required and a researcher must decide where to locate in the trade-off between simplicity and reliability. Computing a multiplier by running one regression and reading the coefficients it is almost surely a recipe for disaster: the economy is too complex to be described by one regression. Conversely, modeling the economy in all details almost certainly entails that there will be too many parameters to be estimated. A choice needs to be made and such a choice is surely a risky one.

In this chapter we shall illustrate all the models that we have used in this book and that we make available for replication. We shall start with an illustrative example and a general discussion to then review one by one the models used chapter by chapter.

204 I Chapter Twelve

WHY SIMULATING MODELS? A SIMPLE EXAMPLE

Consider the simplest possible specification of a model, like the one described in Chapter 5

$$\Delta y_t = \beta_0 + \beta_1 e_t^u + \beta_2 e_{t-1}^u + \gamma_1 e_{t,t-1}^a + \delta_1 e_{t,t+1}^a + u_t$$

$$e_{t,t+1}^a = \varphi_1 e_t^u + v_t$$

$$e_{t+1,t}^a = e_{t,t+1}^a$$

where Δy_t is output growth and the variables on the right-hand side are the unanticipated, announced, and implemented portions of a fiscal correction. To keep matters simple we limit the horizon of plans to one period, do not distinguish between tax-based (TB) and expenditure-based (EB) corrections, and limit the dynamic effects of plans also to one period. The parameters β_1 and β_2, describe the dynamic response of output growth to the unanticipated component of the plan; γ_1 describes the response to the implementation in year t of measures announced in year $t - 1$; δ_1 the response to measures announced in year time t, to be implemented the following year, $t + 1$; and finally β_0 measures the average rate of growth of the economy in absence of fiscal plans. The next two equations describe fiscal plans: the first measures the correlation between the announced and the unanticipated components of a plan; the second simply says that a measure announced, $e_{t+1,t}^a$, is subsequently implemented, showing up as $e_{t,t+1}^a$. Now assume that the data deliver the following estimated parameters:

$$\Delta y_t = 0.02 - 0.8 e_t^u - 0.6 e_{t-1}^u - 0.2 e_{t,t-1}^a - 0.3 \hat{e}_{t,t+1}^a + u_t$$

$$e_{t,t+1}^a = 0.5 \hat{e}_t^u + v_t$$

$$e_{t+1,t}^a = e_{t,t+1}^a$$

Note that the effects of a plan cannot be inferred simply by reading the coefficients of the first equation—because one needs to also take into account the correlation between announcements and unexpected shifts in fiscal variables. In other words, one needs to jointly simulate all three equations in the model and then compute impulse responses. Table 12.1 reports the result of this exercise

TABLE 12.1. A stylized example

	Impulse			Baseline	Alternative	Impulse response		Multiplier
	e_t^u	$e_{t,t-1}^a$	$e_{t,t+1}^a$	Δy_t	Δy_t	Δy_t	y_t	
t	$0.01\frac{2}{3}$	0	$0.01\frac{1}{3}$	0.02	0.013667	−0.00633	−0.00633	−0.633
$t+1$	0	$0.01\frac{2}{3}$	0	0.02	0.015333	−0.004667	−0.011	−1.1
$t+2$	0	0	0	0.02	0.02	0	−0.011	−1.1
$t+3$	0	0	0	0.02	0.02	0	−0.011	−1.1
$t+4$	0	0	0	0.02	0.02	0	−0.011	−1.1
$t+5$	0	0	0	0.02	0.02	0	−0.011	−1.1

The simulation in the table describes the effects of a fiscal correction worth 1% of GDP. Such a correction is implemented with a two-thirds share attributed to the unanticipated component and a one-third share announced at time t to be implemented in the following period. The output multiplier of the plan is −0.6333 in the first period and −1.1 from the second period onwards. These multipliers depend on the coefficients estimated in the first equation but also on the estimate of φ_1 (0.5 in the example). For example, the −0.633 delivered by the simulation in the first period is the sum of the impact effect of the unanticipated component ($-0.8 \cdot 0.01 \cdot \frac{2}{3}$) plus the effect of the announcement ($-0.03 \cdot 0.5 \cdot 0.01 \cdot \frac{2}{3}$).

OUR EMPIRICAL MODELS: AN OVERVIEW

More generally than in the simple case considered so far a model describes the behavior of a set of macro variables, $\mathbf{Y}_t$, as a function of their past values, $\mathbf{Y}_{t-1}$, the past values of a few policy variables $\mathbf{P}_{t-1}$ (in our case the fiscal policy variables) and macroeconomic shocks. Similarly, the dynamics of the policy variables can be decomposed into a "rule"—which describes the response of current policy to past policy and past macroeconomic conditions—and deviations from the rule, our fiscal plans:

$$\mathbf{Y}_t = f_1(\mathbf{Y}_{t-1}, \mathbf{P}_{t-1}, \Theta_1) + f_2(\mathbf{plan}_t, \Theta_2) + \mathbf{u}_{1t} \qquad (12.1)$$

$$\mathbf{P}_t = f_3(\mathbf{Y}_{t-1}, \mathbf{P}_{t-1}, \Theta_3) + f_4(\mathbf{plan}_t, \Theta_4) + \mathbf{u}_{2t} \qquad (12.2)$$

$$\mathbf{plan}_t = g\left(e_{i,t}^u, e_{i,t-1,t}^a, e_{i,t,t+1}^a, \Phi\right) + \mathbf{u}_{3t} \qquad (12.3)$$

Once the variables to be included in $\mathbf{Y}_t$ and $\mathbf{P}_t$ are chosen (a choice, as we already mentioned in Chapter 5, that is limited by the scarcity of data), to use the model to run a simulation we need to decide on a functional form for the functions f_1, f_2, f_3, f_4 and to estimate the parameters $\Theta_1, \Theta_2, \Theta_3, \Theta_4$. Once the model is specified and estimated, the impact of fiscal plans on macroeconomic variables can be computed by constructing an impulse response (IR) computing the difference between two forecasts:

$$IR\left(t, s, d_i\right) = E\left(\mathbf{Y}_{i,t+s} \mid \text{plans}_t; I_t\right) - E\left(\mathbf{Y}_{i,t+s} \mid \text{no plans}_t; I_t\right)$$
$$s = 0, 1, 2, \dots$$

Finally, multipliers can be calculated, as argued by Mountford and Uhlig (2009), Uhlig (2010), and Fisher and Peters (2010), as the integral of the output response divided by the integral of the change in fiscal variables.

THE MODELS USED IN THE LITERATURE TO MEASURE MULTIPLIERS

Beyond the narrative approach discussed in Chapter 4, many other techniques have been developed to deal with the identification, estimation, and simulation of the effects of a shift in taxes or spending.

The VAR Approach

Vector autoregressions (VAR) were one of the first techniques used to identify exogenous shifts in fiscal variables and to simulate their impact on the economy. Blanchard and Perotti (2002) were the first to adopt this empirical strategy.

VARs are systems of equations designed to analyze the linear interdependencies among multiple variables. In other words, rather than a single dynamic equation, VARs include a system of many dynamic equations. Moreover, (structural) VARs can be used to address the reverse causation problem. Structural VARs solve the problem by estimating a dynamic model that projects (linearly) both nonpolicy and policy variables on their past history: innovations in the equations for the policy variables thus represent deviations of these variables from their expected values, conditional on past information. These innovations contain two terms: the contemporaneous response of fiscal policy to the cycle and discretionary policy actions not related to the cycle. These discretionary policy actions are the "exogenous" policy shifts that researchers are interested in. Blanchard and Perotti (2002) recover such discretionary policy actions in two steps: (1) filtering out "the automatic stabilization component" from the VAR innovation, relying on institutional information about the automatic response of taxes, transfers, and spending to the state of the economy (although Caldara and Kamps [2017] show that estimated multipliers are quite sensitive to changes in the identification procedure); and (2) assuming that it takes at least one quarter for fiscal authorities to respond to the state of the economy, so that the current state of the cycle cannot influence the discretionary deviation of policy from the rule, a debatable assumption. Many variations on this theme have been implemented within this general framework.[2]

Once exogenous shifts in taxes or spending are recovered, their impact on macroeconomic variables can be constructed by comparing two different simulations of the VAR model: a baseline simulation and an alternative one. In the baseline simulation, it is assumed that the fiscal authority sticks to its rule; the alternative simulation instead introduces a discretionary deviation from the rule. Simulations of the model under the two different scenarios produce two paths for macroeconomic variables: their difference is the impulse response function that describes the response (over time) of the economy to an exogenous impulse given to policy variables. This approach naturally leads to computing multipliers as the ratio of the discounted sum of the output response to a shift in G or T to the total change in G or T (also discounted) because VAR impulse responses track the entire path of fiscal variables following an initial shift.

There are two main weaknesses in the use of this strategy to identify exogenous shifts in policy variables. First, the exogenous policy shifts depend on the particular specification of the model. For instance, if a relevant variable is omitted, innovations could be contaminated by this misspecification. The second is the validity of the identification assumption that allows the researcher to extract exogenous policy shifts from innovations in policy variables. For instance, Blanchard and Perotti (2002) assume that it takes at least one quarter for fiscal authorities to respond to the state of the economy.

Blanchard and Perotti (2002) estimate a three-variable VAR containing the log of tax revenue, of government spending, and of GDP (all in real per capita terms). This specification is very restrictive: only three variables are considered and the shifts in fiscal variables identified are combinations of unanticipated and announced fiscal corrections, which means that the estimates are obtained under the assumption that the responses to anticipated and unanticipated shifts in fiscal variables are identical. (The assumption that unanticipated and announced policy shifts have identical effects is inevitable if one chooses to identify fiscal innovations within a VAR, since this approach does not allow for the identification of policy announcements, the reason being that the Moving Average representation of a VAR cannot be inverted in the presence of future announced policy shifts). Distinguishing between anticipated and unanticipated shifts in fiscal variables, however, and allowing them to have different effects on output, is crucial for evaluating fiscal multipliers, as argued by Ramey (2011a, b) and confirmed by Mertens and Ravn (2013), who find that they do have different effects on output. In Blanchard and Perotti (2002), taxes are net of transfer payments to individuals and of interest paid by the government, and spending is defined as purchases of goods and services, adding up current and capital spending (transfers are not included in the analysis). Data (for the United States) are quarterly for the period 1947:1 to 1997:4. Multipliers are calculated comparing the peak of the output response to an initial shift in government spending or in taxes. Tax multipliers are close to -1 (between -1.3 and -0.8 depending on whether the variables are defined in first differences or levels) and similar in absolute value to spending multipliers (between 0.9 and 1.3). These results have been confirmed by Fatas and Mihov (2001); Perotti (2005); Galí, López-Salido, and Vallés (2007); and Pappa (2009).

Mountford and Uhlig (2009) estimate a much richer VAR which includes, beyond the two fiscal variables analyzed by Blanchard and Perotti (2002), many more: consumption, real wages, private nonresidential investment, interest rates, materials' prices and the GDP deflator. Data (for the United States) are at a quarterly frequency from 1955 to 2000. Exogenous shifts in government revenue and expenditure are still identified within the VAR model, but also applying the methodology originally introduced by Uhlig (2005) to identify monetary policy shocks, that is, imposing sign restrictions on the effects of VAR innovations. The tax multiplier—defined as the ratio of the response of GDP at a given horizon (one or more quarters after the policy shift) to the initial movement of the fiscal variable—is almost three times larger than that computed by Blanchard and Perotti (2002): 3.57 (with a peak effect after 13 quarters). The deficit-financed spending multiplier is slightly lower than that estimated in Blanchard and Perotti (2002): 0.65 (with a peak effect upon impact). Linearly combining the two, the authors can analyze the effect of a balanced budget tax cut. Comparing these three experiments, they find that a surprise deficit-financed tax cut is the most effective at stimulating the economy, producing the largest present value multiplier (which, instead of measuring the effect of the shift in fiscal variables on impact, considers the cumulated response along the entire path of the response): five dollars of additional GDP for each dollar of cut in government revenue, 5 years after the shock.

Expectational VARs and Ramey's News Variable

Recently some researchers have tried to overcome the problems that arise when exogenous shifts in fiscal variables are identified inside a VAR, in particular the fact that it is impossible to separate announcements from unexpected shifts in policy. They have done so using exogenous shifts identified outside the VAR model, for example, with narrative methods. The approach has been labeled "Expectational VARs."

The outside variable used by Ramey and Shapiro (1998) is a dummy describing military buildups. They identify political events that led to unanticipated military buildups exogenous to the current state of the economy. These are called "war dates." The macroeconomic impact of these "war dates" is then measured by estimating an equation for output growth that includes current and lagged values of war dates (as well as lags of the left-hand-side variable). This single equation approach is a valid approximation to a VAR "full information approach," that is an approach that includes many more variables than just output growth, under the assumption that the measurement error in "war dates" and innovations in the variables that are excluded from the model, for instance interest rates, are orthogonal. A number of follow-up papers (e.g., Edelberg et al. [1999], Burnside et al. [2004], and Cavallo [2005]) have embedded "war dates" in a VAR.[3] These experiments typically found government spending multipliers in the range 0.6–1.5, slightly higher than that found by Blanchard and Perotti (2002).[4]

Barro and Redlick (2011) introduced a second fiscal variable, marginal tax rates, and also allow for multipliers to differ depending on the level of unemployment. Their results cover both periods in which defense spending decreased (e.g., 1946–7 and 1954–5) and periods during which it increased (e.g., World War I, World War II, the Korean War). The estimated multiplier for defense spending (holding average marginal income tax rates fixed) is around 0.7. These estimates are derived under the assumption that the increase in expenditure is deficit financed. The results are obviously different in the case of tax-financed increases in spending. Since an increase in average marginal income tax rates has a significantly negative effect on GDP with an implied multiplier of 1.1, the balanced budget multiplier becomes negative.

Multipliers and the Government Intertemporal Budget Constraint

The response of economic agents to current shifts in fiscal policy depends on their expectations about how future fiscal policy will adjust to such shifts, an observation first made by Bohn (1991). This raises the issue of debt sustainability following a shift in fiscal policy—an issue typically overlooked in the articles discussed in the two previous sections. Chung, Davig, and Leeper (2007) impose debt sustainability on a VAR;

that is, they require that the real value of debt in the hands of the public must always be equal to the expected present value of surpluses. For any given shift in fiscal variables, they therefore can ask whether debt is sustainable. Using data for the United States over the period 1947:2 to 2006:2, they find that for some fiscal shifts, changes in the present value of surpluses are sufficient to guarantee debt sustainability. In other cases expected surpluses, instead, fail to adjust enough to guarantee debt sustainability for given discount rates. In particular, they find robust evidence in favor of a stabilizing role for the primary surplus following shifts in taxes, and similarly robust evidence of a stabilizing role for taxes following a shift in government spending. Conversely, the results point against a stabilizing role of changes in spending following either a shift in taxes or in spending. In all cases the horizon over which debt is stabilized is very long, around 50 years. Present values calculated up to any finite horizon fluctuate wildly, particularly following a shift in government spending or in transfers.

Favero and Giavazzi (2012) estimate a VAR model that includes the narrative tax shocks constructed by the Romers. They then keep track of the dynamics of the debt over GDP ratio in response to one of those shocks, appending to the VAR the identity that defines the change over time of the debt over GDP ratio. Estimated on post-World War II United States data (1950:1–2007:1), the model never delivers "unsustainable debt paths" and it produces multipliers that are very similar to those obtained from a VAR that omits the debt dynamics equation. This equivalence may not hold to other countries outside of the United States, therefore accounting for the debt dynamics in this case would be crucial.

In the same vein, using a standard new-Keynesian model, Corsetti, Meier, and Müller (2012b) analyze the effects of an increase in government spending under a plausible debt stabilizing policy: current increases in spending are accompanied by a subsequent period of spending reversals. They show that accounting for them is of crucial importance for the model to match the stylized facts of fiscal transmission. Their results suggest that for an increase in expenditure to be most effective, policymakers should accompany it with a credible commitment to cut expenditure over the medium term.

Fiscal Policy as an Average Treatment Effect

Impulse responses compute the average effect of a policy shift by simulating the dynamic path of output in the presence and absence of the policy shift. This is a procedure reminiscent of that used to analyze "average treatment effects" in randomized experiments, where researchers split the sample into two subgroups: a "treated" and a "control" group. After the population is randomly assigned to the two groups, a treatment is administered to one group and no treatment (a "placebo" in medical experiments) to the other. The effect of the treatment is then measured by analyzing the differences in outcomes for the two groups. Starting from this intuition, Jordà and Taylor (2016) have studied fiscal multipliers using the logic of treatments. To estimate average treatment effects, they use the set of exogenous shifts in taxes and spending constructed by Devries et al. (2011) and proceed as follows: (1) redefine the fiscal innovations as a 0/1 dummy; (2) estimate a *propensity score* computing the probability with which a correction is expected by regressing it on its own past and other predictors (this step is necessary because the Devries et al. [2011] corrections have been shown by De Cos and Moral-Benito [2016] to be predictable); (3) use the propensity score to compute an Average Treatment Effect, that is, the average difference between output growth in the presence of a fiscal correction (weighted for their predictability, so that more unpredictable corrections carry more weight) and in their absence. They find that average treatment effects of a fiscal consolidation are not very different from those estimated (using the same data but with a different estimation strategy) by Guajardo et al. (2014). The peak effect 5 years after the consolidation is slightly larger than -1, and the cumulative effect after 5 years is about -3.

However, the transformation of shifts in taxes and spending into a 0/1 dummy is not innocuous because it overlooks the fact that there are two sources of identification of narrative adjustments: the timing of a fiscal correction and its size. Transforming fiscal adjustments into a 0/1 dummy neglects size as a source of identification, which is a major limitation of this methodology. Although this transformation is irrelevant in medical experiments, in which patients in the treated group are all administered the same dose of a medicine, it is not irrelevant in economics. This is a problem that VAR-based impulse responses do not have.

Local Multipliers

Nakamura and Steinsson (2014) and Giavazzi and McMahon (2013) studied the effect on state output and state private consumption of procurement contracts signed by the US Department of Defense with companies located in various US states. The identifying assumption is that states differ in the number of procurement contracts they are allocated from the Pentagon in ways that do not depend on their economic conditions, a reasonable but debatable assumption. Funding for such contracts comes from the federal budget and the cost thus falls on federal taxation, an effect that is captured (with many others, including changes in monetary policy, exchange rates, federal regulations) by the time fixed effect included in the estimated regression. The estimated multiplier therefore misses one element that determines consumers' responses to an increase in local defense spending: the anticipation of the taxes that they will need to pay to cover such an expenditure—except for the portion paid through federal taxes, which depends on the size of their state. In other words, the response of consumers takes into account only the fraction of the local defense expenditure that will be paid for by local consumers, but this is only a small part of the financing. For example, think of a large Pentagon project in Rhode Island, a very small state. Rhode Island residents will pay, through their taxes, for just a small fraction of the project. In this literature, the gap between estimated local multipliers and the total multiplier is typically filled by calibrating a model.

Similarly, Chodorow-Reich, Feiveson, Liscow, and Woolston (2012) and Wilson (2012) examined the impact on employment of expenditures related to the 2009 American Recovery and Reinvestment Act (ARRA), exploiting the fact that the distribution of grants was determined in a way that could not be predicted by economic conditions prevailing before 2008. This allows them to estimate state-level effects of the Act for all categories of expenditure covered by ARRA (with the exclusion of unemployment insurance). Shoag (2013) exploits the differential performances of the pension-fund investments of various

US states to generate exogenous shocks to state government spending. He finds large state-level multipliers, around 1.4. A problem with this estimate, however, is that it could be biased if excess returns in pension funds affect GDP, not only through the increase in expenditure following the revenue windfall, but also through a wealth effect on consumers. For a review of what we have learned from the work on Local Multipliers see Chodorow-Reich (2017).

THE MODELS IN CHAPTER 7

Our Baseline Specification

Our baseline specification for the dynamics of Y_t and P_t is a Vector Autoregressive Model (VAR), which in our case would be applied to a panel of 16 countries (the reason for using a panel, as mentioned in Chapter 5, is that plans are rare and estimates for a single country are thus impossible). So we have a panel VAR that in its most parsimonious specification would include the growth rate of per capita output ($\Delta y_{i,t}$) as the only Y_t variable, the change of tax revenues as a fraction of GDP ($\Delta \tau_{i,t}$) and that of primary government spending, also as a fraction of GDP ($\Delta g_{i,t}$) as the two P_t variables:

$$\mathbf{z}_{i,t} = \begin{bmatrix} \Delta y_{i,t} \\ \Delta g_{i,t} \\ \Delta \tau_{i,t} \end{bmatrix}, \mathbf{e}_{i,t} = \begin{bmatrix} e_{i,t}^u \\ e_{i,t-j,t}^a \\ e_{i,t,t+j}^a \end{bmatrix}, \mathbf{a} = \begin{bmatrix} a_1 \\ a_2 \\ a_3 \end{bmatrix} \text{ similarly for } \mathbf{b}$$

$$\Delta y_{i,t} = A_1(L)\,\mathbf{z}_{i,t-1} + \begin{bmatrix} \mathbf{a}'\mathbf{e}_{i,t} & \mathbf{b}'\mathbf{e}_{i,t} \end{bmatrix} \begin{bmatrix} TB_{i,t} \\ EB_{i,t} \end{bmatrix}$$

$$+ \lambda_{1,i} + \chi_{1,t} + u_{1,i,t}$$

$$\Delta g_{i,t} = A_2(L)\,\mathbf{z}_{i,t-1} + \begin{bmatrix} \beta_{11} & \beta_{12} & \beta_{13} & \beta_{14} \end{bmatrix} \begin{bmatrix} g_{i,t}^u \\ g_{i,t-1,t}^a \\ \tau_{i,t}^u \\ \tau_{i,t-1,t}^a \end{bmatrix}$$

$$+ \lambda_{2,i} + \chi_{2,t} + u_{2,i,t}$$

$$\Delta\tau_{i,t} = A_3\left(L\right)\mathbf{z}_{i,t-1} + \begin{bmatrix} \beta_{21} & \beta_{22} & \beta_{23} & \beta_{24} \end{bmatrix}\begin{bmatrix} g_{i,t}^u \\ g_{i,t-1,t}^a \\ \tau_{i,t}^u \\ \tau_{i,t-1,t}^a \end{bmatrix}$$

$$+ \lambda_{3,i} + \chi_{3,t} + u_{3,i,t}$$

The narratively identified exogenous fiscal measures enter the estimation in two ways. In the output growth equation they enter as shifts in the primary budget surplus, $e_{i,t}$; these are then interacted with the type of consolidation, TB or EB. The variable $\mathbf{e}_{i,t}$, has three components $\begin{bmatrix} e_{i,t}^u & e_{i,t-j,t}^a & e_{i,t,t+j}^a \end{bmatrix}$ because, as we discussed, shifts in fiscal variables can be unanticipated, announced, or implementations of previously announced measures.

Differently from the output growth equation, in the two equations for $\Delta g_{i,t}$ and $\Delta\tau_{i,t}$ we explicitly allow for expenditure and revenue corrections to have different coefficients In these equations we include only fiscal shifts implemented in period t, either unexpected or previously announced: future announced corrections do not directly affect the dynamics of revenues and expenditures as their effect is not recorded in national accounts until they are implemented. Each equation includes country, λ_i, and year, χ_t fixed effects. Finally, $u_{j;i;t}$ are unobservable VAR innovations: these are uninteresting for our analysis, as we do not need to extract from them any structural shock.

Interacting the shifts in fiscal variables with the TB and EB dummies allows to decompose fiscal adjustments in two mutually exclusive components, which then allows their effects to be simulated separately. This would not be possible if $g_{i,t}$ and $\tau_{i,t}$ were directly included in the output growth equation because, as already observed, exogenous shifts in taxes and spending are correlated. If we were to include them directly, rather than through orthogonal plans, we could only simulate the "average" adjustment plan, that is, a plan that reproduces the average correlation between changes in taxes and spending observed in the estimation sample. Thus we would no longer be able to study the heterogeneous effect of fiscal adjustments based on their composition. The empirical model also includes fixed effects λ_i and time effects χ_t.

To be able to recover the effect of adjustment plans on the fiscal and macroeconomic variables, the empirical model for $\mathbf{Y}_t$ and $\mathbf{P}_t$ must be accompanied by a set of auxiliary equations describing the response of announcements to contemporaneous corrections and the relative weights of tax and spending measures within a plan. We allow both correlations to be different according to the type of plan, TB versus EB. In other words, we allow for plans to have a different intertemporal and intratemporal structure according to their type.[5] Thus we complete our model for simulation with the following auxiliary regressions:

$$\tau_{i,t}^u = \delta_0^{\text{TB}} e_{i,t}^u * \text{TB}_{i,t} + \delta_0^{\text{EB}} e_{i,t}^u * \text{EB}_{i,t} + \epsilon_{0,i,t} \qquad (12.4)$$

$$g_{i,t}^u = \vartheta_0^{\text{TB}} e_{i,t}^u * \text{TB}_{i,t} + \vartheta_0^{\text{EB}} e_{i,t}^u * \text{EB}_{i,t} + \upsilon_{0,i,t}$$

$$\tau_{i,t,t+j}^a = \delta_j^{\text{TB}} e_{i,t}^u * \text{TB}_{i,t} + \delta_j^{\text{EB}} e_{i,t}^u * \text{EB}_{i,t} + \epsilon_{j,i,t} \quad j = 1, 2$$

$$g_{i,t,t+j}^a = \vartheta_j^{\text{TB}} e_{i,t}^u * \text{TB}_{i,t} + \vartheta_j^{\text{EB}} e_{i,t}^u * \text{EB}_{i,t} + \upsilon_{j,i,t} \quad j = 1, 2$$

where the first two equations describe the average tax (δ) and spending (ϑ) share of EB and TB plans. The next two equations describe the relation between unexpected shifts and those announced for years $t + 1$ and $t + 2$, differentiating between EB and TB plans. (These auxiliary regressions allow us to construct the $e_{i,t,t+j}^a = \tau_{i,t,t+j}^a + g_{i,t,t+j}^a$ needed to compute impulse responses). The coefficients in the equations describing the dynamic evolution of the plans are allowed to vary across the type of plan. This is to capture the fact that, as we shall see, TB plans tend to be front-loaded relative to EB plans because cutting expenditures takes longer than raising taxes. Alternatively, they could be allowed to vary across countries, capturing the possibility that different countries implement fiscal adjustments with different styles when it comes to the correlation between their unexpected and announced components. Both assumptions are interesting: unfortunately the data do not allow us to investigate both at the same time. Most of the results we present in Chapter 7 are obtained assuming plan-specific coefficients—a choice also motivated by consistency with the assumption that fiscal multipliers depend on the type of plan (EB vs TB). We report in Table 12.2 the estimated coefficients for our auxiliary model.

But we shall also show some results that allow country-specific coefficients. The complete model for the dynamics of the macroeconomic

TABLE 12.2. Estimated coefficients

δ_0^{TB}	δ_1^{TB}	δ_2^{TB}	δ_0^{EB}	δ_1^{EB}	δ_2^{EB}
0.7823	0.1552	0.0170	0.3918	−0.0415	0.0072
(0.0175)	(0.0278)	(0.0099)	(0.0104)	(0.0165)	(0.0059)

ϑ_0^{TB}	ϑ_1^{TB}	ϑ_2^{TB}	ϑ_0^{EB}	ϑ_1^{EB}	ϑ_2^{EB}
0.2177	0.1290	0.0305	0.6082	0.1590	0.0364
(0.0175)	(0.0315)	(0.0152)	(0.0104)	(0.0187)	(0.0091)

variables, the fiscal variables and the plans is viable to estimation via a method that takes into account the simultaneous cross-correlations of residuals (for example, Seemingly Unrelated Regressions [SUR]). Stochastic simulation and bootstrap can then be applied to derive impulses responses and the uncertainty surrounding them. A more parsimonious specification of the VAR model can be obtained by estimating directly its Moving Average representation. In this case we would have

$$\Delta y_{i,t} = \alpha + B_1(L)e_{i,t}^u * TB_{i,t} + B_2(L)e_{i,t,t-j}^a * TB_{i,t} + C_1(L)e_{i,t}^u * EB_{i,t}$$
$$+ C_2(L)e_{i,t,t-j}^a * EB_{i,t} + \sum_{j=1}^{2}\gamma_j e_{i,t,j}^a * EB_{i,t} + \sum_{j=1}^{2}\delta_j e_{i,t,j}^a * TB_{i,t}$$
$$+ \lambda_i + \chi_t + u_{i,t}$$
$$e_{i,t,t+j}^a = \varphi_j^{TB}e_{i,t}^u * TB_{i,t} + \varphi_j^{EB}e_{i,t}^u * EB_{i,t} + v_{i,t,t+j} \quad j=1,2 \qquad (12.5)$$

We report the estimated coefficients from model (12.5) in Table 12.3.

There are many potentially omitted variables in the specification of (12.5). However, (1) the correct *measurement* of the effect of a fiscal adjustment only requires that the components of a plan are not correlated with the innovation in the left-hand side variables—and this is our assumption used to identify exogenous fiscal corrections; and (2) the correct *simulation* of the effects of a plan requires only that the plan is not predictable using past values of the right-hand-side variables. Condition (2), nonpredictability of corrections on the basis of past output growth, is discussed in Alesina, Barbiero, Favero, Giavazzi, and Paradisi (2017) The paper—using the procedure developed by Toda and Yamamoto

(1995) that shows no Granger causality on a panel VAR with one lag, and 10% Granger causality on a panel with two lags—shows that GDP does not Granger-cause the narratively identified fiscal consolidations. The Moving Average approach has the advantage of being parsimonious; the VAR compensates the need for more degrees of freedom with several advantages. First, using a VAR which includes changes in revenues and spending (as a fraction of GDP) and tracks the impact of the narratively identified shifts in fiscal variables on total revenues and total spending allows us to check the strength of our narratively identified instruments; for instance, it allows us to verify if, following a positive shift in taxes, revenues indeed increase. Second, in a VAR the estimated coefficients on the narratively identified shifts in fiscal variables measure

TABLE 12.3. Two-block estimation. Baseline Moving Average Representation

Dependent variable: GDP per capita growth			
$e_{i,t}^u * \mathrm{TB}_{i,t}$	−0.949799 (0.125233)	$e_{i,t}^u * \mathrm{EB}_{i,t}$	−0.094089 (0.059393)
$e_{i,t,0}^a * \mathrm{TB}_{i,t}$	−0.733702 (0.159449)	$e_{i,t,0}^a * \mathrm{EB}_{i,t}$	−0.371942 (0.101001)
$e_{i,t-1}^u * \mathrm{TB}_{i,t-1}$	−0.628784 (0.120869)	$e_{i,t-1}^u * \mathrm{EB}_{i,t-1}$	−0.249209 (0.064568)
$e_{i,t-1}^a * \mathrm{TB}_{i,t-1}$	−0.287714 (0.149457)	$e_{i,t-1}^a * \mathrm{EB}_{i,t-1}$	0.06087 (0.103290)
$e_{i,t-2}^u * \mathrm{TB}_{i,t-2}$	−0.105233 (0.119698)	$e_{i,t-2}^u * \mathrm{EB}_{i,t-2}$	0.265 (0.066475)
$e_{i,t-2}^a * \mathrm{TB}_{i,t-2}$	−0.171947 (0.207754)	$e_{i,t-2}^a * \mathrm{EB}_{i,t-2}$	0.089771 (0.104005)
$e_{i,t-3}^u * \mathrm{TB}_{i,t-3}$	−0.331351 (0.129430)	$e_{i,t-3}^u * \mathrm{EB}_{i,t-3}$	0.073684 (0.062918)
$e_{i,t-3}^a * \mathrm{TB}_{i,t-3}$	−0.829834 (0.334179)	$e_{i,t-3}^a * \mathrm{EB}_{i,t-3}$	0.107686 (0.109019)
$(e_{i,t,1}^a + e_{i,t,2}^a) * \mathrm{TB}_{i,t}$	0.267816 (0.112263)	$(e_{i,t,1}^a + e_{i,t,2}^a) * \mathrm{EB}_{i,t}$	−0.348291 (0.078104)

φ_1^{TB}	φ_2^{TB}	φ_1^{EB}	φ_2^{EB}
0.284212 (0.053105)	0.047558 (0.021784)	0.117178 (0.031600)	0.043429 (0.012962)

the effect on output growth of the component of such adjustments that is orthogonal to lagged included variables: thus the estimated multipliers are not affected by the possible predictability of plans on the basis of the lagged information included in the VAR. Note that the narrative strategy adopted to identify exogenous fiscal corrections means that they can be predicted by past components of the deficit. This is fine because consistent estimates of fiscal multipliers require only that innovations in output growth and the components of fiscal adjustment plans are not correlated—an assumption that is not violated by predictability from past information. Simulation instead could be a problem, as the simulated shift in fiscal policy should not be those that agents have already predicted. The results in Chapter 7 are based on the more parsimonious MA representation. We use both models in Chapter 9 and find that they deliver very similar impulse responses, thus confirming that the predictability of fiscal plans on the basis of past deficits has a negligible empirical effect.

Predictability of Plans

Fiscal adjustments identified by the narrative approach are predictable by construction, either by their own past or by past economic data and this predictability could be a threat to their exogeneity. This point has been made by De Cos and Moral-Benito (2016) and Jordà and Taylor (2016) with reference to the narrative data constructed by Devries et al. (2011) and on which we have built—with many extensions—our dataset. Let us go through these arguments in turn.

First, finding that narratively identified fiscal "shocks" are predictable is not surprising: predictability is a feature of plans that contain the implementation in year t of measures that had been decided on in previous years and thus are by construction predictable. Assume you overlook announcements and plans and consider only the shifts in fiscal variables happening in year t, that is, $\widetilde{e}_t = e_t^u + e_{t-j,t}^a$, where the second term on the right-hand side measures the realization in year t of shifts in fiscal variables that had been announced j years before. Guajardo et al. (2014) analyzed the fiscal "shocks" $\widetilde{e}_t$ and found them to be predictable by their own past. As we explained in Chapter 5, within a plan policy announcements are correlated with unanticipated policy shifts.

Under the null, that the e_t^u are not correlated over time (and considering for simplicity one-year plans), $Cov(\widetilde{e}_t, \widetilde{e}_{t-1}) = \phi_1 Var(e_{t-1}^u)$.[6] Finding $Cov(\widetilde{e}_t, \widetilde{e}_t - 1) \neq 0$ is therefore not surprising. In other words, predictability of $\widetilde{e}_t$ from their own past is a feature of multiyear fiscal plans and is properly dealt with by analyzing plans rather than "shocks" such as $\widetilde{e}_t$. Predictability of $\widetilde{e}_t$ by past economic data raises a separate issue. De Cos and Moral-Benito (2016) show that if the $\widetilde{e}_t$ are described by a dummy variable that takes the value of 1 when $\widetilde{e}_t \neq 0$, they are predictable based on information available at time $(t-1)$. This observation, however, does not take into account the fact that there are two sources of identification of narrative adjustments: the *timing* of a fiscal correction and its *size*. Transforming fiscal adjustments into a 0/1 dummy neglects the importance of size as a source of identification. Second, predictability is different from exogeneity. To understand this, think of the following example (see Colacito, Hoffmann, and Phan [2016]). Seasonal temperatures have significant and systematic effects on the economy, both at the aggregate level and across a wide cross section of economic sectors. This effect is particularly strong during the summer: in the United States, for example, a 1 degree Fahrenheit increase in the average summer temperature is associated with a reduction in the annual growth rate of state-level output of 0.15 to 0.25 percentage points. Summer temperature is predictable, but this does not make it endogenous. In our context, what matters to avoid endogeneity is that narrative fiscal corrections are independent of the current state of the cycle: this is the criterion that drives narrative identification.

An Alternative Specification

Finally, as discussed in the concluding section of Chapter 5, we could have chosen an alternative specification. Instead of interacting the change in the primary deficit with the two dummies (EB and TB), we could have *directly* introduced unexpected, announced, and implemented changes in taxes and spending into the estimated regression, and from there derive multipliers for taxes and spending directly. However, this approach has an important drawback. Using τ_t and g_t directly in the empirical model would require estimating, in the second block, a much larger number of φ_j parameters: between announced and unexpected changes in taxes (and in spending) and all cross correlations, for example between announced changes in taxes and unexpected changes in spending, etc. In other words, since changes in taxes and in expenditures are correlated in the plans in our sample, it would be wrong to interpret the coefficients on taxes and spending as partial derivatives: wrong in the sense that we would be studying a style of fiscal actions that does not reflect what the countries actually did, at least in our sample. Constructing EB and TB plans is a way of greatly simplifying the estimation because the two type of plans are mutually exclusive.

In any case, a possible specification for this alternative model could be

$$\Delta y_{i,t} = \alpha + B_1(L)\tau_{i,t}^u + B_2(L)\tau_{i,t,t-j}^a + C_1(L)g_{i,t}^u + C_2(L)g_{i,t,t-j}^a$$

$$+ \sum_{j=1}^{2}\gamma_j\tau_{i,t,j}^a + \sum_{j=1}^{2}\delta_j g_{i,t,j}^a + \lambda_i + \chi_t + u_{i,t} \tag{12.6}$$

$$\tau_{i,t}^u = \delta_0^{TB}e_{i,t}^u * TB_{i,t} + \delta_0^{EB}e_{i,t}^u * EB_{i,t} + \epsilon_{0,i,t} \tag{12.7}$$

$$g_{i,t}^u = \vartheta_0^{TB}e_{i,t}^u * TB_{i,t} + \vartheta_0^{EB}e_{i,t}^u * EB_{i,t} + \upsilon_{0,i,t}$$

$$\tau_{i,t,j}^a = \delta_j^{TB}e_{i,t}^u * TB_{i,t} + \delta_j^{EB}e_{i,t}^u * EB_{i,t} + \epsilon_{j,i,t} \quad j=1,2$$

$$g_{i,t,j}^a = \vartheta_j^{TB}e_{i,t}^u * TB_{i,t} + \vartheta_j^{EB}e_{i,t}^u * EB_{i,t} + \upsilon_{j,i,t} \quad j=1,2$$

In this alternative specification, the first bloc describes the macroeconomic variables directly as a function of the exogenous corrections in taxes and spending, rather than as a function of TB and EB based corrections. The second bloc models the intratemporal and the intertemporal structure of fiscal plans. Note that in this specification both the intratemporal and the intertemporal dimension of plans need to be modeled, because $\tau_{i,t}^u$ and $g_{i,t}^u$ are correlated and their effects cannot be simulated independently. Another way to say this is that we have an identification problem that is solved projecting $\tau_{i,t}^u$ and $g_{i,t}^u$ on $e_{i,t}^u * TB_{i,t}$ and $e_{i,t}^u * EB_{i,t}$, respectively. Because $e_{i,t}^u * TB_{i,t}$ and $e_{i,t}^u * EB_{i,t}$ are by construction mutually exclusive, it is natural to simulate the effect of one component keeping the other at zero (when EB $=1$, TB $=0$ by construction). One could avoid this identification problem only if $\tau_{i,t}^u$ and $g_{i,t}^u$ were orthogonal to each other, which is not the case in our sample. If we overlooked this, the estimated coefficients in the first bloc of the system could not

TABLE 12.4. Two-block estimation. Alternative MA Representation

		Dependent variable: Real GDP per capita growth		
τ_t^u	−0.495994		g_t^u	−0.405841
	(0.122127)			(0.128105)
$\tau_{t,0}^a$	−0.864720		$g_{t,0}^a$	−0.348672
	(0.182199)			(0.160364)
τ_{t-1}^u	−0.235163		g_{t-1}^u	−0.458218
	(0.123533)			(0.135375)
$\tau_{t-1,0}^a$	−0.432061		$g_{t-1,0}^a$	0.376504
	(0.186349)			(0.167767)
τ_{t-2}^u	−0.263732		$g_{t-2,0}^u$	0.694599
	(0.129703)			(0.136117)
$\tau_{t-2,0}^a$	−0.312234		$g_{t-2,0}^a$	0.260049
	(0.206196)			(0.167913)
τ_{t-3}^u	−0.418055		g_{t-3}^u	0.280307
	(0.133359)			(0.131676)
$\tau_{t-3,0}^a$	0.100652		$g_{t-3,0}^a$	−0.141484
	(0.216779)			(0.177044)
$\tau_{t,t+1}^a + \tau_{t,t+2}^a$	−0.499966		$g_{t,t+1}^a + g_{t,t+2}^a$	−0.178579
	(0.143745)			(0.117367)

be interpreted as partial derivatives. The estimated coefficients from the alternative specification are reported in Table 12.4

FISCAL ADJUSTMENTS AND THE DYNAMICS OF DEBT OVER GDP

Simulating the effects of fiscal adjustments on the dynamics of the debt over GDP ratio (the debt ratio for short) requires a more structured empirical model. Our general description of the empirical model we used to simulate the effects of fiscal plans as follows: the model describes the behavior of a set of macro variables, $\mathbf{Y}_t$, as a function of their past values, $\mathbf{Y}_{t-1}$; the past values of a few policy variables $\mathbf{P}_{t-1}$; and macroeconomic shocks. Similarly, the dynamics of the policy variables can be decomposed into a "rule"—which describes the response of current policy to past policy and past macroeconomic conditions—and deviations from the rule, some of which are our fiscal plans. The dynamics of the debt ratio, d, for country i is

$$d_{it} = \frac{1 + i_{i,t}}{(1 + x_{i,t})} d_{i,t-1} + g_{i,t} - \tau_{i,t} + u_{6,i,t}$$

$$x_{it} \equiv \Delta p_{i,t} + \Delta y_{i,t} + \Delta p_{i,t} \Delta y_{i,t}$$

where i_{it} is the nominal average net cost of financing the debt, x_{it} nominal output growth, Δp_{it} is GDP inflation, $\tau_{i,t}$ is tax revenue as a fraction of GDP, and $g_{i,t}$ is primary government spending, also as a fraction of GDP. $u_{6,i,t}$ is a stock-flow adjustment, namely a term that tracks the difference between the actual change in the debt ratio and the change associated with the variables in the foregoing equation. The need for stock-flow adjustment arises, for example, in the presence of revenue from sales or purchases of financial and nonfinancial assets; revaluations, in the case the debt is valued at market prices; debt write-offs, and so forth, all items that do not enter the definition of the primary surplus $(g_{i,t} - \tau_{i,t})$.

To track the effect on the debt ratio of austerity plans the model must be extended so that $\mathbf{Y}_t = (\Delta y_{i,t}, \Delta p_{it}, i_{it}, d_{it})$, $\mathbf{P}_t = (\Delta g_{i,t}, \Delta \tau_{i,t})$. We therefore adopt the following specification:

$$\mathbf{z}_{i,t} = \begin{bmatrix} \Delta y_{i,t} \\ \Delta p_{i,t} \\ i_{i,t} \\ \Delta g_{i,t} \\ \Delta \tau_{i,t} \end{bmatrix}, \mathbf{e}_{i,t} = \begin{bmatrix} e_{i,t}^u \\ e_{i,t-j,t}^a \\ e_{i,t,t+j}^a \end{bmatrix}, \mathbf{a}_i = \begin{bmatrix} a_{1,i} \\ a_{2,i} \\ a_{3,i} \end{bmatrix} \text{ similarly for } \mathbf{b}_i$$

$$\Delta y_{i,t} = A_1(L) \mathbf{z}_{i,t-1} + \begin{bmatrix} \mathbf{a}_1' \mathbf{e}_{i,t} & \mathbf{b}_1' \mathbf{e}_{i,t} \end{bmatrix} \begin{bmatrix} TB_{i,t} \\ EB_{i,t} \end{bmatrix} + \lambda_{1,i} + \chi_{1,t} + u_{1,i,t}$$

$$\Delta p_{i,t} = A_2(L) \mathbf{z}_{i,t-1} + \begin{bmatrix} \mathbf{a}_2' \mathbf{e}_{i,t} & \mathbf{b}_2' \mathbf{e}_{i,t} \end{bmatrix} \begin{bmatrix} TB_{i,t} \\ EB_{i,t} \end{bmatrix} + \lambda_{2,i} + \chi_{2,t} + u_{2,i,t}$$

$$i_{i,t} = A_3(L) \mathbf{z}_{i,t-1} + \begin{bmatrix} \mathbf{a}_3' \mathbf{e}_{i,t} & \mathbf{b}_3' \mathbf{e}_{i,t} \end{bmatrix} \begin{bmatrix} TB_{i,t} \\ EB_{i,t} \end{bmatrix} + \lambda_{3,i} + \chi_{3,t} + u_{3,i,t}$$

$$\Delta g_{i,t} = A_4\,(L)\,\mathbf{z}_{i,t-1} + \begin{bmatrix} \beta_{11} & \beta_{12} & \beta_{13} & \beta_{14} \end{bmatrix} \begin{bmatrix} g_{i,t}^{u} \\ g_{i,t-1,t}^{a} \\ \tau_{i,t}^{u} \\ \tau_{i,t-1,t}^{a} \end{bmatrix}$$

$$+\ \lambda_{4,i} + \chi_{4,t} + u_{4,i,t}$$

$$\Delta \tau_{i,t} = A_5\,(L)\,\mathbf{z}_{i,t-1} + \begin{bmatrix} \beta_{21} & \beta_{22} & \beta_{23} & \beta_{24} \end{bmatrix} \begin{bmatrix} g_{i,t}^{u} \\ g_{i,t-1,t}^{a} \\ \tau_{i,t}^{u} \\ \tau_{i,t-1,t}^{a} \end{bmatrix}$$

$$+\ \lambda_{5,i} + \chi_{5,t} + u_{5,i,t}$$

$$d_{i,t} = \frac{1 + i_{i,t}}{\left(1 + x_{i,t}\right)} d_{i,t-1} + g_{i,t} - \tau_{i,t} + u_{6,i,t}$$

$$x_{i,t} \equiv \Delta p_{i,t} + \Delta y_{i,t} + \Delta p_{i,t}\Delta y_{i,t}$$

No modification is required for the bloc that models the fiscal plans. Thus, estimation and simulation of this extended model can then be implemented using exactly the same techniques described for the baseline VAR in Chapter 5.

TB VERSUS EB AUSTERITY IN A GENERAL EQUILIBRIUM MODEL

Standard new Keynesian models with less than perfectly flexible prices cannot explain our empirical results on the difference between TB and EB consolidations. These models predict that spending cuts are always recessionary (see, e.g., DeLong and Summers [2012], Galí et al. [2007]) and that the multiplier for government spending is larger (in absolute value) than that for taxes. Recent research (see, e.g., Christiano, Eichenbaum, and Rebelo [2011], Eggertsson [2011]) finds that this result is amplified at the zero lower bound. These models concentrate on the demand side: the output effects of fiscal policy, however, also depend on wealth effects; on intertemporal substitution effects; on the effects of distortions on the economy; and on the nature of public spending, in particular if it is a substitute for or a complement to private spending. These channels operate differently in the case of tax increases as opposed to expenditure cuts. When taxes are lump sum, and when agents derive no benefits from public spending, a reduction in government spending raises private wealth because future expected taxes fall. Private consumption increases and (if leisure and consumption are normal goods) labor supply falls. If labor demand does not change when government spending changes, then hours worked decrease, the real wage increases, and output falls. For output to increase after a reduction in government spending, taxes need to be distortionary, and the intertemporal substitution elasticity must be sufficiently high. Intuitively, this happens because when the intertemporal substitution elasticity is high, the wealth effect produced by a cut in government spending is small relative to the substitution effect generated by the reduction in distortionary taxes.

Alesina et al. (2017) extend the basic neo-Keynesian model with tax distortions by introducing TB and EB fiscal plans. They investigate the mechanism that could explain heterogeneity in the output effect of such plans, finding that the persistence of shifts in fiscal variables is the key to explaining the observed heterogeneous effects of different plans. EB plans are the least recessionary the longer lived is the reduction in government spending. Symmetrically, TB plans are more recessionary the longer lasting is the increase in tax burdens.

To grasp the intuition, think in terms of a simple supply and demand framework such as the one shown in Figures 12.1 and 12.2. Assume that the government budget is always balanced through compensating changes in nondistortionary transfers. A cut in government expenditure has two effects. The demand curve shifts inward, due to the direct effect of lower demand from the government. The supply curve also shifts inward: following a cut in government spending, consumers feel richer because they expect higher transfers in the future. This lowers labor supply, which in turn leads to an increase in firms' marginal costs. The shifts in aggregate supply and demand are functions of the persistence of fiscal adjustments: higher persistence implies both higher demand and higher supply elasticities, because the long-term nature of fiscal shocks makes consumers more sensitive to changes in prices, and firms more

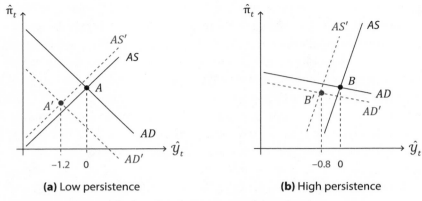

Figure 12.1. The output effect of a cut in government spending.

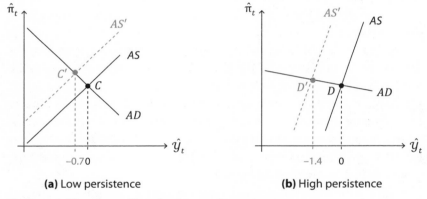

Figure 12.2. The output effect of an increase in wage taxes.

aggressive in their price settings. On the other hand, the present value of transfers increases with the persistence of spending cuts. The result is that aggregate demand reacts less, but labor supply falls more because of the wealth effect. As shown in Figure 12.1, when persistence increases, the demand shift due to a cut in government expenditure starts to be dominated by the supply shift due to lower labor supply. However, the demand effect falls faster than the supply effect, so the government spending multiplier decreases with persistence.

Symmetrically, in the case of an increase in wage taxes, the multiplier increases with persistence. An increase in wage taxes has a direct effect only on aggregate supply. This is because a wage tax creates a wedge in the labor market but does not distort demand directly. As in the case of reductions in government consumption, higher persistence raises the elasticities of both supply and demand. However, it is clear that now the shift in supply dominates: as persistence rises, this shift amplifies. To put it simply, a persistent increase in labor taxes makes the static substitution effect between labor and leisure more permanent and this increases the wage tax multiplier.

RECONSIDERING BLANCHARD AND LEIGH (2014) IN CHAPTER 8

Blanchard and Leigh (2014, hereafter BL) address the stability of fiscal multipliers, investigating the relation between the International Monetary Fund growth forecast errors and the total amount of fiscal consolidations expected to be implemented in 2011, based on IMF forecasts. In practice, they run an ordinary least squares (OLS) regression on a cross section of 27 advanced economies, employing a cyclically adjusted measure of changes in the structural budget balance

$$\left(\frac{Y_{i,2011} - Y_{i,2009}}{Y_{i,2009}} - \frac{Y^f_{i,2011} - Y_{i,2009}}{Y_{i,2009}} \right) = \alpha + \beta \left(\frac{F^f_{i,2011}}{Y^{f,pot}_{i,2011}} - \frac{F_{i,2009}}{Y^{pot}_{i,2009}} \right) + \epsilon_i$$

The variable on the left hand side is the difference between the actual cumulated real GDP growth (year-over-year) during 2010–11 (based on the latest data) and the forecast prepared for the April 2010 IMF World Economic Outlook (WEO). This variable is regressed on the forecasted change in the general government fiscal balance as a percent of potential GDP during 2010–1 prepared for the same issue of the WEO.

Under the null hypothesis—that fiscal multipliers used for forecasting were accurate—the coefficient β should be 0. They found instead an estimated parameter equal to -1.095 (t-statistic $= -4.294$). This result suggests that for every additional percentage point of GDP of fiscal consolidation, GDP was about 1% lower than forecasted. They interpret the result as implying that fiscal multipliers in 2011 were higher than

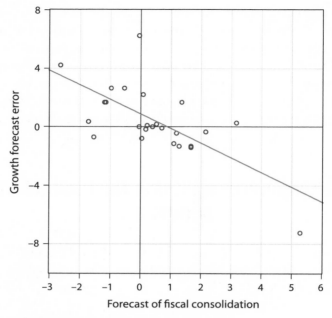

Figure 12.3. Blanchard and Leigh argument.

those predicted by forecasters: "Stronger planned fiscal consolidation has been associated with lower growth than expected, with the relation being particularly strong, both statistically and economically, early in the crisis."

Figure 12.3 illustrates the main result by plotting Growth Forecast errors (forecast errors for real GDP growth in 2010 and 2011 relative to forecasts made in the spring of 2010) versus Fiscal Consolidation Forecasts (forecasts of Fiscal Consolidation for 2010 and 2011 made in spring of 2010). The slope of the regression line, which is −1, illustrates the main point by the authors.

A closer look at Figure 12.3 suggests that for several countries in the sample what was forecasted was in fact a negative consolidation, that is, a fiscal expansion. It is therefore interesting to see if separating consolidations and expansions makes a difference. In columns 1 and 2 of Table 12.5 we compare (using the BL data) the results of the baseline model estimated by BL with one in which fiscal consolidations are interacted with a dummy identifying expansions and contractions.

TABLE 12.5. Blanchard and Leigh Regressions

	Baseline	Model 1	Model 2	Model 3	Model 4
const	0.775 (2.03)	1.319 (2.24)	1.014 (1.74)	0.195 (0.46)	0.817 (1.24)
$\left(\dfrac{F^f_{i,2011}}{Y^{f,pot}_{i,2011}} - \dfrac{F_{i,2009}}{Y^{pot}_{i,2009}}\right)$	−1.095 (−4.29)				
$\left(\dfrac{F^f_{i,2011}}{Y^{f,pot}_{i,2011}} - \dfrac{F_{i,2009}}{Y^{pot}_{i,2009}}\right) * D^{EXP}$		−0.394 (−0.65)	−0.461 (−0.74)		−0.507 (−0.79)
$\left(\dfrac{F^f_{i,2011}}{Y^{f,pot}_{i,2011}} - \dfrac{F_{i,2009}}{Y^{pot}_{i,2009}}\right) * (1 - D^{EXP})$		−1.401 (−3.95)	−1.183 (−3.55)		−0.922 (−1.86)
$\Delta 10Y_{i,2007/2009}$			−0.6433 (−4.06)	−0.95 (−2.42)	−0.675 (−3.07)
$\Delta 10Y_{i,2009/2011}$				−0.20 (−6.48)	−0.0647 (−1.08)
R^2	0.49	0.53	0.62	0.51	0.63
No. of obs.	26	26	24	24	24

Note: Model 1 separates expansions from contractions, Model 2 adds pre-austerity yields, Model 3 considers only pre-austerity and contemporaneous yields, Model 4 adds pre-austerity and contemporaneous yields.

While the first column of the table exactly replicates the results of BL, the second column illustrates that the bulk of the evidence is indeed generated by the episodes of fiscal consolidation, thus refining the conclusions of BL.

Note that in columns 1 and 2 the only regressor used to explain growth forecast errors are the forecasts of fiscal consolidation constructed in BL; it is therefore in principle possible that the fiscal adjustment variable acts as an instrument for other shocks that hit the economies during 2010–11. In this case the results obtained with this specification might change when one includes in the regression other variables that were in the information set of the forecasters and whose effect on output might have changed during the crisis. In fact, BL conducted an extensive analysis of potential variables included in forecasters' information set but omitted in these regressions: sovereign debt, financial sector stress, banking crises, fiscal consolidation in trading partners, precrisis external imbalances, and household debt overhang. Their main finding is that their main result is robust to these alternative specifications. However, they did not consider long-term yields on government bonds. Yields are a natural candidate to test the effect of potential omitted variables.

First, they fluctuated in an important way during the subprime loan crisis. Hence including the change in interest rates in the period preceding 2010–11 could be an interesting way of testing that a change in the response of growth to fluctuations in long-term interest rates could also be responsible for the observed forecast errors. Second, the level of long-term interest rates was relatively low at the beginning of 2010 before the (unexpected) explosion of the Greek crisis. Over the course of 2011, long-term interest rates in some countries in the sample increased sharply and a large difference emerged between the realized level of long-term rates and the level expected at the beginning of 2010. If these prediction errors—that is, prediction errors on yields—were correlated with the planned fiscal consolidation in 2010, then the BL coefficient would also capture the output effect of the surprise increase in long-term rates. In this case, it would be hard to interpret it as a measure of the underestimation of the size of the fiscal multiplier and the policy implications of the correlation observed in BL would change rather drastically. Note that this interpretation is not implausible because if the subprime loan crisis induced an increase in the volatility of long-term rates and in the price of risk, high-debt and high-risk countries were forced to implement a fiscal adjustment as soon as their economies started recovering from the effects of the subprime loan crisis. Such a fiscal correction would have reduced the risk in a worst case scenario in which some new shocks would have caused long-term rates to spike again: a worst case scenario that was in fact sparked by the Greek announcement during 2010 that their deficit had been vastly underestimated.

To take into account the effect of changes in long-term interest rates, in column 3 of the table 12.5 we add, as a further regressor $\Delta 10Y_{i,2007/2009}$, the change in the yield to maturity of 10Y government bonds only between the end of 2007 and the end of 2009. All the regressors in this specification were in the information set of the forecasters. Both coefficients on $\Delta 10Y_{i,2007/2009}$ and $\left(\dfrac{F^f_{i,2011}}{Y^{f,pot}_{i,2011}} - \dfrac{F_{i,2009}}{Y^{pot}_{i,2009}} \right)$ are significant, thus pointing to the coexistence of two potentially separate channels explaining the GDP growth forecast errors. In column 4 of the same table we only consider as regressors the change in the yield to maturity of 10Y government bonds between the end of 2007 and the end of 2009 and between the end of 2011 and the beginning of 2010. This specification illustrates that (1) the argument applied by BL to the instability of fiscal multipliers could be also applied to the effects on growth of the change in long-term interest rates, as confirmed by the significance of the coefficient on $\Delta 10 Y_{i,2007/2009}$; (2) shocks to long-term interest rates over the period 2010–11 played an important role in determining the forecast error for output growth over the same period, as demonstrated by the significance of the coefficient on $\Delta 10 Y_{i,2009/2011}$. Interestingly when fiscal adjustment and fluctuations in interest rates (both before and during the forecast period) are considered, as in column 5, the coefficient on $\Delta 10 Y_{i,2007/2009}$ remains significant while both the coefficients on $\Delta 10 Y_{i,2009/2011}$ and $\left(\frac{F_{i,2011}^f}{Y_{i,2011}^{f,pot}} - \frac{F_{i,2009}}{Y_{i,2009}^{pot}} \right)$ become insignificant, proving the existence of correlation among these two variables. Therefore, the correlation between fiscal adjustments and fluctuations in long-term rate over 2010 and 2011 questions the interpretation that attributes the significance of the coefficient on fiscal adjustments in column 2 to the mismeasurement of the fiscal multipliers.[7]

We further assess these results by considering, as dependent variables, rather than the forecast errors constructed by BL, the forecast errors conditional on the implementation of fiscal adjustment plans, thus based on the methodology adopted throughout the book. We use our results in Chapter 8 to construct a panel of 11 economies over two periods (2010–11 and 2012–13):

$$\left(\frac{Y_{i,t} - Y_{i,t-2}}{Y_{i,t-2}} - \frac{Y_{i,t}^f - Y_{i,t-2}}{Y_{i,t-2}} \right) = \alpha + \beta_1 e_{it-2} + \beta_2 e_{it-2,t-1,t}^a$$

$$+ \beta_3 \Delta 10 Y_{i,t-4/t-2} + \varepsilon_{it}$$

$$t = 2011, 2013$$

The results of the estimation of this model are reported in Table 12.6.

Whereas in columns 1 and 2 we consider only the impact on growth forecast errors of fiscal adjustments e_{it-2} and of their announcements $e_{it-2,t-1,t}^a$, in column 3 and 4 the effect of pre-austerity long-term interest rates changes is also assessed. The evidence reported confirms that the instability of the fiscal multipliers becomes much weaker when the role of the fluctuations in long-term interest rates before the forecast period and of other shocks (as captured by the time effects in column 4) is considered.

TABLE 12.6. Our Model

	Baseline	Model 1	Model 2	Model 2 FE
const	1.066	1.205	1.08	0.624
	(1.3)	(1.53)	(1.25)	(1.16)
e_{it-2}	−1.090	−0.812	−0.748	−0.291
	(−2.95)	−0.812	−0.748	−0.291
$e^a_{it-2,t-1,t}$		−0.538	−0.449	−0.379
		(−3.52)	(−1.13)	(−0.72)
$\Delta 10 Y_{i,t-4/t-2}$			−0.098	−0.587
			(−0.27)	(−2.48)
R^2	0.29	0.34	0.34	0.29
No. of obs.	22	22	22	22

THE MODEL OF "HOW" AND "WHEN" IN CHAPTER 9

To allow for the impact of a fiscal adjustment to depend on the state of the economy, two ingredients are necessary: an indicator for the state of the economy and a model in which the dynamics of all variables depend on the state of the economy. This is the approach adopted by Auerbach and Gorodnichenko (2012, 2013a, 2013b) to produce different fiscal multipliers in expansion and recession. In practice we need to reconsider once more our general framework and choose a different specification for the relevant variables and the relevant functional forms f describing the relationships among them.

Consider the case in which one wants to allow the f functions to depend on the state of the economy. This is measured using a logistic function $F(s_{i,t})$ (where the index i refers to the country) that smooths the distribution of output growth, $\Delta y_{i,t-j}$ $(j = 1, 2, ...)$ and transforms it into a variable ranging between 0 and 1. The transition between states of the economy happens smoothly, with $F(s_{i,t})$ being the weight given to recessions and $1 - F(s_{i,t})$ the weight given to expansions. $F(s_{i,t})$ is

$$F(s_{i,t}) = \frac{\exp(-\gamma_i s_{i,t})}{1 + \exp(-\gamma_i s_{i,t})}, \quad \gamma_i > 0, \tag{12.8}$$

$$s_{i,t} = \left(\mu_{i,t} - E\left(\mu_{i,t}\right)\right) / \sigma\left(\mu_{i,t}\right) \tag{12.9}$$

$$\mu_{i,t} = \frac{\Delta y_{i,t-1} + \Delta y_{i,t-2}}{2} \tag{12.10}$$

where $\mu_{i,t}$ is the moving average (and $s_{i,t}$ its standardized version) of output growth during the 2 years preceding the shift in fiscal policy and γ_i are the country-specific parameters of the logistic function. An economy is defined to be in recession if $F(s_{i,t}) > 0.8$. The parameters γ_i are calibrated to match actual recession probabilities in the countries in our sample: that is, the percentage of years in which growth is negative over the sample, which consists of yearly data from 1979 to 2014. In other words, we calibrate γ_i so that country i spends x_i percent of time in a recessionary regime. $Pr(F(s_{i,t}) > 0.8) = x_i$, where x_i is the ratio of the number of years of negative GDP growth for country i to the total number of years in the sample.

Next we specify a model for the dynamics of three variables—the growth rate of per capita output ($\Delta y_{i,t}$); the change of tax revenues as a fraction of GDP ($\Delta \tau_{i,t}$); and that of primary government spending, also as a fraction of GDP ($\Delta g_{i,t}$)—as a function of the state of the economy. In this specification, taxes and spending enter in two ways: as endogenous variables in the model—in this case they are total government spending and total revenue, which includes both their exogenous and endogenous components—and as narratively identified shifts in taxes and spending, which are exogenous

$$\Delta y_{i,t} = (1 - F(s_{i,t}))A_1^E (L) \, \mathbf{z}_{i,t-1} + F(s_{i,t})A_1^R (L) \, \mathbf{z}_{i,t-1}$$

$$+ \lambda_{1,i} + \chi_{1,t} + u_{1,i,t} \qquad (12.11)$$

$$\Delta g_{i,t} = (1 - F(s_{i,t}))A_2^E (L) \, \mathbf{z}_{i,t-1} + F(s_{i,t})A_2^R (L) \, \mathbf{z}_{i,t-1}$$

$$+ \lambda_{2,i} + \chi_{2,t} + u_{2,i,t}$$

$$\Delta \tau_{i,t} = (1 - F(s_{i,t}))A_3^E (L) \, \mathbf{z}_{i,t-1} + F(s_{i,t})A_3^R (L) \, \mathbf{z}_{i,t-1}$$

$$+ \lambda_{3,i} + \chi_{3,t} + u_{3,i,t}$$

$$\mathbf{u}_{i,t} = \begin{bmatrix} u_{1,i,t} \\ u_{2,i,t} \\ u_{3,i,t} \end{bmatrix} \sim N(0, \Sigma_t)$$

$$\Sigma_t = \Sigma_E(1 - F(s_{t-1})) + \Sigma_R F(s_{t-1})$$

where $\mathbf{z}_{it} : [\Delta y_{i,t}, \Delta g_{i,t}, \Delta \tau_{i,t}]$. Auerbach and Gorodnichenko identify structural shocks to fiscal variables from VAR innovations using the approach of Blanchard and Perotti (2002). They then derive impulse responses to such shocks in the state of recession and expansion.

To allow simultaneously for nonlinearities related to the "How" and the "When," Alesina et al. (2018) have adopted a specification that includes the observed (narratively identified) fiscal measures directly, rather than identifying them from VAR innovations. In practice one replaces the standard VAR specification described in Chapter 5 with a nonlinear Smooth Transition VAR specification (STAR).

$$\mathbf{z}_{i,t} = \begin{bmatrix} \Delta y_{i,t} \\ \Delta g_{i,t} \\ \Delta \tau_{i,t} \end{bmatrix}, \mathbf{e}_{i,t} = \begin{bmatrix} e^u_{i,t} \\ e^a_{i,t-j,t} \\ e^a_{i,t,t+j} \end{bmatrix}, \mathbf{a} = \begin{bmatrix} a_1 \\ a_2 \\ a_3 \end{bmatrix} \text{ similarly for } \mathbf{b}, \mathbf{c}, \mathbf{d}$$

$$\Delta y_{i,t} = (1 - F(s_{i,t}))A_1^E(L)\,\mathbf{z}_{i,t-1} + F(s_{i,t})A_1^R(L)\,\mathbf{z}_{i,t-1}$$

$$+ \begin{bmatrix} 1 - F(s_{i,t}) \\ F(s_{i,t}) \end{bmatrix}' \begin{bmatrix} \mathbf{a}'\mathbf{e}_{i,t} & \mathbf{b}'\mathbf{e}_{i,t} \\ \mathbf{c}'\mathbf{e}_{i,t} & \mathbf{d}'\mathbf{e}_{i,t} \end{bmatrix} \begin{bmatrix} TB_{i,t} \\ EB_{i,t} \end{bmatrix}$$

$$+ \lambda_{1,i} + \chi_{1,t} + u_{1,i,t}$$

$$\Delta g_{i,t} = (1 - F(s_{i,t}))A_2^E(L)\,\mathbf{z}_{i,t-1} + F(s_{i,t})A_2^R(L)\,\mathbf{z}_{i,t-1}$$

$$+ \begin{bmatrix} 1 - F(s_{i,t}) \\ F(s_{i,t}) \end{bmatrix}' \begin{bmatrix} \beta_{11} & \beta_{12} & \beta_{13} & \beta_{14} \\ \beta_{15} & \beta_{16} & \beta_{17} & \beta_{18} \end{bmatrix} \begin{bmatrix} g^u_{i,t} \\ g^a_{i,t-1,t} \\ \tau^u_{i,t} \\ \tau^a_{i,t-1,t} \end{bmatrix}$$

$$+ \lambda_{2,i} + \chi_{2,t} + u_{2,i,t}$$

$$\Delta \tau_{i,t} = (1 - F(s_{i,t}))A_3^E(L)\,\mathbf{z}_{i,t-1} + F(s_{i,t})A_3^R(L)\,\mathbf{z}_{i,t-1} +$$

$$+ \begin{bmatrix} 1 - F(s_{i,t}) \\ F(s_{i,t}) \end{bmatrix}' \begin{bmatrix} \beta_{21} & \beta_{22} & \beta_{23} & \beta_{24} \\ \beta_{25} & \beta_{26} & \beta_{27} & \beta_{28} \end{bmatrix} \begin{bmatrix} g^u_{i,t} \\ g^a_{i,t-1,t} \\ \tau^u_{i,t} \\ \tau^a_{i,t-1,t} \end{bmatrix}$$

$$+ \lambda_{3,i} + \chi_{3,t} + u_{3,i,t}$$

$$\tau_{i,t}^u = \delta_0^{\mathrm{TB}} e_{i,t}^u * \mathrm{TB}_{i,t} + \delta_0^{\mathrm{EB}} e_{i,t}^u * \mathrm{EB}_{i,t} + \epsilon_{0,i,t}$$

$$g_{i,t}^u = \vartheta_0^{\mathrm{TB}} e_{i,t}^u * \mathrm{TB}_{i,t} + \vartheta_0^{\mathrm{EB}} e_{i,t}^u * \mathrm{EB}_{i,t} + \upsilon_{0,i,t}$$

$$\tau_{i,t,t+j}^a = \delta_j^{\mathrm{TB}} e_{i,t}^u * \mathrm{TB}_{i,t} + \delta_j^{\mathrm{EB}} e_{i,t}^u * \mathrm{EB}_{i,t} + \epsilon_{j,i,t} \quad j = 1,2$$

$$g_{i,t,t+j}^a = \vartheta_j^{\mathrm{TB}} e_{i,t}^u * \mathrm{TB}_{i,t} + \vartheta_j^{\mathrm{EB}} e_{i,t}^u * \mathrm{EB}_{i,t} + \upsilon_{j,i,t} \quad j = 1,2$$

As it is the case with the VAR of Chapter 5, the narratively identified exogenous fiscal measures enter the estimation in two ways. In the output growth equation, they enter as shifts in $e_{i,t}$, the primary budget deficit. These are then interacted with the type of consolidation, TB or EB. The variable $\mathbf{e}_{i,t}$ has three components $\left[e_{i,t}^u \; e_{i,t-j,t}^a \; e_{i,t,t+j}^a \right]$ because shifts in fiscal variables can be unanticipated, announced, or an implementation of previously announced measures.

Unlike the output growth equation, in the two equations for $\Delta g_{i,t}$ and $\Delta \tau_{i,t}$ we allow for expenditure and revenue corrections to have different coefficients. Note that only the part of a narratively identified fiscal correction that is implemented in period t can affect the growth rates of revenues and expenditures: this is because future announced corrections do not directly affect total revenues and total expenditures; they are determined either by discretionary policy actions or by the endogenous response to fluctuations in output, not by announcements.

In the model, nonlinearities with respect to the state of the economy and with respect to the composition of a fiscal plan affect per capita output growth, both on impact and through the dynamic response of the economy to a consolidation plan. On impact, the possible nonlinearities associated with a consolidation plan—stemming from its composition and from the state of the economy—are described by the coefficient vectors $\mathbf{a}, \mathbf{b}, \mathbf{c}, \mathbf{d}$ in the first equation of the model.

The structure of the fiscal adjustment plans is unaltered. The impulse responses reported in Figure 12.4 are constructed simulating the full model. They allow us to measure the effect of EB and TB plans adopted during an expansion or a recession.

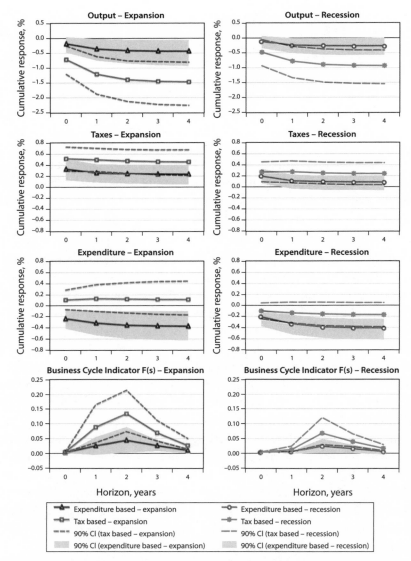

Figure 12.4. Impulse responses of output, taxes, spending and $F(s)$. *Source:* Alesina et al. (2018). *Note:* Allowing for heterogeneity between EB and TB plans and across states of the cycle.

Nonlinearities Related to Public Debt

When measuring the impact of fiscal adjustment it might be important to consider the possibility that the state of the economy is determined by the level of public debt. A fiscal consolidation began when debt is so high that investors consider it no longer sustainable could have different effects than one implemented when debt is rather low and/or stable. Following up on work by Ilzetzki, Mendoza, and Végh (2013), Huidrom et al. (2016) studied the relationship between fiscal multipliers and the fiscal position of the government in a panel of advanced and developing (19 advanced and 15 developing) economies using data at quarterly frequency over the period 1980:1–2014:1. They estimated a panel VAR in which lagged variables (real government consumption, the only fiscal instrument, real GDP, the real effective exchange rate, and the current account balance as a share of GDP) are interacted with a (lagged) moving average of the government debt over GDP ratio. Spending shocks are identified assuming that government consumption does not react contemporaneously to any other variable included in the VAR. Impulse responses show that government consumption multipliers do depend on the level of the debt ratio: multipliers tend to be as large as one when the fiscal position is strong (low debt over GDP ratio) and negative when the fiscal position is weak. These authors suggest that two channels could be at work: an interest rate channel, through which higher borrowing costs crowd out private investment; and a Ricardian channel, through which households reduce consumption in anticipation of future fiscal adjustment.

However, nonlinearities related to debt can be naturally studied by considering a STAR specification based on the VAR model with debt studied and illustrated in Chapter 7.

$$
\mathbf{z}_{i,t} = \begin{bmatrix} \Delta y_{i,t} \\ \Delta p_{i,t} \\ i_{i,t} \\ \Delta g_{i,t} \\ \Delta \tau_{i,t} \end{bmatrix}, \mathbf{e}_{i,t} = \begin{bmatrix} e^u_{i,t} \\ e^a_{i,t-j,t} \\ e^a_{i,t,t+j} \end{bmatrix}, \mathbf{a}_i = \begin{bmatrix} a_{1,i} \\ a_{2,i} \\ a_{3,i} \end{bmatrix}
$$

similarly for $\mathbf{b}_i, \mathbf{c}_i, \mathbf{d}_i$

$$\Delta y_{i,t} = (1 - F(s_{i,t}))A_1^E (L)\, \mathbf{z}_{i,t-1} + F(s_{i,t})A_1^R (L)\, \mathbf{z}_{i,t-1}$$

$$+ \begin{bmatrix} 1 - F(s_{i,t}) \\ F(s_{i,t}) \end{bmatrix}' \begin{bmatrix} \mathbf{a}_1' \mathbf{e}_{i,t} & \mathbf{b}_1' \mathbf{e}_{i,t} \\ \mathbf{c}_1' \mathbf{e}_{i,t} & \mathbf{d}_1' \mathbf{e}_{i,t} \end{bmatrix} \begin{bmatrix} \mathrm{TB}_{i,t} \\ \mathrm{EB}_{i,t} \end{bmatrix}$$

$$+ \lambda_{1,i} + \chi_{1,t} + u_{1,i,t} \qquad\qquad (12.12)$$

$$\Delta p_{i,t} = (1 - F(s_{i,t}))A_Z^E (L)\, \mathbf{z}_{i,t-1} + F(s_{i,t})A_Z^R (L)\, \mathbf{z}_{i,t-1}$$

$$+ \begin{bmatrix} 1 - F(s_{i,t}) \\ F(s_{i,t}) \end{bmatrix}' \begin{bmatrix} \mathbf{a}_2' \mathbf{e}_{i,t} & \mathbf{b}_2' \mathbf{e}_{i,t} \\ \mathbf{c}_2' \mathbf{e}_{i,t} & \mathbf{d}_2' \mathbf{e}_{i,t} \end{bmatrix} \begin{bmatrix} \mathrm{TB}_{i,t} \\ \mathrm{EB}_{i,t} \end{bmatrix}$$

$$+ \lambda_{2,i} + \chi_{2,t} + u_{2,i,t}$$

$$i_{i,t} = (1 - F(s_{i,t}))A_3^E (L)\, \mathbf{z}_{i,t-1} + F(s_{i,t})A_3^R (L)\, \mathbf{z}_{i,t-1}$$

$$+ \begin{bmatrix} 1 - F(s_{i,t}) \\ F(s_{i,t}) \end{bmatrix}' \begin{bmatrix} \mathbf{a}_3' \mathbf{e}_{i,t} & \mathbf{b}_3' \mathbf{e}_{i,t} \\ \mathbf{c}_3' \mathbf{e}_{i,t} & \mathbf{d}_3' \mathbf{e}_{i,t} \end{bmatrix} \begin{bmatrix} \mathrm{TB}_{i,t} \\ \mathrm{EB}_{i,t} \end{bmatrix}$$

$$+ \lambda_{3,i} + \chi_{3,t} + u_{3,i,t}$$

$$\Delta g_{i,t} = (1 - F(s_{i,t}))A_4^E (L)\, \mathbf{z}_{i,t-1} + F(s_{i,t})A_4^R (L)\, \mathbf{z}_{i,t-1}$$

$$+ \begin{bmatrix} 1 - F(s_{i,t}) \\ F(s_{i,t}) \end{bmatrix}' \begin{bmatrix} \beta_{11} & \beta_{12} & \beta_{13} & \beta_{14} \\ \beta_{15} & \beta_{16} & \beta_{17} & \beta_{18} \end{bmatrix} \begin{bmatrix} g_{i,t}^u \\ g_{i,t-1,t}^a \\ \tau_{i,t}^u \\ \tau_{i,t-1,t}^a \end{bmatrix}$$

$$+ \lambda_{4,i} + \chi_{4,t} + u_{4,i,t}$$

$$\Delta \tau_{i,t} = (1 - F(s_{i,t}))A_5^E (L)\, \mathbf{z}_{i,t-1} + F(s_{i,t})A_5^R (L)\, \mathbf{z}_{i,t-1}$$

$$+ \begin{bmatrix} 1 - F(s_{i,t}) \\ F(s_{i,t}) \end{bmatrix}' \begin{bmatrix} \beta_{21} & \beta_{22} & \beta_{23} & \beta_{24} \\ \beta_{25} & \beta_{26} & \beta_{27} & \beta_{28} \end{bmatrix} \begin{bmatrix} g_{i,t}^u \\ g_{i,t-1,t}^a \\ \tau_{i,t}^u \\ \tau_{i,t-1,t}^a \end{bmatrix}$$

$$+ \lambda_{5,i} + \chi_{5,t} + u_{5,i,t}$$

$$d_{i,t} = \frac{1 + i_{i,t}}{(1 + x_{i,t})} d_{i,t-1} + g_{i,t} - \tau_{i,t} + u_{6,i,t}$$

$$x_{i,t} \equiv \Delta p_{i,t} + \Delta y_{i,t} + \Delta p_{i,t} \Delta y_{i,t}$$

$$\tau_{i,t}^u = \delta_0^{\mathrm{TB}}\, e_{i,t}^u *\mathrm{TB}_{i,t} + \delta_0^{\mathrm{EB}}\, e_{i,t}^u *\mathrm{EB}_{i,t} + \epsilon_{0,i,t}$$

$$g_{i,t}^{u} = \vartheta_{0}^{TB}\, e_{i,t}^{u} * TB_{i,t} + \vartheta_{0}^{EB} e_{i,t}^{u} * EB_{i,t} + \upsilon_{0,i,t}$$

$$\tau_{i,t,t+j}^{a} = \delta_{j}^{TB}\, e_{i,t}^{u} * TB_{i,t} + \delta_{j}^{EB} e_{i,t}^{u} * EB_{i,t} + \epsilon_{j,i,t} \quad j = 1,2$$

$$g_{i,t,t+j}^{a} = \vartheta_{j}^{TB}\, e_{i,t}^{u} * TB_{i,t} + \vartheta_{j}^{EB} e_{i,t}^{u} * EB_{i,t} + \upsilon_{j,i,t} \quad j = 1,2$$

Using a nonlinear model specified along these lines, Mei (2016) simultaneously studies two sources of nonlinearity: one associated with the composition of narratively identified fiscal plans (TB or EB adjustments) and one related to the growth rate of the debt over GDP ratio. For the latter, the two regimes to which the model attaches probabilities are high debt growth and stable debt (rather than expansion and recessions, as we did earlier in this chapter). More specifically, the model identifies a high debt growth regime as when the debt ratio increased by at least 3 percentage points on average in the 2 years preceding the fiscal correction. This threshold changes slightly in each country to reflect historical country-specific debt dynamics. Debt is instead defined as "stable" when it did not vary on average in the two years preceding the consolidation. Simulation of the model produces the impulse response functions reported in Figure 12.5.

The asymmetry between EB and TB adjustments is confirmed, independent of the state of debt growth, and is observed in both scenarios. When debt growth is relatively high, fiscal adjustments are less contractionary than when the debt over GDP ratio is stable. Interestingly, and differently from the results in Huidrom et al. (2016), the possibility of expansionary austerity for EB-based plans is a remote one also in the state of high debt growth.

Using an innovative and creative technique to derive impulse response functions, Barnichon and Matthes (2015) found that the multiplier associated with a negative shock to government spending is substantially above 1, while it is well below 1 in the case of a positive spending shock. Multipliers also could depend on the size of the government: cutting 1% of expenditure when it represents 57% of GDP, as in France, is very different than for a country like Ireland where the government spends only 30% of GDP. These are very interesting questions and remain a topic for future research.

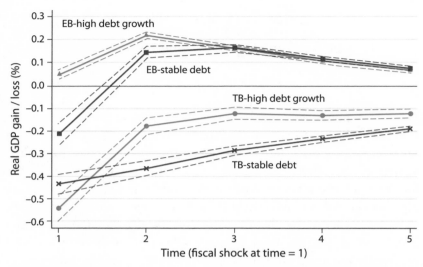

Figure 12.5. Impulse response: high vs. stable debt growth. *Source:* Mei (2016). *Note:* Real GDP generalized impulse response in high debt growth and stable debt scenarios. The initial values of *F* are respectively 0.8 (red simulations) and 0.5 (blue simulations). Red triangle = EB, high debt growth; red circle = TB, high debt growth; blue square = EB, stable debt; blue cross = TB, stable debt.

WHO ADJUSTS AND WHO WINS: MORE DETAILS ON THE MODEL FOR CHAPTER 10

Who Adjusts?

The variable "share_tenure" is the remaining number of years in office the government has divided by the total legislated duration of the term. As an example, a government in Italy in its first year in office will have a share_tenure of 0.8, because it still has four years to go (unless it gets kicked out earlier) on a total term of 5 years. We use this ratio, rather than the simple number of years left in office, because the duration of the executive term varies in the countries of our sample. We use an indicator variable (dummy) for coalition governments: that is, a dummy taking a value of 1 when the government is formed by a coalition of parties and otherwise 0. This variable is motivated by the literature on delayed stabilization that predicts that more divided governments will fail to promptly stabilize budget deficits.

TABLE 12.7. Probability of a new plan

	(1) New positive plans	(2) TB new positive plans	(3) EB new positive plans
Coalition dummy	−0.0327 (0.04)	−0.0746** (0.03)	0.0262 (0.04)
Share of tenure	0.1356** (0.06)	0.0991** (0.04)	0.0055 (0.06)
Right-wing cabinet dummy	0.1010** (0.04)	0.0711** (0.03)	0.0043 (0.04)
Lagged deficit	−0.0556*** (0.01)	−0.0074* (0.00)	−0.0424*** (0.01)
Lagged GDP growth per capita	−0.0460*** (0.01)	−0.0127** (0.01)	−0.0217** (0.01)
Observations	509	509	509

Note: Standard errors in parentheses. ***$p<0.01$, **$p<0.05$, *$p<0.1$.

We also use a dummy for a right-wing cabinet. It equals 1 if the main government party is center right and 0 if the government is center-left.

Table 12.7 presents the results of our probit specification; we jointly evaluate the effects of these three variables on the probability of introducing a new plan of fiscal consolidation. In the first column, the dependent variable is a dummy with a value of one whenever new measures of fiscal restraint are introduced and implemented immediately or are announced for the future. It equals 0 when there is no fiscal consolidation in that year, or when the measures undertaken in that year are simply the execution of a plan announced previously. In the second and the third columns we further distinguish among new TB or EB plans. In all three columns we add to the specification as economic controls the deficit and GDP growth in period $t − 1$.

The share_tenure is an important predictor of fiscal consolidations. The higher the share of years that a government still has in office—that is, the further off are the next scheduled elections—the higher is the probability that a government will implement a fiscal correction. This holds true even after controlling for lagged deficit. Looking at the second column, this result seems to be particularly driven by TB consolidations. We observe that coalition governments seem to implement fiscal

TABLE 12.8. Probability of a new large plan

	(1) New positive large plans	(2) TB new positive large plans	(3) EB new positive large plans
Coalition dummy	0.0151	−0.0081	0.0175
	(0.02)	(0.01)	(0.02)
Share of tenure	0.0592**	0.0338**	0.0226
	(0.03)	(0.01)	(0.02)
Right-wing cabinet dummy	0.0001	0.0049	−0.0046
	(0.02)	(0.01)	(0.02)
Lagged deficit	−0.0201***	−0.0020*	−0.0151***
	(0.00)	(0.00)	(0.00)
Lagged GDP growth per capita	−0.0115***	−0.0036*	−0.0070**
	(0.00)	(0.00)	(0.00)
Observations	509	509	509

Note: Standard errors in parentheses. ***p <0.01, **p <0.05, *p <0.1.

restraints less often than single-party governments: the coefficient of the dummy is always negative and is strongly significant in the case of TB plans. Right-wing governments appear to initiate fiscal corrections more often than left and center governments. However, contrary to the common belief about right-wing government preferences regarding fiscal policy, we find that they tend to mostly implement consolidations based on tax hikes.

As a robustness check (Table 12.8), we repeat our analysis, redefining our dependent variable in order to capture only the largest fiscal adjustments in our sample—those larger than the 70th percentile. The right-wing and coalition dummies lose statistical significance, but share_tenure still has explanatory power, although its marginal effect is smaller.

Who Wins?

We measure the change in government with a dummy: at time t it is equal to one if the political orientation of the government has changed in either the second semester of year t or the first semester of year $t + 1$. We obtain similar results (available from the authors) if we use any change in government cabinet (either a change in the political orientation or in the prime minister) as our dependent variable. The analysis has three different checks, shown in the three regression tables below, namely Tables 12.9, 12.10, and 12.11. Throughout the analysis we include as additional explanatory variables the level of GDP growth per capita in the previous year, the growth in the unemployment rate, the inflation rate (GDP deflator), the number of years the government has been in charge, and two political controls: whether the government is right wing and whether it is formed by a coalition. The first specification focuses on the association between the probability of a government being followed by another with different political ideology (either in regularly scheduled or unanticipated elections), and the same set of explanatory variables that were used to explain output.

We find that the probability of losing the office is a function of past expected and unexpected shocks that are part of previous fiscal plans up to 3 years back. It is also a function of current expected and unexpected shocks and of announcements about the next two years made in the current year or in previous years. One way of intepreting this specification is as follows: on the one hand, when judging the government, electors take into account what the government has done in the current and previous years. They distinguish its current decisions (unexpected shocks) from what it has just implemented, but had decided on earlier (anticipated shocks). On the other hand, the government is evaluated in light of its announced policies that are to be implemented in the near future. Each shock (expected and unexpected) is presumed to have different effects on the outcome, conditional on whether it is part of an EB or TB plan. Table 12.9 shows this analysis both with and without economic controls (first and second column respectively).

In the second column we see a seemingly significant finding: that an unexpected current contractionary measure within an EB plan predicts a higher probability of being replaced in office. However, a more detailed analysis shows that this result is not robust to the exclusion of two observations for Italy: the years 1991 and 1995. Qualitatively, this is similar to other findings reported in column 2: the effects of announcements within a TB plan, or of expected shocks in an EB plan 2 years earlier or in a TB plan 3 years earlier, are not robust.

TABLE 12.9. Change in ideology, all shocks (Contemporaneous and announcements. Classification by total composition of the plan.)

	(1) Full sample w/o controls	(2) Full sample	(3) Govt terminations	(4) Regular elections
$e^u_{i,t} * EB_{i,t}$	0.0498**	0.0433**	0.0965	0.4012*
	(0.02)	(0.02)	(0.07)	(0.21)
$e^u_{i,t} * TB_{i,t}$	−0.0292	−0.037	0.1371	−0.484
	(0.04)	(0.04)	(0.28)	(0.75)
$e^a_{i,t,0} * EB_{i,t}$	0.0331	0.0278	0.0994	−0.2391
	(0.04)	(0.04)	(0.15)	(0.29)
$e^a_{i,t,0} * TB_{i,t}$	0.0316	0.0322	0.5894	1.0337
	(0.07)	(0.07)	(0.46)	(1.03)
$e^a_{i,t,1} * EB_{i,t} + e^a_{i,t,2} * EB_{i,t}$	−0.0409	−0.0424	−0.0413	0.1806
	(0.03)	(0.03)	(0.10)	(0.23)
$e^a_{i,t,1} * TB_{i,t} + e^a_{i,t,2} * TB_{i,t}$	0.1287**	0.1235**	0.7575*	1.0373
	(0.06)	(0.06)	(0.44)	(0.94)
$e^u_{i,t-1} * EB_{i,t-1}$	0.0113	0.0122	0.0073	
	(0.02)	(0.02)	(0.08)	
$e^u_{i,t-1} * TB_{i,t-1}$	−0.0207	−0.0174	0.016	
	(0.03)	(0.03)	(0.14)	
$e^a_{i,t-1,0} * EB_{i,t-1}$	−0.0679	−0.0547	−0.0081	
	(0.05)	(0.05)	(0.17)	
$e^a_{i,t-1,0} * TB_{i,t-1}$	−0.0699	−0.064	−0.6507	
	(0.10)	(0.10)	(0.49)	
$e^u_{i,t-2} * EB_{i,t-2}$	−0.0345	−0.0277	−0.1003	
	(0.03)	(0.03)	(0.13)	
$e^u_{i,t-2} * TB_{i,t-2}$	−0.0094	0.0038	0.0333	
	(0.03)	(0.03)	(0.13)	
$e^a_{i,t-2,0} * EB_{i,t-2}$	−0.0781*	−0.0753*	−0.1929	
	(0.04)	(0.04)	(0.14)	
$e^a_{i,t-2,0} * TB_{i,t-2}$	−0.0627	−0.0416	0.2185	
	(0.10)	(0.10)	(0.32)	
$e^u_{i,t-3} * EB_{i,t-3}$	−0.0061	−0.0016	0.0389	
	(0.03)	(0.02)	(0.10)	
$e^u_{i,t-3} * TB_{i,t-3}$	0.0155	0.0198		
	(0.03)	(0.05)		
$e^a_{i,t-3,0} * EB_{i,t-3}$	−0.0195	−0.0103		
	(0.04)	(0.04)		
$e^a_{i,t-3,0} * TB_{i,t-3}$	−0.4639**	−0.4303**		
	(0.22)	(0.22)		
GDP growth per capita		0.0035	−0.0048	−0.0046
		(0.01)	(0.03)	(0.03)
Unempl. rate (yearly variation)		0.0018	0.0078*	0.0104*
		(0.00)	(0.01)	(0.01)
Inflation rate		0.0026	0.0119	−0.028
		(0.00)	(0.01)	(0.03)
Years from gov. appointment	0.0652***	0.0625***		
	(0.01)	(0.01)		
Coalition cabinet dummy		0.0380*	0.0804	0.0847
		(0.02)	(0.09)	(0.12)
Right wing cabinet dummy		−0.0066	0.0101	
		(0.05)	(0.23)	
Observations	527	517	175	87

Note: Standard errors in parentheses. ***$p < 0.01$, **$p < 0.05$, *$p < 0.1$.

TABLE 12.10. Change in ideology, contemporaneous shocks (Classification by composition of the contemporaneous total shock.)

	(1) Full Sample w/o controls	(2) Full Sample	(3) Govt Terminations	(4) Regular Elections
$e_{i,t}^{u} * \widehat{\text{EB}}_{i,t}$	0.022 (0.03)	0.012 (0.03)	0.0222 (0.08)	0.0000 (0.00)
$e_{i,t}^{u} * \widehat{\text{TB}}_{i,t}$	0.0546** (0.02)	0.0518** (0.03)	0.5860*** (0.21)	0.0000 (0.00)
$e_{i,t,0}^{a} * \widehat{\text{EB}}_{i,t}$	0.0045 (0.04)	−0.0055 (0.04)	0.1149 (0.14)	0.0000 (0.00)
$e_{i,t,0}^{a} * \widehat{\text{TB}}_{i,t}$	0.0525 (0.06)	0.0394 (0.06)	−0.1768 (0.35)	0.0000 (0.00)
$e_{i,t-1}^{u} * \widehat{\text{EB}}_{i,t-1}$	0.0593** (0.03)	0.0683** (0.03)	0.1888* (0.10)	
$e_{i,t-1}^{u} * \widehat{\text{TB}}_{i,t-1}$	−0.0206 (0.03)	−0.0104 (0.03)	−0.0052 (0.12)	
$e_{i,t-1,0}^{a} * \widehat{\text{EB}}_{i,t-1}$	−0.0251 (0.04)	−0.0166 (0.04)	0.07 (0.18)	
$e_{i,t-1,0}^{a} * \widehat{\text{TB}}_{i,t-1}$	−0.1123 (0.12)	−0.0784 (0.11)	−0.2637 (0.32)	
$e_{i,t-2}^{u} * \widehat{\text{EB}}_{i,t-2}$	−0.0849** (0.04)	−0.0764** (0.04)	−0.3518** (0.14)	
$e_{i,t-2}^{u} * \widehat{\text{TB}}_{i,t-2}$	−0.0232 (0.03)	−0.0227 (0.03)	−0.0659 (0.11)	
$e_{i,t-2,0}^{a} * \widehat{\text{EB}}_{i,t-2}$	−0.1390*** (0.05)	−0.1298** (0.05)	−0.2043 (0.14)	
$e_{i,t-2,0}^{a} * \widehat{\text{TB}}_{i,t-2}$	−0.0872 (0.10)	−0.0621 (0.09)	0.0073 (0.35)	
$e_{i,t-3}^{u} * \widehat{\text{EB}}_{i,t-3}$	0.0384 (0.03)	0.0379 (0.03)		
$e_{i,t-3}^{u} * \widehat{\text{TB}}_{i,t-3}$	−0.0208 (0.03)	−0.0421 (0.05)		
$e_{i,t-3,0}^{a} * \widehat{\text{EB}}_{i,t-3}$	0.004 (0.04)	0.0101 (0.04)		
$e_{i,t-3,0}^{a} * \widehat{\text{TB}}_{i,t-3}$	−0.0992 (0.10)	−0.0801 (0.10)		
GDP growth per capita		0.0038 (0.01)	−0.0055 (0.02)	0.0000 (0.00)
Unempl. rate (yearly variation)		0.0020* (0.00)	0.0074* (0.00)	0.0000 (0.00)
Inflation rate		0.003 (0.00)	0.0101 (0.01)	0.0000 (0.00)
Years from gov. appointment	0.0701*** (0.01)	0.0663*** (0.01)		
Coalition cabinet dummy		0.0397* (0.02)	0.0498 (0.08)	0.0000 (0.00)
Right wing cabinet dummy		0.0003 (0.05)	0.0406 (0.25)	
Observations	527	517	175	87

Note: Marginal effects reported. Standard errors in parentheses. ***$p <0.01$, **$p <0.05$, *$p <0.1$.

TABLE 12.11. Change in ideology, cumulative new plans

	(1) Sum of plans	(2)	(3) Ideology	(4)
	Govt terminations	Regular elections	Govt terminations	Regular elections
Exp. based new plans	0.0006 −0.026	−0.0183 −0.04		
Tax based new plans	0.0111 −0.044	−0.1322 −0.09		
Unempl. rate (avg. of mandate yearly var.)	0.0101** −0.005	0.0137 −0.008	0.0099* −0.005	0.0135 −0.009
GDP growth per capita (avg. of mandate)	−0.0374 −0.028	−0.0189 −0.047	−0.0374 −0.028	−0.0155 −0.047
Inflation rate (avg. of mandate)	0.0167 −0.012	−0.0076 −0.022	0.0171 −0.012	−0.0065 −0.022
Coalition cabinet dummy	0.0437 −0.078	0.0899 −0.111	0.0502 −0.078	0.0867 −0.111
Right wing cabinet dummy	0.0879 −0.21		0.0995 −0.217	
Exp. based new plans (mandate avg.)			−0.0031 −0.047	0.003 −0.137
Tax based new plans (mandate avg.)			0.0884 −0.103	−0.4448 −0.308
Observations	175	87	175	87

Note: Marginal effects reported. Standard errors in parentheses. ***$p < 0.01$, **$p < 0.05$, *$p < 0.1$

The second specification (Table 12.10) frames the event of a change in the ideology of the government as a function of the measures (both expected and unexpected) that have been implemented only in the current year or the three previous years. Here, each shock is presumed to have a different effect, not in light of the total direction of the plan it is part of (EB or TB plans), but of the total direction of the measures implemented in the same year. For example, an unexpected current shock in expenditures in a plan in which there are announced future larger shock in taxes would appear as a TB shock in the previous specification, but as an EB shock in this specification.

Therefore, we can think of this case in two ways: as a robustness check of the previous, not robust, results as to the definition of shocks; and as a test of voters' reaction to a more plausible set of scenarios. That is, voters are more likely informed about present and past shocks than about announcements for the future. Moreover, they are more likely to perceive the quality of the shock according to the overall quality of the present shocks, which are more salient than future ones.

As a result of this different classification of shocks, the seemingly significant findings of column 1 are quite different from those of the previous case, showing that TB shocks predict a government's higher probability of being replaced while earlier EB shocks do not. We have earlier seen a positive association between contractionary shocks coming from a mainly EB plan and the probability of being replaced. But as before, this second result is due to a few observations: in particular, it relies only on Italy in 1995 and vanishes if we exclude it from the sample. The two negative coefficients on mainly EB measures taken 2 years before also lose significance as soon as we drop Italy or Belgium, while the positive coefficient on the expenditure side, unexpected measures taken the year before, reverts to statistical zero after dropping Germany. The same story can be told for the robustness of the results reported in the third column, restricting the analysis to only those years in which a government change actually happened. There, only 2-year-old unexpected EB shocks seem to predict a lower probability of the government being replaced with an ideologically different one.

While the message of the first two specifications is that no robust relationship can be found between fiscal adjustments and government change, a third more synthetic and intuitive specification (Table 12.11) confirms this. Now the sample is the list of all 16 countries' governments since 1981, with the exclusion of preunitary Germany and post-2010 United States. The outcome variable is a dummy that is 1 if the government of a country is followed by one with a different ideology and otherwise 0. The economic controls include unemployment variation, GDP per capita, and inflation, all measured as the average of the mandate of the government. The political controls capture whether the government is a coalition or not, and whether it is right wing or not. The explanatory variable is either the sum of new adjustment plans that have been decided by the government or the per-year-of-mandate average size of new plans decided by it. Both alternative explanatory variables, sum or average, are duplicated according to the overall composition of the cumulative new adjustment plans: if in its mandate the government has implemented or announced a total of spending cuts larger than tax increases, then the adjustment is classified as expenditure based.

Table 12.11 demonstrates that governments that undertake either TB or EB adjustment plans do not seem to be replaced by an adverse party more frequently than those who do not do this. This is also true when we restrict the analysis to governments that end at the time scheduled, as in column 4 (i.e., excluding early elections).

Note that the controls used in the regressions for estimating the probability of a new plan (Tables 12.7 and 12.8) are different from those explaining the probability of a turnover (Table 12.9 and 12.10) and also from those explaining the turnover as a function of the overall government performance (Table 12.11). This is because the controls used in the explanation of turnover (per capita GDP growth, yearly variation of unemployment rate, inflation rate) are believed to be endogenous to fiscal plans (given that we show estimates of the effects of plans on GDP in other chapters of this book). Therefore, they cannot be used to explain the probability of a plan taking place. Because the selection criterion of exogenous fiscal plans often has made us record deficit-driven consolidations, we include the lagged deficit as an explanatory variable of fiscal plans. Moreover, it can be shown that lagged GDP growth predicts the event of a plan, although not its size: therefore we include it. On the other hand, lagged deficit and GDP growth are not included in the explanation of the probability of turnover because the latter is strongly correlated with current GDP, included as a control, and the former with the lagged values of the fiscal shocks. For consistency, the final specification (i.e., the change in ideology as a function of the overall government performance during its tenure) requires using the same controls as the previous specification, averaged by the years the government has been in charge. In any event, our results are very robust to these alternative specifications and controls.

In summary, fiscal adjustments do not systematically predict replacement of governments with their rivals.

NOTES

CHAPTER 2. THEORY

1. See Alesina and Drazen (1991) and Blanchard (1990) for models of this type; Alesina, Ardagna, and Galasso (2010) for some evidence; and Alesina and Passalacqua (2016) for a survey.

2. See, e.g., four papers in the May 2011 issue of the *American Economic Review* (pp. 471–491) based on the symposium "Micro versus macro labor supply elasticities": Chetty, Guren, Manoli, and Weber (2011), Chang, Kim, Kwon, and Rogerson (2011), Blundell, Bozio, and Laroque (2011) and Ljungqvist and Sargent (2011). Baxter and King (1993) offers a theoretical discussion.

3. See Alesina, Glaeser, and Sacerdote (2005) for a discussion of hours worked in the United States versus Europe and also Rogerson (2006) and Bick, Bruggemann, and Fuchs-Schundeln (2016).

CHAPTER 3. EXPANSIONARY AND RECESSIONARY AUSTERITY UP TO THE FINANCIAL CRISIS OF 2008

1. Not all tables report all three types of measures. For instance, Austria in 1979–1983 (Table 3.1) used only "Unexp" measures, while Belgium in 1982–4 used all three types of measures.

2. Unlike most countries, where GDP and GNP are virtually synonymous, the gap between Irish GDP and GNP is enormous. According to estimates from the Irish Economic and Social Research Institute the value of Irish GDP in 2015 was €213bn, but the value of GNP was almost 15pc smaller, at just €182bn. GNP is GDP plus net receipts from abroad. The problem with GDP for Ireland is that it includes the undistributed profits of foreign-owned multinationals. This has the effect of artificially boosting the value of Irish economic output, since those profits belong not to Irish residents, but to the multinationals' overseas shareholders. They also fluctuate over time: Fitzgerald (2015) calculated that the undistributed profits of reregistered companies had risen from €1.5bn, or 1.2pc of GNP, in 2009 to €7.4bn, or 5.5pc of GNP, by 2012.

3. Differently from all the other countries (for which we used the OECD Economic Outlook n.97) the source for the data on the effective exchange for Ireland is the BIS dataset because a long enough time series for Ireland is not available in the OECD database. In the statistical analysis we will present later in the book, whenever the exchange rate is involved, Ireland is dropped from the sample.

CHAPTER 4. MEASURING THE EFFECTS OF FISCAL POLICY

1. See Riera-Crichton, Vegh, and Vuletin (2016) for an extensive survey and also Leeper, Traum, and Walker (2015).

2. The authors measure tax multipliers as the present value of the output response over a 3-year horizon and obtain that result for deficit-financed tax changes. When they

instead compute impact multipliers, that is the response of the economy to an increase in taxes at a specific horizon, they find a maximum of -3.6 at quarter 13.

3. See Woodford (2011) and Drautzburg and Uhlig (2015).

4. Lambertini et al. (2005) report that spending cuts increase the probability that an adjustment is successful. Many of them occurred in periods of either high debt-to-GDP ratio or after very high rates of debt accumulation. Alesina and Perotti (1997a) construct a measure of cyclically adjusted defict, estimating the elasticity of taxes and expenditures to macroeconomic variables such as the unemployment rate.

5. Giavazzi and Pagano (1995) study whether and how the size and persistence of an adjustment make a difference.

6. Giavazzi, Jappelli, and Pagano (2000) find that tax hikes during large contractions do not increase national savings—a result which is at odds with the basic Keynesian model that suggests that an increase in one dollar of taxes reduces private savings by less than one dollar (since some of the reduction is translated into lower consumption) and results in a net increase in national savings.

7. While most results used data from OECD countries, some studies (Gupta, Clements, Baldacci, and Mulas-Granados [2005]) analyzed the experience of low income countries and found that countries with a higher share of spending dedicated to wages experience lower growth and that on average fiscal adjustments in those countries were not harmful, especially if conducted through a reduction in current expenditure.

8. In a similar vein, Fisher and Peters (2010) use excess stock market returns of defense contractors as an instrument for military spending, assuming that the stock market moves on news that a military contract has been signed. This instrument, however, has less explanatory power for defense spending than Ramey's news variable.

9. Furno (2015) has extended the Romers' analysis, distinguishing between shifts in personal and in corporate taxes. He finds heterogeneous responses of output and of its main components to the announcement of changes in the two types of taxes.

CHAPTER 5. FISCAL PLANS

1. We shall use a Seemingly Unrelated Regression (SUR) estimator to take into account the simultaneous cross-country correlations of residuals. More details are in Chapter 12.

CHAPTER 6. THE DATA

1. https://ec.europa.eu/info/business-economy-euro/economic-and-fiscal-policy coordination/eu-economic-governance-monitoringprevention-correction/stability-and -growth-pact/stability-and-convergence-programmes_en.

2. They do not drive our results. In a few episodes the motivation for expansionary measures introduced to partially offset the consolidation is not clear: in those cases, we did not include them. One example is Japan in 1997: according to the IMF, the Japanese budget was aimed at reversing some of the exceptional expansionary measures adopted in previous years: it did so both by cutting expenditures and raising taxes. Based on this description, we would categorize the measures as exogenous and record their estimated impact on public finances as computed by the IMF Staff Reports (1997). But in the same document, we found evidence of an expansionary measure which

decreased the total amount of the consolidation launched that year, but did not offset it completely.

3. One example is the United States in 1983, when the federal government introduced exogenous tax cuts to be implemented in the current year but also announced (exogenous) tax increases to be implemented in 1985, 1986, and 1988. Even though the total size of the 1983 measures was expansionary, based on our criterion we recorded only the announcement of tax increases and excluded the tax cuts.

4. This example is extracted from the excel file *Appendix Tables_new_xlsx* of the online appendix.

5. The precise thresholds used to decide on the episode classification are described in *AppendixNotes.docx* of the online appendix. Note that to avoid the need to assign ambiguous cases to one of these categories, we leave room for an episode to be *not classified* (n.c.).

CHAPTER 7. THE EFFECTS OF AUSTERITY

1. The growth rate of real per capita is constructed as follows: $dy_{i,t} = log\left(\frac{y_{i,t}}{y_{i,t-1}}\right) - log\left(\frac{popt_{i,t}}{popt_{i,t-1}}\right)$. The same applies for all other variables.

2. There is a puzzle, however, in the response of consumer confidence during periods of EB austerity. Confidence recovers and turns positive by year 3, while consumption does not.

3. Overlooking plans results in much wider confidence intervals. Note that Guajardo et al. (2014) report, in their Figure 9, *one standard error* bands, with 64% confidence intervals.

4. See also "Productivity Commission Inquiry" Report, no. 33, 2005. Australian Government.

5. The coefficient on the index is 0.04 with an associated standard error of 0.08; the McFadden R^2 is 0.002.

6. Mei (2016) investigated whether the output effects of fiscal consolidation plans change depending on the dynamics of the debt over GDP ratio dynamics before the consolidation starts. Using a nonlinear model à la Auerbach and Gorodnichenko (2013a), it confirms that TB adjustments have significantly more negative effects on GDP than EB ones. Moreover, the dynamics of public debt seem to matter: both TB and EB adjustments are associated with smaller output losses when debt has increased rapidly before the fiscal shift.

7. Croce et al. (2012) examine the effects of corporate taxation on firms' decisions, and hence on asset prices. Shocks to government expenditure generate tax risks for firms, and the extent of this uncertainty depends on the government's financing policy and on its ability to pin down long-run tax dynamics.

8. This also may affect net exports. De Almeida Bandeira, Pappa, Sajedi, and Vella (2016), analyzing a model of a monetary union, studied fiscal consolidation in a two-sector economy, public and private, where the private sector is more productive. They showed that when the nominal interest rate is constrained at its lower bound, a fiscal consolidation induces a positive wealth effect. This increases demand and reallocates workers toward the private sector. Together, the two effects boost private activity.

CHAPTER 8. EUROPEAN AUSTERITY DURING THE GREAT RECESSION

1. See "IMF Fiscal Implications of the Global Economic and Financial Crisis," June 2009, p. 12.

2. Data on the share of articles regarding the fiscal consolidation debate were gathered from Factiva from January 2006 to January 2014. The extent to which fiscal policy was debated in the media is measured by the number of articles concerning fiscal policy divided by the total number of published articles. Data are monthly, and the plotted series is a 5-year centered moving average of the measure in our sample. The numbers along the vertical axis are the percentage over total articles published. Using the archive Factiva, we searched for keywords connected to fiscal policy and debt: "austerity," "fiscal consolidation," "fiscal compact," "Maastricht," "excessive deficit procedure," "public debt," "fiscal policy," "budget deficit," and "debt crisis." We collected monthly data for the countries in our sample from January 2006 to January 2014. We normalized the absolute number of articles, dividing by the total number of published articles, measured by searching the most common word for each country (e.g. "the" for English-speaking countries). We selected the first five national newspapers for circulation in every country excluding sports newspapers, free newspapers, and tabloids.

3. Minor changes were made in 2011 for a total estimated cumulative effect of 2.5 £bn. In addition, in 2013, further measures for a total of 3.3 £bn were implemented, including some in the area of National Insurance contributions, both public and private and both for employers and employees, and reductions in tax relief on pension contributions. In 2014, small expansionary measures were announced.

4. The Irish economy is better described through its GNP rather than its GDP, as we discussed in Chapter 3.

5. The labor market reform inaugurated in 2012 was directed against the high unemployment rate (almost 15%). The reform provided higher connections between unemployed people and labor demand by, for instance, planning 30,000 group interviews in 2012, and higher qualifications for the long-term unemployed augmenting training courses' places by 157,000. The reform also incentivized employers by extending and simplifying the Employer Jobs Incentive Scheme (PRSI) which conceded exemptions from the payment of social insurance contributions.

6. On June 12, 2014 the government allowed the Programme to lapse without disbursement of the final tranche of EUR 2.6 billion in assistance. On May 30, the Constitutional Court had ruled several important consolidation measures in the 2014 budget as unconstitutional. This ruling opened a budgetary gap of 0.4% of GDP vis-à-vis the deficit target of 4% in 2014, with follow-on effects in 2015, which the government had committed to replace with measures of equivalent size and quality so as to achieve the agreed budgetary targets. There were, however, further rulings expected from the Court on 2014 measures and 2015 budgetary plans, which could widen the gap. Accordingly, the government decided to wait for these further rulings so as to address the implied budgetary gap in a comprehensive manner. When it became clear that the Court's next rulings would come well after the scheduled end of the Programme at the end of June, the Government decided not to ask for a further extension but to allow the Programme to lapse and without formal conclusion of the 12th review. This decision was publicly announced by the government on June 12, followed by a joint statement by the EC, ECB, and IMF. (*European Economy*, Occasional Papers 202, October, 2014).

7. The 10 European countries are Austria, Belgium, Denmark, Germany, France, Ireland, Italy, Portugal, Spain, and the United Kingdom. Data on postcrisis austerity measures have been revised after this projection excercise was first published in Alesina, Barbiero, Favero, Giavazzi, and Paradisi (2015) as new documents became available. Measures for 2014 have also been added to our sample.

In particular, a Bank of Spain document has become available reporting in detail the expenditure reduction measures implemented in the period of interest, part of them resulting from the expenditure review plan 2011–13. This reduced the amount of exogenous spending cuts that we record. Thus the 2013 and 2014 episodes switch from spending based to tax based. For Italy the only differences came from the intertemporal allocation of some announcements: this produced a switch in 2010 from a tax- to a spending-based plan. We learned that in Ireland many unexpected measures had in fact been announced, but this did not cause any switch in the main component. For Portugal we now record, from 2012 onwards, announcements made in 2011 that were not included in the previous version, but this also does not imply changes in the main component.

8. More precisely, the model simulations assume that fiscal policy affects GDP only relatively to the level of the country fixed-effect: this may lead to an overestimation of growth. Absent any fiscal shock, our model predicts that the growth in a country is equal to the average growth it experienced in 1980–2007. If 2007 financial crisis marked a structural downward change in growth, the average of our sample will be higher than it. As a result, when the fiscal adjustment is small, if a structural break occurred, our prediction will be steadily higher than the actual data.

9. Note that in the case of Spain the burst of the housing bubble contributed to the recession and high unemployment above and beyond the effects of the fiscal adjustments.

10. We refer to Gourinchas et al. (2017) for a detailed description of the Greek experience.

11. *n.c.* refers to items that are not classified, that is, for which we do not have sufficient information to classify them. As an example, according to Occasional Paper No. 61 issued by the European Commission, the first Economic Adjustment Plan agreed on by Greece and the "Troika" introduced "Unidentified expenditure cuts" of 4.2 €bn to be implemented in 2013 that would have been specified in the future. In November 2012 such cuts were identified as savings in pension expenditures.

12. From the second revision of the first adjustment plan in November 2010, we report this sentence: "The Government committed to respect the 2011 ESA deficit target of EUR 17 billion. With higher than expected starting deficit and debt levels and somewhat lower growth prospects, larger consolidation efforts are needed to reach initial deficit targets and to put the debt ratio on a downward path from 2013 onwards." (Occasional Paper No. 72, European Commission December 2010).

13. These measures were introduced in November 2012 for 2013, so we consider them unexpected in 2013.

14. Blanchard and Leigh control for the value of CDS contracts on government bonds at the time of the forecast. During the euro area crisis, however, controlling for CDSs is not like controlling for long-term interest rates, because bond prices, differently from CDS contracts, reflect not only default risk but also re-denomination risk. Thus during the crisis CDS moved less than long-term bonds.

CHAPTER 9. WHEN AUSTERITY?

1. E.g., Barro and Redlick (2011); Auerbach and Gorodnichenko (2012, 2013b); Fazzari, James, and Panovska (2015); Caggiano et al. (2015).

2. Some "New Keynesian Dynamic Stochastic General Equilibrium models" (DGSE) also come to this conclusion, suggesting that multipliers can be higher during a recession than they are in normal times, e.g., Cogan et al. (2010); Christiano, Eichenbaum, and Rebelo (2011); Coenen et al. (2012).

3. Another dimension on which the paper is a step forward, relative to Blanchard and Perotti (2002), is by improving the measure of unanticipated shocks to fiscal policy. In particular, to purge fiscal variables of the components that were predictable, they use quarterly forecasts of fiscal and aggregate variables from the University of Michigan's Research Seminar in Quantitative Economics (RSQE) macroeconometric model, the Survey of Professional Forecasters (SPF), and the forecasts prepared by the staff of the Federal Reserve Board for the meetings of the Federal Open Market Committee.

4. They also use a different measure of slack—unemployment rather than output growth—and experiment with two different identification schemes: the Blanchard–Perotti scheme, and an updated version of Ramey's 2011b military news variable (both discussed in Chapter 4).

5. Caggiano et al. (2015) also allow for the state of the economy to change following a shift in fiscal policy: They find higher multipliers in downturns than in booms, but the result depends upon "extreme" events, that is, deep recessions and strong expansionary periods.

6. The response of the indicator $F(s_t)$ is computed as the difference between its simulated values after a fiscal adjustment that starts in a recession (expansion) and its simulated values in the absence of a fiscal adjustment, starting in the same regime. Note that in these experiments, $F(s_t)$ is a time-varying variable; it would be a constant if we had assumed, as Auerbach and Gorodnichenko (2012, 2013a, 2013b) do, that the state of the economy remains constant for 20 periods following the shift in fiscal policy. We discuss this case later in this chapter.

7. As an alternative, one can check for the stability of the results after removing the observations at the ZLB from the sample: that is, removing euro area countries in 2013 and 2014, the United States from 2008, and Japan from 1996 onward. The results of this exercise are very similar to the baseline case, confirming that observations at the ZLB do not influence the main findings significantly.

CHAPTER 10. AUSTERITY AND ELECTIONS

1. Australia, Austria, Belgium, Canada, Denmark, Finland, France, Germany, Greece, Ireland, Italy, Japan, Netherlands, Norway, Portugal, Spain, Sweden, United Kingdom, and United States. The fiscal and macroeconomic data of Alesina et al. (2013) are taken from the OECD Economic Outlook Database no. 84. In their analysis, the authors focus on 1975–2008.

2. Alesina and Drazen (1991); Persson and Tabellini (1999); Alesina et al. (2010).

3. Alesina, Ardagna, and Trebbi (2006) present a battery of tests on electoral reform in a large sample of countries which are consistent with the empirical implications of the war of attrition model.

4. The pathbreaking paper was Weingast, Shepsle, and Johnsen (1981). More recently see Battaglini and Coate (2008) and the survey by Alesina and Passalacqua (2016)

5. See the volume edited by Poterba and von Hagen (1999) for an extensive discussion of budget institutions.

CHAPTER 12. THE MODELS IN OUR BOOK

1. There are several approaches to experimenting with empirical models, but the validity of such experiments requires that a number of conditions be satisfied. First, empirical reduced form models need to be simulated keeping all parameters constant. The estimated parameters in a reduced form model could depend on the particular policy rule followed. A simulation keeping parameters constant can be constructed only by considering deviations from a policy rule. This guarantees that the empirical evidence is robust to the Lucas (1976) critique. Such deviations must satisfy three further conditions for the researcher to be able to make valid inferences on their effect (see Lucas [1976]): (1) they must be exogenous relative to the estimation of the model parameters; (2) they must be uncorrelated with other structural macroeconomic shocks—which allows one to assess their effect keeping all other shocks constant; (3) they should not mix anticipated with unanticipated shifts in policy variables. Condition (1) allows identification of the relevant information from the observed correlation in the data: if we can identify fiscal actions that are exogenous with respect to current fluctuations in output, then we can measure the output effect of fiscal policy analyzing the response of output to such policy actions. Condition (2) allows simulation of the effect of a shift in fiscal policy muting other potential sources of macroeconomic fluctuations (i.e. shifts in technology, or in monetary policy, or in consumers' preferences), so that their effect can be assessed by keeping all the other shocks constant. Condition (3) allows discrimination between the response of economic agents to changes in the information set, from their response to the implementation of fiscal measures.

2. See Barro (1981); Blanchard and Watson (1986); Rotemberg and Woodford (1992); Ahmed and Rogers (1995); Blanchard and Perotti (2002); Fatas and Mihov (2001); Perotti (2005); Galí, López-Salido, and Vallés (2007); Mountford and Uhlig (2009); Pappa (2009); and Caldara and Kamps (2017).

3. Fisher and Peters (2010) has created a forward-looking news variable which is alternative to "war dates." He constructed it using innovations in the excess returns in the shares of defense contractors.

4. Ramey (2011b), however, shows that the innovations identified within a standard VAR are predictable from "war dates." Correcting for this effect, impulse responses become even more similar.

5. Alternatively we could have allowed the intertemporal structure of plans to be country- rather than plan-specific (see Alesina, Favero, and Giavazzi [2015]).

6. Since $Cov\left((e_t^u + e_{t-1,t}^a), (e_{t-1}^u + e_{t-2,t-1}^a)\right) = Cov\left((e_t^u + \phi_1 e_{t-1}^u + v_{t-1,1}), (e_{t-1}^u + e_{t-2,t-1}^a)\right)$

7. Note that the sample of the regressions including long-term rates features two fewer observation than the original BL. This is due to the fact that data on long-term yields are not available for Cyprus and Malta. The exclusion of these two countries does not affect the baseline results in BL.

REFERENCES

Ahmed, S. and J. H. Rogers (1995). Government budget deficits and trade deficits: Are present value constraints satisfied in long-term data? *Journal of Monetary Economics 36*(2), 351–374.

Alesina, A. and S. Ardagna (1998). Tales of fiscal adjustment. *Economic Policy 13*(27), 489–585.

Alesina, A. and S. Ardagna (2010). Large changes in fiscal policy: Taxes versus spending. In *Tax Policy and the Economy,* Volume 24, pp. 35–68. National Bureau of Economic Research.

Alesina, A. and S. Ardagna (2013). The design of fiscal adjustments. *Tax Policy and the Economy,* Volume 27, pp. 19–68.

Alesina, A., S. Ardagna, and V. Galasso (2010). The euro and structural reforms. In A. Alesina and F. Giavazzi (Eds.), *Europe and the Euro,* pp. 57–98. University of Chicago Press and National Bureau of Economic Research.

Alesina, A., S. Ardagna, R. Perotti, and F. Schiantarelli (2002, June). Fiscal policy, profits, and investment. *American Economic Review 92*(3), 571–589.

Alesina, A., S. Ardagna, and F. Trebbi (2006). Who adjusts and when? The political economy of reforms. *IMF Staff Papers 53*, 1–49.

Alesina, A., G. Azzalini, C. Favero, F. Giavazzi, and A. Miano (2018). Is it the "how" or the "when" that matters in fiscal adjustments? *IMF Economic Review 66*(1), 144–188.

Alesina, A., O. Barbiero, C. Favero, F. Giavazzi, and M. Paradisi (2015). Austerity in 2009-13. *Economic Policy 30*(83), 383–437.

Alesina, A., O. Barbiero, C. Favero, F. Giavazzi, and M. Paradisi (2017, May). The effects of fiscal consolidations: Theory and evidence. Working Paper 23385, National Bureau of Economic Research.

Alesina, A., D. Carloni, and G. Lecce (2013). The electoral consequences of large fiscal adjustments. In A. Alesina and F. Giavazzi (Eds.), *Fiscal Policy after the Financial Crisis,* pp. 531–570. National Bureau of Economic Research.

Alesina, A. and A. Drazen (1991). Why are stabilizations delayed? *American Economic Review 81*(5), 1170–1188.

Alesina, A., C. Favero, and F. Giavazzi (2015). The output effect of fiscal consolidation plans. *Journal of International Economics 96*, 519–542.

Alesina, A., E. Glaeser, and B. Sacerdote (2005). Work and leisure in the United States and Europe: Why so different? *NBER Macroeconomics Annual 20*, 1–64.

Alesina, A. and A. Passalacqua (2016). The political economy of government debt. In J. B. Taylor and H. Uhlig (Eds.), *Handbook of Macroeconomics,* Volume 2, pp. 2599–2651. Elsevier.

Alesina, A. and R. Perotti (1997a). Fiscal adjustments in OECD countries: Composition and macroeconomic effects. IMF Staff Papers 44, 210–248.

Alesina, A. and R. Perotti (1997b). The welfare state and competitiveness. *American Economic Review 87*(5), 921–939.

Alesina, A., R. Perotti, J. Tavares, M. Obstfeld, and B. Eichengreen (1998). The political economy of fiscal adjustments. *Brookings Papers on Economic Activity 1998*(1), 197–266.

Ardagna, S. and F. Caselli (2014). The political economy of the Greek debt crisis: A tale of two bailouts. *American Economic Journal: Macroeconomics 6*(4), 291–323.

Auerbach, A. J. and Y. Gorodnichenko (2012). Measuring the output responses to fiscal policy. *American Economic Journal: Economic Policy 4*(2), 1–27.

Auerbach, A. J. and Y. Gorodnichenko (2013a). Fiscal multipliers in recession and expansion. In *Fiscal Policy after the Financial Crisis*, pp. 63–98. National Bureau of Economic Research.

Auerbach, A. J. and Y. Gorodnichenko (2013b). Output spillovers from fiscal policy. *American Economic Review 103*(3), 141–146.

Banks, G. (2004). Structural reform Australian-style: Lessons for others? Technical report, Organisation for Economic Co-operation and Development.

Barnichon, R. and C. Matthes (2015, May). Stimulus versus austerity: The asymmetric government spending multiplier. CEPR Discussion Paper 10584.

Baron, D. P. and J. A. Ferejohn (1989). Bargaining in legislatures. *The American Political Science Review 83*(4), 1181–1206.

Barro, R. J. (1981, December). Output effects of government purchases. *Journal of Political Economy 89*(6), 1086–1121.

Barro, R. J. (1984). *Macroeconomics*. Wiley.

Barro, R. J. (2001). Economic growth in East Asia before and after the financial crisis. Working paper 8330, National Bureau of Economic Research.

Barro, R. J. and C. J. Redlick (2011). Macroeconomic effects from government purchases and taxes. *The Quarterly Journal of Economics 126*(1), 51–102.

Battaglini, M. and S. Coate (2008, March). A dynamic theory of public spending, taxation, and debt. *American Economic Review 98*(1), 201–236.

Baxter, M. and R. G. King (1993, June). Fiscal policy in general equilibrium. *American Economic Review 83*(3), 315–334.

Ben Zeev, N. and E. Pappa (2015). Multipliers of unexpected increases in defense spending: An empirical investigation. *Journal of Economic Dynamics and Control 57*(C), 205–226.

Bick, A., B. Bruggemann, and N. Fuchs-Schundeln (2016). Hours worked in Europe and the US: New data, new answers. IZA Discussion Paper 10179, Institute for the Study of Labor (IZA).

Blanchard, O. J. (1990). Comments on Giavazzi and Pagano. NBER Chapters in NBER *Macroeconomics Annual* 1990, Vol. 5.

Blanchard, O. J. and D. Leigh (2014, June). Learning about fiscal multipliers from growth forecast errors. *IMF Economic Review 62*(2), 179–212.

Blanchard, O. J. and R. Perotti (2002). An empirical characterization of the dynamic effects of changes in government spending and taxes on output. *The Quarterly Journal of Economics 117*(4), 1329–1368.

Blanchard, O. J. and M. Watson (1986). Are business cycles all alike? In R. J. Gordon (Ed.), *The American Business Cycle: Continuity and Change*, pp. 123–156. Chicago: University of Chicago Press.

Bloom, N. (2009, 05). The impact of uncertainty shocks. *Econometrica 77*(3), 623–685.

Blundell, R., A. Bozio, and G. Laroque (2011, May). Labor supply and the extensive margin. *American Economic Review 101*(3), 482–486.

Bohn, H. (1991). Budget balance through revenue or spending adjustments? *Journal of Monetary Economics 27*(3), 333–359.

Brender, A. and A. Drazen (2008, December). How do budget deficits and economic growth affect reelection prospects? Evidence from a large panel of countries. *American Economic Review 98*(5), 2203–2220.

Buchanan, J. M. and R. E. Wagner (1977). *Democracy in Deficit: The Political Legacy of Lord Keynes*. New York: Academic Press.

Burnside, C., M. Eichenbaum, and J. D. M. Fisher (2004, March). Fiscal shocks and their consequences. *Journal of Economic Theory 115*(1), 89–117.

Caggiano, G., E. Castelnuovo, V. Colombo, and G. Nodari (2015). Estimating fiscal multipliers: News from a non-linear world. *The Economic Journal 125*(584), 746–776.

Cairns, A. C. (1994). An election to be remembered: Canada 1993. *Canadian Public Policy/Analyse de Politiques 20*(3), 219–234.

Caldara, D. and C. Kamps (2017). The analytics of SVARS: A unified framework to measure fiscal multipliers. *Review of Economic Studies 84*(3), 1015–1040.

Caminada, K. and K. Goudswaard (2009). Effectiveness of poverty reduction in the EU: A descriptive analysis. *Poverty & Public Policy 1*(2), 1–49.

Cavallo, M. (2005). Government employment expenditure and the effects of fiscal policy shocks. Federal Reserve Bank of San Francisco Working Paper 16, 2005.

Chang, Y., S.-B. Kim, K. Kwon, and R. Rogerson (2011, May). Interpreting labor supply regressions in a model of full- and part-time work. *American Economic Review 101*(3), 476–481.

Chetty, R., A. Guren, D. Manoli, and A. Weber (2011, May). Are micro and macro labor supply elasticities consistent? A review of evidence on the intensive and extensive margins. *American Economic Review 101*(3), 471–475.

Chodorow-Reich, G. (2017). Geographic cross-section fiscal spending multipliers: What have we learned? Working paper 23577. National Bureau of Economic Research.

Chodorow-Reich, G., L. Feiveson, Z. Liscow, and W. G. Woolston (2012, April). Does state fiscal relief during recessions increase employment? Evidence from the American Recovery and Reinvestment Act. *American Economic Journal: Economic Policy 4*(3), 118–145.

Christiano, L., M. Eichenbaum, and S. Rebelo (2011). When is the government spending multiplier large? *Journal of Political Economy 119*(1), 78–121.

Chung, H., T. Davig, and E. M. Leeper (2007, 06). Monetary and fiscal policy switching. *Journal of Money, Credit and Banking 39*(4), 809–842.

Cloyne, J. (2013). Discretionary tax changes and the macroeconomy: New narrative evidence from the United Kingdom. *American Economic Review 103*(4), 1507–1528.

Coenen, G., C. J. Erceg, C. Freedman, D. Furceri, M. Kumhof, R. Lalonde, D. Laxton, J. Lindé, A. Mourougane, D. Muir, S. Mursula, C. de Resende, J. Roberts, W. Roeger, S. Snudden, M. Trabandt, and J. Veld (2012, January). Effects of fiscal stimulus in structural models. *American Economic Journal: Macroeconomics 4*(1), 22–68.

Cogan, J. F., T. Cwik, J. B. Taylor, and V. Wieland (2010, March). New Keynesian versus old Keynesian government spending multipliers. *Journal of Economic Dynamics and Control 34*(3), 281–295.

Colacito, R., B. Hoffmann, and T. Phan (2016). Temperature and growth: A panel analysis of the United States. IDB Working Paper Series IDB-WP-676, Inter-American Development Bank.

Corsetti, G., A. Meier, and G. J. Müller (2012a). Fiscal stimulus with spending reversals. *Review of Economics and Statistics 94*(4), 878–895.

Corsetti, G., A. Meier, and G. J. Müller (2012b, October). What determines government spending multipliers? *Economic Policy 27*(72), 521–565.

Croce, M. H. Kung, T. Nguyen, and L. Schmid (2012). Fiscal policy and asset prices. *Review of Financial Studies 25*(9).

Daveri, F., G. Tabellini, S. Bentolila, and H. Huizinga (2000). Unemployment, growth and taxation in industrial countries. *Economic Policy 15*(30), 47–104.

de Almeida Bandeira, G., E. Pappa, R. Sajedi, and E. Vella (2016). Fiscal consolidation in a low inflation environment: Pay cuts versus lost jobs. Staff working paper no. 628, Bank of England.

De Cos, P. H. and E. Moral-Benito (2016). On the predictability of narrative fiscal adjustments. *Economics Letters 143*, 69–72.

DeLong, J. B. and L. H. Summers (2012). Fiscal policy in a depressed economy. *Brookings Papers on Economic Activity 43*(1), 233–297.

Devries, P., A. Pescatori, D. Leigh, and J. Guajardo (2011, June). A new action-based dataset of fiscal consolidation. IMF Working Paper 11/128, International Monetary Fund.

Drautzburg, T. and M. Uhlig (2015). Fiscal stimulus and distortionary taxation. *Review of Economic Dynamics 18*(4), 894–920.

Edelberg, W., M. Eichenbaum, and J. D. Fisher (1999, January). Understanding the effects of a shock to government purchases. *Review of Economic Dynamics 2*(1), 166–206.

Edwards, S. (1989). Exchange rate misalignment in developing countries. *The World Bank Research Observer 4*(1), 3–21.

Eggertsson, G. B. (2011, May). What fiscal policy is effective at zero interest rates? In D. Acemoglu and M. Woodford (Eds.), *NBER Macroeconomics Annual 2010*, Volume 25, pp. 59–112. Chicago: University of Chicago Press.

Erceg, C. J. and J. Lindé (2013). Fiscal consolidation in a currency union: Spending cuts vs. tax hikes. *Journal of Economic Dynamics and Control 37*(2), 422–445.

Evans, M. K. (1969). Reconstruction and estimation of the balanced budget multiplier. *The Review of Economics and Statistics 51*(1), 14–25.

Fatas, A. and I. Mihov (2001). The effects of fiscal policy on consumption and employment: Theory and evidence. CEPR Discussion Paper No. 2760.

Favero, C. and F. Giavazzi (2012, May). Measuring tax multipliers: The narrative method in fiscal VARS. *American Economic Journal: Economic Policy 4*(2), 69–94.

Favero, C., F. Giavazzi, and J. Perego (2011). Country heterogeneity and the international evidence on the effects of fiscal policy. *IMF Economic Review 59*(4), 652–682.

Fazzari, S. M., M. James, and I. Panovska (2015). State-dependent effects of fiscal policy. *Studies in Nonlinear Dynamics & Econometrics 19*(3), 285–315.

Fisher, J. D. and R. Peters (2010). Using stock returns to identify government spending shocks. *The Economic Journal 120*(544), 414–436.

Fitzgerald, J. (2015). Problems interpreting the national accounts in a globalised economy – Ireland. *Quarterly Economic Commentary: Special Articles.*

Furno, F. (2015). The macroeconomic effects of tax policy in the US: Disaggregating taxes. Working paper, Bocconi.

Galí, J., J. D. López-Salido, and J. Vallés (2007). Understanding the effects of government spending on consumption. *Journal of the European Economic Association* 5(1), 227–270.

Gechert, S. (2015). What fiscal policy is most effective? A meta-regression analysis. *Oxford Economic Papers* 67(3), 553–580.

Giavazzi, F., T. Jappelli, and M. Pagano (2000, June). Searching for non-linear effects of fiscal policy: Evidence from industrial and developing countries. *European Economic Review* 44(7), 1259–1289.

Giavazzi, F. and M. McMahon (2013). The household effects of government spending. In *Fiscal Policy after the Financial Crisis*, pp. 103–141. Chicago: University of Chicago Press.

Giavazzi, F. and M. Pagano (1990). Can severe fiscal contractions be expansionary? Tales of two small European countries. In *NBER Macroeconomics Annual 1990, Volume 5*, pp. 75–122. National Bureau of Economic Research.

Giavazzi, F. and M. Pagano (1995, November). Non-Keynesian effects of fiscal policy changes: International evidence and the Swedish experience. CEPR Discussion Paper 1284.

Gil Martin, S. (2017). An overview of Spanish labour market reforms, 1985–2002. Working paper 02-17, CSIC.

Gourinchas, P.-O., T. Philippon, and D. Vayanos (2017, September). The analytics of the Greek crisis. In M. Eichenbaum and J. A. Parker (Eds.), *NBER Macroeconomics Annual 2016*, Volume 31, pp. 1–81. Chicago: University of Chicago Press.

Guajardo, J., D. Leigh, and A. Pescatori (2014, August). Expansionary austerity? International evidence. *Journal of the European Economic Association* 12(4), 949–968.

Gupta, P., D. Mishra, and R. Sahay (2007). Behavior of output during currency crises. *Journal of International Economics* 72(2), 428–450.

Gupta, S., B. Clements, E. Baldacci, and C. Mulas-Granados (2005). Fiscal policy, expenditure composition, and growth in low-income countries. *Journal of International Money and Finance* 24(3), 441–463.

Hall, R. E. (1986). The role of consumption in economic fluctuations. In R. J. Gordon (Ed.), *The American Business Cycle: Continuity and Change*, pp. 237–255. University of Chicago Press for the National Bureau of Economic Research.

Hall, R. E. (2009). By how much does GDP rise if the government buys more output? *Brookings Papers on Economic Activity* 40(2 (Fall)), 183–249.

Honohan, P. (1992). Fiscal adjustment in Ireland in the 1980s. *Economic and Social Review* 23(3), 285–314.

Huidrom, R., M. A. Kose, J. J. Lim, and F. L. Ohnsorge (2016, June). Do fiscal multipliers depend on fiscal positions? CAMA Working Paper 2016-35, Centre for Applied Macroeconomic Analysis, Crawford School of Public Policy, The Australian National University.

Ilzetzki, E., E. G. Mendoza, and C. A. Végh (2013). How big (small?) are fiscal multipliers? *Journal of Monetary Economics* 60(2), 239–254.

Jordà, O. and A. M. Taylor (2016). The time for austerity: Estimating the average treatment effect of fiscal policy. *The Economic Journal* 126(590), 219–255.

Kaplan, G. and G. L. Violante (2014). A model of the consumption response to fiscal stimulus payments. *Econometrica 82*(4), 1199–1239.

Krugman, P. and L. Taylor (1978). Contractionary effects of devaluation. *Journal of International Economics 8*(3), 445–456.

Lambertini, L. and J. Tavares (2005). Exchange rates and fiscal adjustments: Evidence from the OECD and implications for the EMU. *Contributions to Macroeconomics 5*(1), 1–28.

Lane, P. R. and R. Perotti (2003). The importance of composition of fiscal policy: Evidence from different exchange rate regimes. *Journal of Public Economics 87*(9), 2253–2279.

Leeper, E. M. (2010). Monetary science, fiscal alchemy. Proceedings—Economic Policy Symposium—Jackson Hole, Federal Reserve Bank of Kansas City.

Leeper, E. M., N. Traum, and T. B. Walker (2015, July). Clearing up the fiscal multiplier morass: Prior and posterior analysis. NBER Working Paper 21433, National Bureau of Economic Research, Inc.

Lemoine, M. and J. Lindé (2016, May). Fiscal consolidation under imperfect credibility. Working Paper Series 322, Sveriges Riksbank (Central Bank of Sweden).

Ljungqvist, L. and T. J. Sargent (2011, May). A labor supply elasticity accord? *American Economic Review 101*(3), 487–491.

Lucas, R. E. (1976). Econometric policy evaluation: A critique. In *Carnegie-Rochester Conference Series on Public Policy*, Volume 1, pp. 19–46. Philadelphia: Elsevier.

McDermott, C. J. and R. F. Wescott (1996). An empirical analysis of fiscal adjustments. *International Monetary Fund Staff Papers 43*(4), 725–754.

Mei, P. (2016). Debt dynamics and fiscal consolidation plans. Working paper, Bocconi.

Mertens, K. and M. O. Ravn (2013). The dynamic effects of personal and corporate income tax changes in the United States. *American Economic Review 103*(4), 1212–1247.

Mertens, K. and M. O. Ravn (2014). A reconciliation of SVAR and narrative estimates of tax multipliers. *Journal of Monetary Economics 68*(S), S1–S19.

Morley, S. A. (1992). On the effect of devaluation during stabilization programs in LDCS. *Review of Economics and Statistics*, 21–27.

Mountford, A. and H. Uhlig (2009). What are the effects of fiscal policy shocks? *Journal of Applied Econometrics 24*(6), 960–992.

Nakamura, E. and J. Steinsson (2014, March). Fiscal stimulus in a monetary union: Evidence from us regions. *American Economic Review 104*(3), 753–792.

Ong, J. (2006). A new effective exchange rate index for the Canadian dollar. *Bank of Canada Review 2006*(Autumn), 41–46.

Owyang, M. T., V. A. Ramey, and S. Zubairy (2013). Are government spending multipliers greater during periods of slack? Evidence from twentieth-century historical data. *American Economic Review 103*(3), 129–134.

Pappa, E. (2009). The effects of fiscal shocks on employment and the real wage. *International Economic Review 50*(1), 217–244.

Passarelli, F. and G. Tabellini (2017). Emotions and political unrest. *Journal of Political Economy 125*(3), 903–946.

Perotti, R. (1999). Fiscal policy in good times and bad. *The Quarterly Journal of Economics 114*(4), 1399–1436.

Perotti, R. (2005). Estimating the effects of fiscal policy in OECD countries. CEPR Discussion Paper No. 4842, CEPR.

Perotti, R. (2013). The "austerity myth": Gain without pain? In A. Alesina and F. Giavazzi (Eds.), *Fiscal Policy after the Financial Crisis*, 8, pp. 307–354. National Bureau of Economic Research.

Perotti, R. (2014, May). Defense government spending is contractionary, civilian government spending is expansionary. NBER Working Paper 20179, National Bureau of Economic Research.

Persson, T. and G. Tabellini (1999). Political economics and macroeconomic policy. In J. B. Taylor and M. Woodford (Eds.), *Handbook of Macroeconomics*, Volume 1C, pp. 1397–1482. Elsevier.

Ponticelli, J. and H.-J. Voth (2011). Austerity and anarchy: Budget cuts and social unrest in Europe 1919–2009. CEPR Discussion Paper 8513, Centre for Economic Policy Research.

Poterba, J. M. and J. von Hagen (Eds.) (1999). *Fiscal Institutions and Fiscal Performance* (1st ed.). Chicago: University of Chicago Press.

Ramey, V. A. (2011a, September). Can government purchases stimulate the economy? *Journal of Economic Literature 49*(3), 673–685.

Ramey, V. A. (2011b). Identifying government spending shocks: It's all in the timing. *The Quarterly Journal of Economics 126*(1), 1–50.

Ramey, V. A. (2016, February). Macroeconomic shocks and their propagation. NBER Working Paper 21978, National Bureau of Economic Research.

Ramey, V. A. and M. D. Shapiro (1998). Costly capital reallocation and the effects of government spending. In *Carnegie-Rochester Conference Series on Public Policy*, Volume 48, pp. 145–194. Philadelphia: Elsevier.

Ramey, V. A. and S. Zubairy (2018). Government spending multipliers in good times and in bad: Evidence from U.S. historical data. *Journal of Political Economy 126*(2), 850–901.

Riera-Crichton, D., C. A. Vegh, and G. Vuletin (2016). Tax multipliers: Pitfalls in measurement and identification. *Journal of Monetary Economics 79*, 30–48.

Rogerson, R. (2006). Understanding differences in hours worked. *Review of Economic Dynamics 9*(3), 365–409.

Romer, C. D. and J. Bernstein (2009). The job impact of the American recovery and reinvestment plan. Technical report, Office of the President-Elect.

Romer, C. D. and D. H. Romer (1989). Does monetary policy matter? A new test in the spirit of Friedman and Schwartz. *NBER Macroeconomics Annual 4*, 121–170.

Romer, C. D. and D. H. Romer (2009). Do tax cuts starve the beast? The effect of tax changes on government spending. *Brookings Papers on Economic Activity 40*(1 (Spring), 139–214.

Romer, C. D. and D. H. Romer (2010, June). The macroeconomic effects of tax changes: Estimates based on a new measure of fiscal shocks. *American Economic Review 100*(3), 763–801.

Romer, C. D. and D. H. Romer (2016, Mar). Transfer payments and the macroeconomy: The effects of social security benefit increases, 1952–1991. *American Economic Journal: Macroeconomics 8*(4), 1–42.

Rotemberg, J. J. and M. Woodford (1992). Oligopolistic pricing and the effects of aggregate demand on economic activity. *Journal of Political Economy 100*(6), 1153–1207.

Shoag, D. (2013). Using state pension shocks to estimate fiscal multipliers since the great recession. *American Economic Review 103*(3), 121–124.

Tanzi, V. and L. Schuknecht (2000). *Public Spending in the 20th Century: A Global Perspective*. Cambridge: Cambridge University Press.

Toda, H. Y. and T. Yamamoto (1995). Statistical inference in vector autoregressions with possibly integrated processes. *Journal of Econometrics 66*(1), 225–250.

Uhlig, H. (2005, March). What are the effects of monetary policy on output? Results from an agnostic identification procedure. *Journal of Monetary Economics 52*(2), 381–419.

Uhlig, H. (2010, May). Some fiscal calculus. *American Economic Review 100*(2), 30–34.

Von Hagen, J., A. H. Hallett, and R. Strauch (2002). Budgetary consolidation in Europe: quality, economic conditions, and persistence. *Journal of the Japanese and International Economies 16*(4), 512–535.

Weingast, B. R., K. A. Shepsle, and C. Johnsen (1981). The political economy of benefits and costs: A neoclassical approach to distributive politics. *Journal of Political Economy 89*(4), 642–664.

Wilson, D. J. (2012, April). Fiscal spending jobs multipliers: Evidence from the 2009 American Recovery and Reinvestment Act. *American Economic Journal: Economic Policy 4*(3), 251–282.

Woodford, M. (2011). Simple analytics of the government expenditure multiplier. *American Economic Journal: Macroeconomics 3*(1), 1–35.

Zettelmeyer, J., E. Kreplin, and U. Panizza (2017). Does Greece need more official debt relief? If so, how much? Working Paper No. 17-6, Peterson Institute for International Economics.

INDEX

accompanying policies, 11, 17–18, 26–27, 195; empirical model and, 71; expenditure-based vs. tax-based adjustments and, 4, 63, 105–12, 116, 198–99; IMF narrative dataset and, 63. *See also* exchange rate movements; monetary policy; structural reforms

aggregate demand: business cycle and, 23; expansionary austerity and, 5; expenditure-based vs. tax-based plans and, 5, 12–13, 113, 115, 199; popular anti-austerity argument and, 17, 19; positively affected by austerity implementation, 22; private investment and, 12, 115; in simple Keynesian model, 19; uncertainty and, 23, 113, 199

aging of populations, 15, 20, 119

Albuquerque, Maria Luís, 138

alternative specification, 112–13, 220–22

American Recovery and Reinvestment Act: fiscal multipliers related to, 50, 51; state-level effects of, 213

announced measures: in constructing fiscal plans, 65; defined, 30; in empirical model, 71, 204–5; intertemporal correlations and, 70; in VAR approach, 208, 209, 215

austerity: arguments about deficits and, 3, 194–95, 200; defined, 1; delay in implementing, 17, 22, 188–89; intertwined with other public issues, 200; past policy mistakes leading to, 1–2, 194, 198; two types of, 3–5, 7, 9–10 (*see also* EB vs. TB fiscal adjustments). *See also* expansionary austerity; recessionary austerity

austerity policies after financial crisis of 2008, 3. *See also* European austerity during 2010–14

austerity policies up to financial crisis of 2008, 31; expansionary examples of, 29, 31–42; recessionary examples of, 30–31, 42–49

austerity programs, multiyear, 11, 23–24; different countries' styles of, 12, 24, 70, 71, 216; limitations of elementary Keynesian

model and, 195; of most European countries starting in 2010, 121, 123. *See also* fiscal plans, multiyear

Australia: dataset of fiscal measures, 1993–96, 84, 85, 86, 87, 88–89; product market reforms of 1995, 109

Austria: expansionary austerity in 1980s, 31–32, 33; fiscal consolidations, 2010–14, 144; macroeconomic variables for 1979–85, 33

bail-in, 123

banking crises: in Greece, 149; in Ireland, 123, 127, 129, 130, 131, 147; need for European austerity programs and, 117, 201; recessions attributed to austerity and, 158

bank levy, in UK austerity program, 127

banks: distressed in Europe after financial crisis, 120, 122; government bonds on balance sheets of, 149, 158, 201; recapitalization of, 197, 201

Belgium: business cycle in relation to consolidation plans, 163; expansionary austerity in 1980s, 32, 34–37, 56; fiscal consolidations 2010–14, 144; large debt in 1970s and 1980s, 2; macroeconomic variables for 1980–89, 36

budgetary rules and institutions, 192

bureaucracy, and implementation of policy, 192

business confidence: of investors, 2, 199; response to CIB, TRB, and TB plans, 102, 104, 105; response to EB and TB plans, 100, 101, 116, 196. *See also* confidence

business cycle: early literature on fiscal consolidations and, 58–59; EB vs. TB fiscal adjustments and, 163, 165, 166, 169, 170, 174, 236; endogeneity problem and, 10, 160–61; fiscal multipliers related to, 161–63, 232, 256n2, 256n5; fiscal policies of euro area economies and, 121–22; methodological choices on timing of austerity and, 169–71, 174; timing of austerity

direct tax based (DB) fiscal plans, 78, 87, 90, 91, 93, 105
distortionary taxes, 26, 225
doom loop, 158
Draghi, Mario, 202

EB (expenditure-based) fiscal plans: average low output losses from, 116; classification of, 82–87, 90, 91, 93; defined, 67; ideological opposition to, 194; three types of government expenditures in, 25
EB vs. TB fiscal adjustments: business cycle at introduction of plan and, 163, 165, 166, 169, 170, 174, 235, 236; in case studies up to 2008 financial crisis, 29–30; components of aggregate demand and, 12 (*see also* private investment); confidence of consumers and investors and, 4–5, 22–23, 100, 101, 113–14, 116, 196, 199; debt over GDP ratio and, 4, 13, 110, 111, 161, 196, 239–40, 253n6; early literature on multipliers and, 57, 58, 59, 63; exchange rate movements and, 4, 97, 106–9, 116, 197, 198–99; expectations and, 4–5, 20–21, 199; explanations for the difference, 4–5, 113–16, 198–200; fiscal plans divided according to, 66–67, 68, 71, 74, 75, 90; in general equilibrium models, 115, 224–27; governmental variables and, 241–42; incentive effects and, 24–26; monetary policy and, 63, 97, 99, 100, 105, 116, 198; persistence of spending or tax changes and, 115, 225–27; recessionary effects and, 9–10, 12, 62; replacement of government and, 178, 243, 244, 245, 246, 247–48; response of output to, 96–97, 116; simple Keynesian model and, 18–20; structural reforms and, 110, 116, 199; summary of results on, 3–5, 10–13, 116, 195–97; use of TB despite greater costs, 188–92; at zero lower bound, 7–8, 115, 170–74, 224
Ecofin (Economic and Financial Affairs Council): Portuguese austerity program and, 136
economic growth: debt too large to reduce by means of, 2; delay of austerity measures and, 22; high debt as impediment to, 2; timing of austerity plan and, 23. *See also* GDP growth; output
electoral effects of austerity: conventional wisdom on, 8, 175, 192–93, 198; examples of specific countries, 185–89; existing evidence

on, 176–80; fiscal plans and, 180–83; not systematically leading to defeat, 10, 175, 198; reelection despite social protests, 188; timing relative to next election and, 180–81, 193, 241–42. *See also* politics
empirical models: dynamics of debt ratio and, 222–24; fiscal multipliers measured with, 71, 203, 206; models used in the literature, 206–14; nonlinearities in, 234–26, 238–40, 253n6; overview of basic features, 70–71, 204–6; panel regression in, 72; parameter φ in, 70, 71; simplicity vs. accuracy of, 10–11, 203; simulating European postcrisis fiscal consolidations, 142–47; simulations with, 71, 204–5; two blocs of, 70; validity of experiments with, 256n1. *See also* VAR (vector autoregressions)
employment: American Recovery and Reinvestment Act and, 213; labor market regulation and, 26–27. *See also* labor market reforms; unemployment
endogeneity problem, 10, 160–61. *See also* exogenous shifts in fiscal variables; reverse causation problem
entitlement programs: future taxes and, 4–5, 20–21, 196, 199; monetary policy and, 97
episode of fiscal adjustment: classification of, 90–91, 93; defined, 75
euro: deficits reduced in order to join, 73, 194; low interest rates in first decade of, 118; unconventional monetary policy and, 202
European austerity during 2010–14, 117–59; aftermath of financial crisis and, 117, 118–22; arguments about, 3, 194–95; comparison to US, 141, 142, 146; counterfactual experiments on GDP response, 147–48; critiqued as possibly too severe, 117, 141, 157–58, 197, 201; deep recessions associated with, 141, 158–59, 197; electoral events following, 183, 187, 188–89; expansionary in Ireland and UK, 6; fiscal multipliers possibly higher than expected, 118, 157–58, 197; Greek economy and, 148–57, 198, 255nn11–13; in Ireland 2010–14, 127–31, 143, 147, 188, 255n7; in Italy 2011–12, 138–41, 143, 147, 148, 255n7; necessity of, 2, 117, 201–2; in Portugal 2010–14, 67–69, 134–38, 143, 146, 147, 254n6, 255n7; before recovery from Great Recession, 159, 160; revised data based on

Italy: austerity program in 2011–12, 26, 138–41, 143, 147, 148, 255n7; elections of 2013, 187, 188; fiscal consolidation 1989–92, 57; fiscal plan for consolidation of 1991–93, 69; government during main austerity push in 2011–13, 188; high debt to GDP ratio before crisis, 118; large debt in 1970s and 1980s, 1–2; temporary deficit reduction measures in, 24, 69

Japanese budget of 1997, 252n2
Juncker, Jean-Claude, 8

Kenny, Enda, 188
Keynesian model, simple, 18–20; based on much smaller government, 18; effects not covered by, 20, 195; fiscal multipliers and, 19, 50–51, 60, 188; liquidity constrained consumers in, 21; tax increases and, 19, 60, 252n6. See also new-Keynesian approach

labor market reforms: accompanying austerity plans, 26–27, 195; in Irish austerity program, 129, 254n5; not explaining difference between EB and TB plans, 110, 116, 199; in Portuguese austerity program, 138
labor market regulations, 26–27
labor markets: effects of austerity on, 115, 225. See also unionized economies
labor taxes: consequences of increase in, 5, 24–25; effects of persistent increase in, 115, 226–27; reducing incentive to work, 24
lagged output growth, 169–70, 241, 242, 248, 256n6
legislatures, preferring tax increases to spending cuts, 191–92
liquidity constrained consumers, 21, 22; fiscal multipliers and, 63
liquidity trap, 19
local multipliers, 213–14

Medicare, 20. See also entitlement programs
Merkel, Angela, 123
military spending, 59–60, 252n8; expectational VAR and, 209–10; local, 213–14. See also wars
minimum wages, 26
models. See empirical models
monetary policy: accompanying fiscal austerity plans, 4, 11, 17–18, 26, 27, 195; counterfactual simulation constraining

interest rates, 105; country-level fiscal policies and, 172; EB vs. TB adjustments and, 63, 97, 99, 100, 105, 116, 198; empirical model and, 70, 105; endogenous reaction of, 97; narrative approach to, 61; unconventional, 3, 27, 202; VAR model and, 209. See also interest rates; zero lower bound
Monti, Mario, 140
Mulroney, Brian, 37
multipliers. See fiscal multipliers
multiyear austerity programs. See austerity programs, multiyear; fiscal plans, multiyear

narrative approach, 59–63; dataset based on, 73, 76, 94 (see also fiscal measures); predictability of plans and, 219–20; VAR model and, 209–10
narrative identification, 61, 76; nonlinearity and, 239; state-of-economy analysis and, 234, 235
National Reform Programmes, 79
natural disasters, debt resulting from, 1, 2
n.c. (not classified) fiscal measures, 86–87; in Greek fiscal consolidation, 153, 255n11
neoclassical economic models, 19
net exports: defined, 95; depreciation of exchange rate and, 27; increased during UK austerity program, 127; response to CIB, TRB, and TB plans, 102; response to EB and TB plans, 97, 99, 106, 196–98, 199; sometimes increasing with fiscal contraction, 58. See also trading partners
Netherlands, dropped from sample, 78
new-Keynesian approach, 20; EB vs. TB consolidations and, 224–26; to government spending increase with debt stabilization, 211
news variable: of Fisher and Peters, 257n3; of Ramey, 59, 252n8
nonlinear models, 234–36, 238–40, 253n6

Obama, Barack, 50. See also American Recovery and Reinvestment Act
OECD (Organisation for Economic Co-operation and Development) economies: arguments about austerity in, 3; average time in recession, 162; database of, 93; dataset for 16 countries in, 9, 73–78 (see also fiscal measures); Economic Surveys of, 77; electoral effect of austerity in, 176; IMF

OECD (cont.)
    narrative dataset for, 62; income inequality
    in, 189; index of labor market reforms, 110;
    index of product market reforms, 110;
    regulations of product, services, and labor
    markets in, 26–27; two types of austerity in,
    3–4; VAR model for 16 countries in,
    214–19
Omnibus Budget Reconciliation Acts
    (OBRAs), 73
optimal taxation, 194
output: cost of austerity and, 1; defined, 95;
    endogeneity problem and, 10; exchange rate
    devaluations and, 106–7; response to CIB,
    TRB, and TB plans, 102; response to EB
    and TB plans, 96–97, 116; sustained by
    structural reforms, 116; in VAR model for
    16 countries, 214. See also economic growth;
    GDP growth
output growth, lagged, 169–70, 241, 242, 248,
    256n6

Papandreou, George, 149
Passos Coelho, Pedro, 188
payroll taxes. See labor taxes
pension-fund investments, and state-level
    multipliers, 213–14
pension reform: with small savings in short
    run, 26; unions' opposition to, 189
pension systems: future taxes and, 20;
    intergenerational redistribution and, 200.
    See also social security systems
persistence of changes in taxes and
    expenditures, 115, 225–27
Pinto Balsemão, Francisco, 47
policy variables, 205–6; dynamics of debt ratio
    and, 222–23; VARs and, 208–9, 214, 216,
    222–23. See also fiscal policy
politics: of delay in initiating fiscal adjust-
    ments, 188–89; of spending cuts vs. tax
    increases, 191. See also electoral effects of
    austerity
Portugal: austerity program in 2010–14, 67–69,
    134–38, 143, 146, 147, 254n6, 255n7; fiscal
    consolidation in 1984–6, 57; macro-
    economic variables for 1980–87, 48;
    recessionary austerity program of 1983,
    47–49; three elections after financial crisis,
    187, 188
poverty, and redistributive effects of austerity,
    189–90

private investment: avoiding delay of austerity
    measures and, 22; confidence and, 2,
    113–14, 199; crowded out by higher
    government debt, 237; crowded out by war
    spending, 59; data on, 92, 93; defined, 95; as
    driver of difference between TB and EB
    austerity, 12, 114, 116; expansionary
    austerity and, 5; future taxes and, 21, 22;
    Greece's collapse of, 154; large fiscal
    consolidations and, 57; response to CIB,
    TRB, and TB plans, 102–3; response to EB
    and TB plans, 97, 98, 114, 116, 196; strongly
    reacting to government spending cuts, 58
product market reforms: EB vs. TB
    adjustments and, 110, 116, 199; liberalizing
    earlier regulations, 27, 195; in Portuguese
    austerity program, 138
public debt: accumulated in 1970s and 1980s,
    1–2, 194; argument that it's not really a
    problem, 194, 200; of European countries
    2007–10, 118–21, 200; left to future
    generations, 15–16, 189; level of, and impact
    of fiscal adjustment, 237, 238–40. See also
    debt crises; debt dynamics; debt over GDP
    ratio

quantitative easing, 27

rainy-day reserve funds, 1
Rajoy, Mariano, 188
Ramey's news variable, 59, 252n8
real estate bubbles: depth of some countries'
    recessions and, 197; financial crisis of 2008
    and, 2, 117, 118; in Ireland of early 2000s,
    29, 128; in Spain, 29, 131–32, 255n9
recapitalization of banks, 197, 201
recessionary austerity: EB vs. TB adjustments
    and, 10, 12, 62; in Europe after euro crisis,
    123; in Europe after financial crisis, 141,
    158–59, 197; up to financial crisis of 2008,
    20–30, 42–49
recessions: anti-austerity argument about, 17;
    fiscal multipliers in, 7; income inequality
    increased by, 188; need to run deficits
    during, 1; probability of being in, $F(s)$, 162,
    164–70, 256n6; simple Keynesian model
    and, 18–19; in state-of-economy analysis,
    232–36
recessions, austerity implemented during, 6–8,
    23, 121, 122, 160–61; in dataset of fiscal
    consolidations, 59; higher output cost than

during an expansion, 170; with large difference between EB and TB austerity, 197–98; oversampled by construction, 6–7, 161

redistribution: consequences of austerity and, 188–90; of debt to future generations, 189, 200

reverse causation problem, 10, 30, 58–59, 160–61; addressed with VARs, 207

Romer and Romer methodology, 59, 60–61, 76

Sarkozy, Nicolas, 123

services markets: liberalization of, 18, 195; regulations of 1970s and 1980s, 26

simple Keynesian model. *See* Keynesian model, simple

Smooth Transition VAR (STAR), 234–36, 238–39

Soares, Mario, 47

social security systems: incentive effects and, 25–26; intergenerational redistribution and, 189; reforms of, 26. *See also* pension systems

Socrates, José, 186

Spain: austerity measures in 1990s, 41–42, 43–44; austerity program in 2009–14, 131–34, 143, 147–48, 255n7; elections from 2008 to 2016, 187, 188; labor market reform of 1994, 109; macroeconomic variables for 1990–2001, 44; overinvested in infrastructure, 190; real estate bubble in, 29, 131–32

spending cuts: as measured in fiscal plans, 67. *See also* EB (expenditure-based) fiscal plans

Stability and Convergence Programmes, 77, 79

Stability and Growth Pact, and Greek budget deficits, 149

state-of-economy analysis, 232–36

stimulating the economy, with deficit-financed tax cut, 209

Stimulus Program. *See* American Recovery and Reinvestment Act

structural reforms, 18, 110, 195; EB vs. TB plans and, 110, 116, 199; in Irish austerity program, 129; in Portuguese austerity program, 138; in Spanish austerity program, 134; in UK austerity program, 127. *See also* labor market reforms; product market reforms; supply-side reforms

subprime loan crisis, long-term bond yields during, 230

sudden stop: in Greece's economy in 2010, 149–51; in Italy's economy in 2011, 138, 139–40; in Portugal's economy in 2011, 134, 136

supply side of economy: contractionary effect of tax increase and, 115; incentives and, 17, 24–26; simple Keynesian model and, 19–20, 195; spending cuts or tax hikes and, 5, 17, 199–200

supply-side reforms, 4, 110. *See also* structural reforms

Sweden: fiscal consolidation 1983–89, 57; reelection of leader after four years of austerity, 183, 186

tax amnesties, temporary, in Italy, 24, 69

tax-based plans. *See* EB vs. TB fiscal adjustments; TB (tax-based) fiscal plans

tax cuts: deficit-financed, 209; United States 1947–2007, 76; United States 1983, 253n3

tax distortions, 26, 225

tax evasion, 26; in Greece, 149; Italian measures against, 140

tax increases: in simple Keynesian model, 19, 60, 252n6. *See also* TB (tax-based) fiscal plans

tax reforms, 11, 26, 27

TB (tax-based) fiscal plans: Australia's product market reforms of 1995 and, 109; classification of, 82–87, 90, 92, 93, 102–5; defined, 67; electoral consequences of, 178, 183; more costly than EB plans regardless of business cycle, 160; recessionary response to, 95, 97, 102–3, 116, 196; used despite superiority of spending cuts, 188–92. *See also* EB vs. TB fiscal adjustments

timing of austerity plans: delay in implementation, 17, 22, 188–89; early in government's term of office, 193; methodological choices in analysis of, 169–71, 174; trading partners and, 7, 122, 157; at zero lower bound, 7–8, 157, 160, 161, 174, 197. *See also* business cycle; recessions, austerity implemented during

trading partners: negative spillovers between, 197; timing of austerity plans and, 7, 122, 157. *See also* net exports

transfer-based (TRB) fiscal plans, 10, 78, 87, 102–5

transfers, reductions in: long-lasting effects of, 57, 196; similar to cutting government